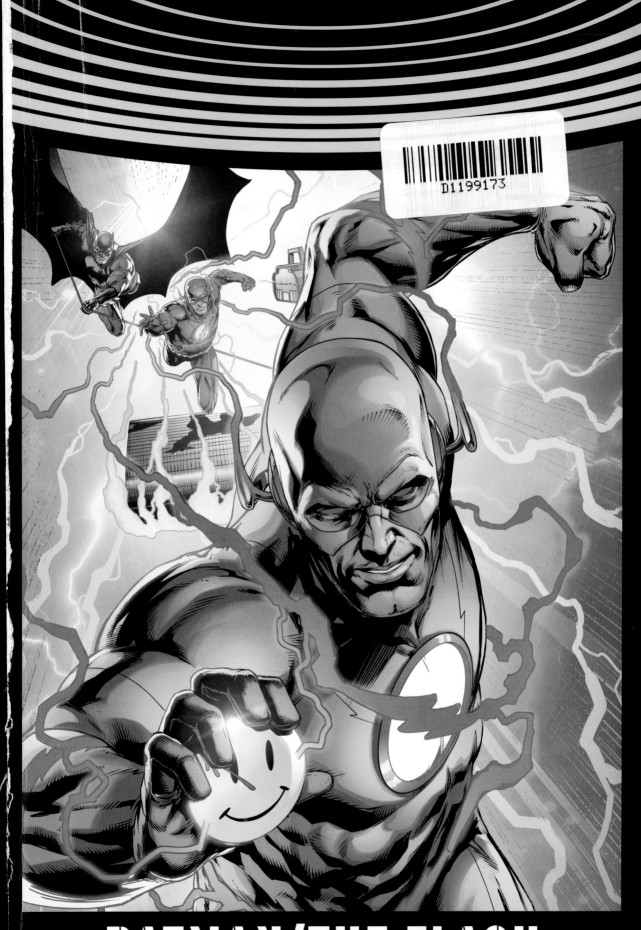

BATMAN/THE FLASH
THE BUTTON DELUXE EDITION

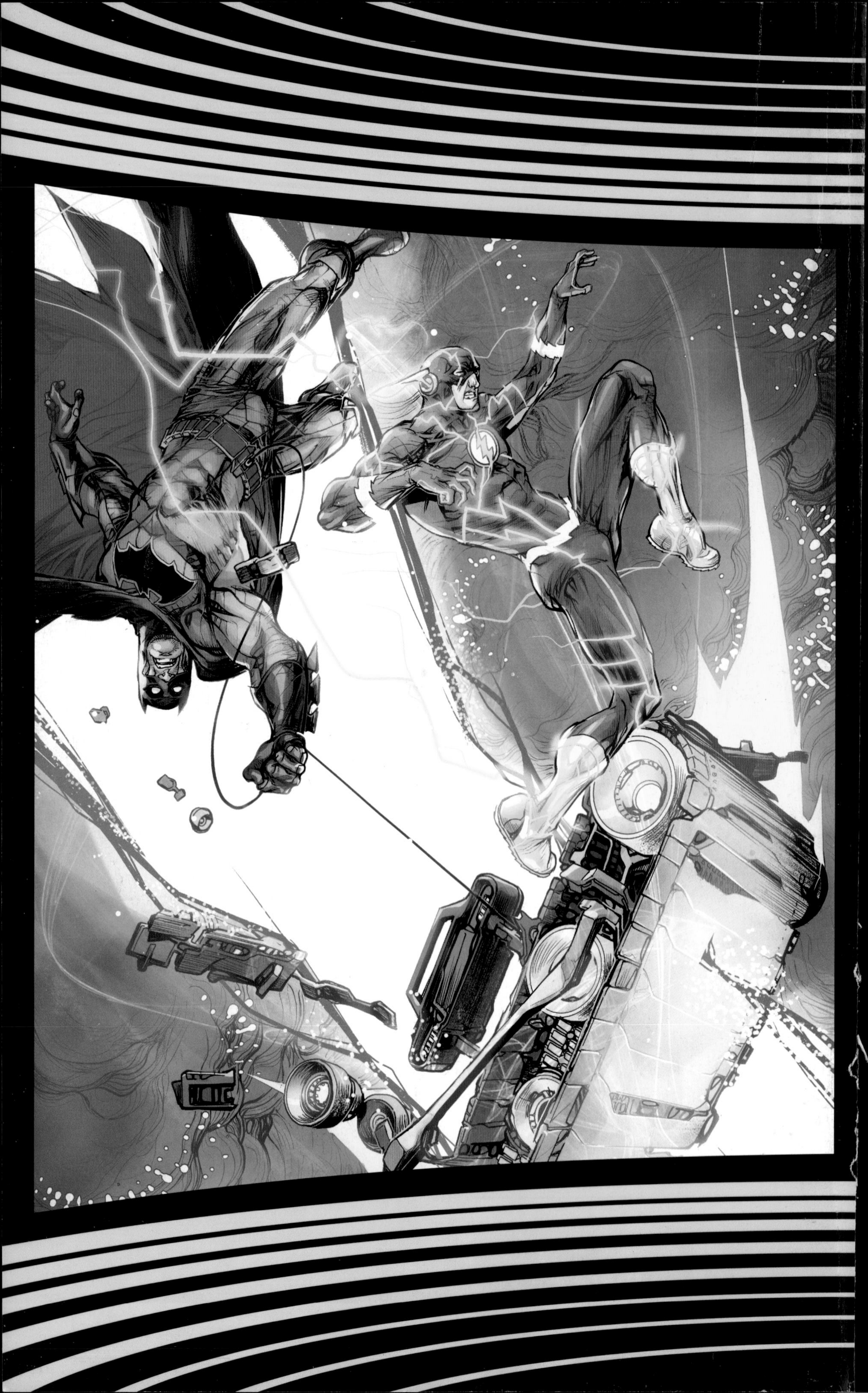

BATMAN/THE FLASH
THE BUTTON DELUXE EDITION

JOSHUA WILLIAMSON * **TOM KING**
writers

JASON FABOK * **HOWARD PORTER**
artists

BRAD ANDERSON * **HI-FI**
colorists

DERON BENNETT * **STEVE WANDS**
letterers

JASON FABOK and **BRAD ANDERSON**
collection cover artists

MIKEL JANÍN
international edition collection cover artist

BATMAN created by **BOB KANE** with **BILL FINGER**

Special thanks to **GEOFF JOHNS**

BRIAN CUNNINGHAM MARK DOYLE Editors - Original Series ✳ **REBECCA TAYLOR** Associate Editor - Original Series ✳ **AMEDEO TURTURRO** Assistant Editor - Original Series
JEB WOODARD Group Editor - Collected Editions ✳ **ROBIN WILDMAN** Editor - Collected Edition
STEVE COOK Design Director - Books ✳ **DAMIAN RYLAND** Publication Design

BOB HARRAS Senior VP - Editor-in-Chief, DC Comics

DIANE NELSON President ✳ **DAN DiDIO** Publisher ✳ **JIM LEE** Publisher ✳ **GEOFF JOHNS** President & Chief Creative Officer
AMIT DESAI Executive VP - Business & Marketing Strategy, Direct to Consumer & Global Franchise Management ✳ **SAM ADES** Senior VP - Direct to Consumer
BOBBIE CHASE VP - Talent Development ✳ **MARK CHIARELLO** Senior VP - Art, Design & Collected Editions
JOHN CUNNINGHAM Senior VP - Sales & Trade Marketing ✳ **ANNE DePIES** Senior VP - Business Strategy, Finance & Administration
DON FALLETTI VP - Manufacturing Operations ✳ **LAWRENCE GANEM** VP - Editorial Administration & Talent Relations
ALISON GILL Senior VP - Manufacturing & Operations ✳ **HANK KANALZ** Senior VP - Editorial Strategy & Administration
JAY KOGAN VP - Legal Affairs ✳ **THOMAS LOFTUS** VP - Business Affairs
JACK MAHAN VP - Business Affairs ✳ **NICK J. NAPOLITANO** VP - Manufacturing Administration
EDDIE SCANNELL VP - Consumer Marketing ✳ **COURTNEY SIMMONS** Senior VP - Publicity & Communications
JIM (SKI) SOKOLOWSKI VP - Comic Book Specialty Sales & Trade Marketing ✳ **NANCY SPEARS** VP - Mass, Book, Digital Sales & Trade Marketing

BATMAN/THE FLASH: THE BUTTON—DELUXE EDITION

Published by DC Comics. Compilation and all new material Copyright © 2017 DC Comics. All Rights Reserved. Originally published in single magazine form in BATMAN 21-22, THE FLASH 21-22. Copyright © 2017 DC Comics. All Rights Reserved. All characters, their distinctive likenesses and related elements featured in this publication are trademarks of DC Comics. The stories, characters and incidents featured in this publication are entirely fictional. DC Comics does not read or accept unsolicited submissions of ideas, stories or artwork.

DC Comics, 2900 West Alameda Ave., Burbank, CA 91505. Printed by Transcontinental Interglobe, Beauceville, QC, Canada. 9/8/17. First Printing.
ISBN: 978-1-4012-7644-7
International Edition ISBN: 978-1-4012-7679-9

Library of Congress Cataloging-in-Publication Data is available.

The Flash, a.k.a. Jay Garrick, created by Gardner Fox
Superman created by Jerry Siegel and Joe Shuster
By special arrangement with the Jerry Siegel family

PEFC Certified
Printed on paper from
sustainably managed
forests and controlled
sources
PEFC/01-31-106   www.pefc.org

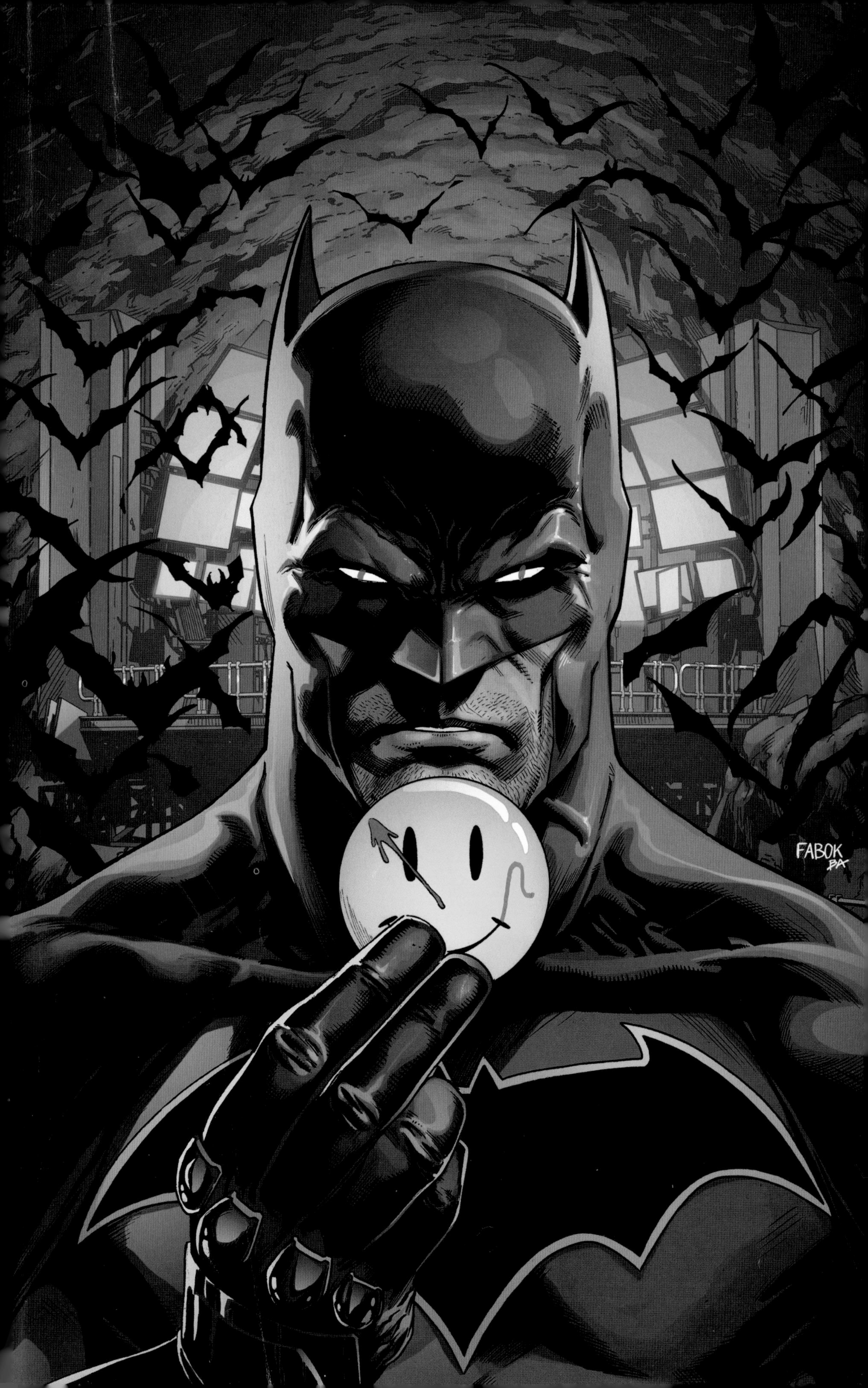
FABOK
BA

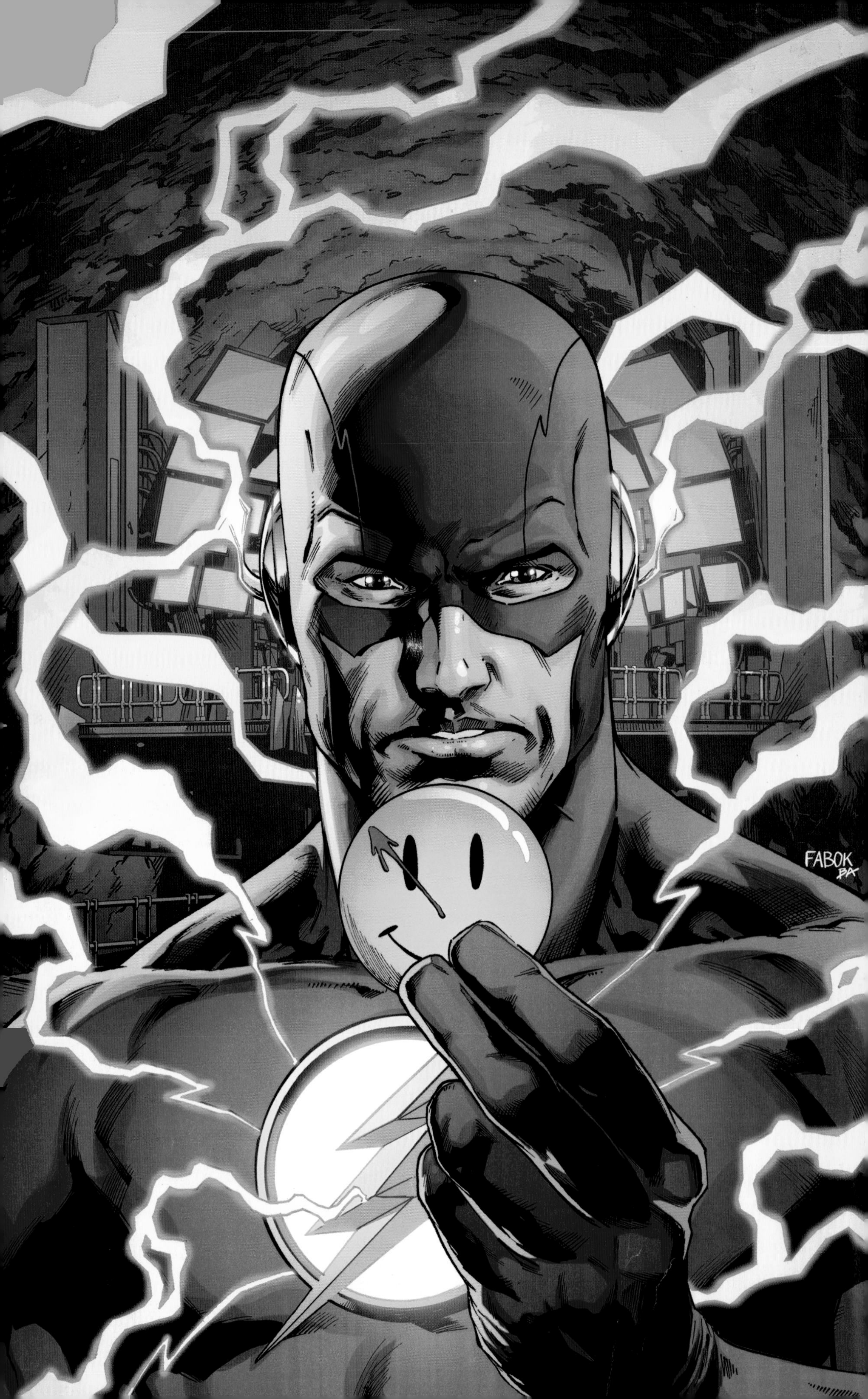
FABOK
BA

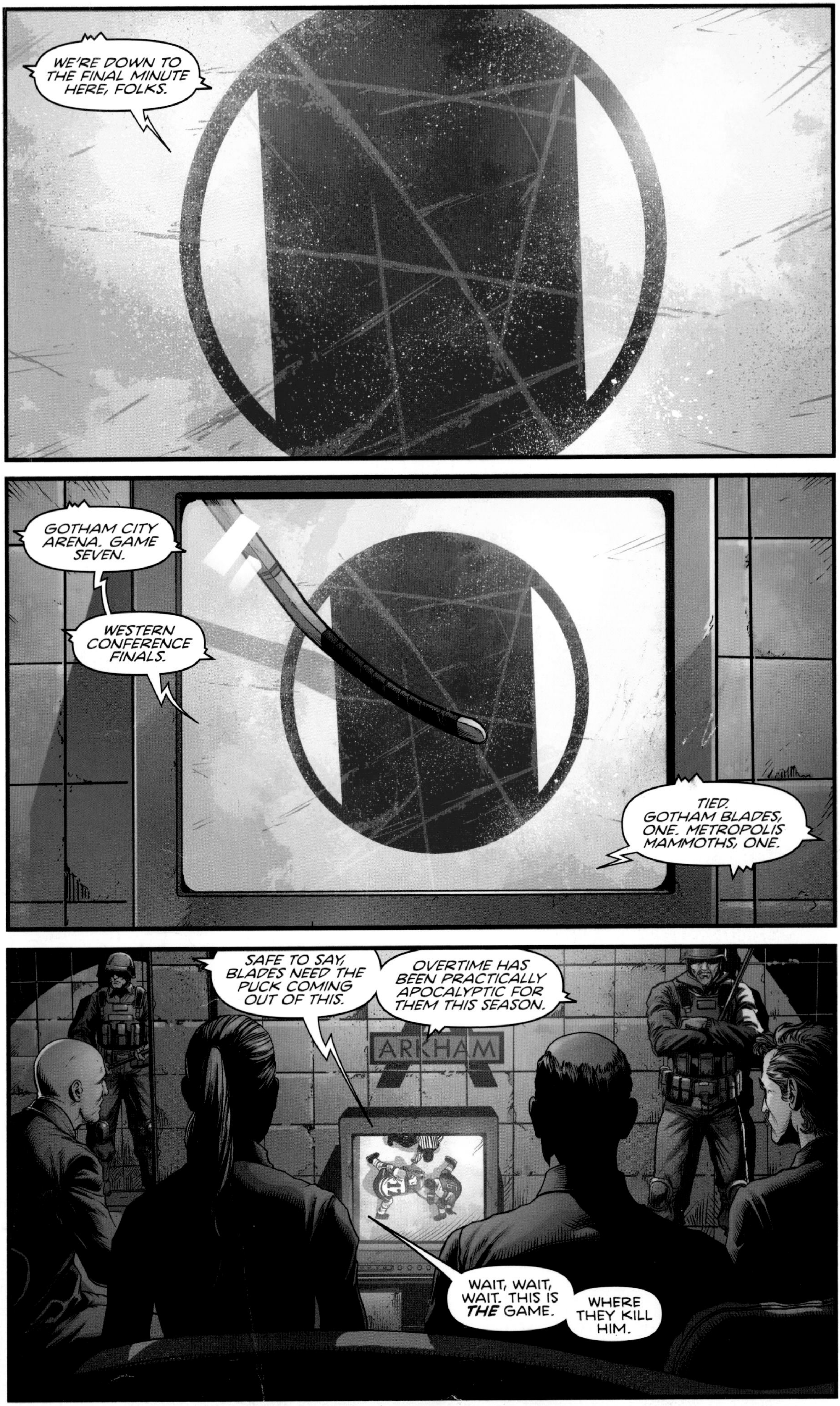
WE'RE DOWN TO THE FINAL MINUTE HERE, FOLKS.
GOTHAM CITY ARENA. GAME SEVEN.
WESTERN CONFERENCE FINALS.
TIED. GOTHAM BLADES, ONE. METROPOLIS MAMMOTHS, ONE.
SAFE TO SAY, BLADES NEED THE PUCK COMING OUT OF THIS.
OVERTIME HAS BEEN PRACTICALLY APOCALYPTIC FOR THEM THIS SEASON.
ARKHAM
WAIT, WAIT, WAIT. THIS IS *THE* GAME.
WHERE THEY KILL HIM.

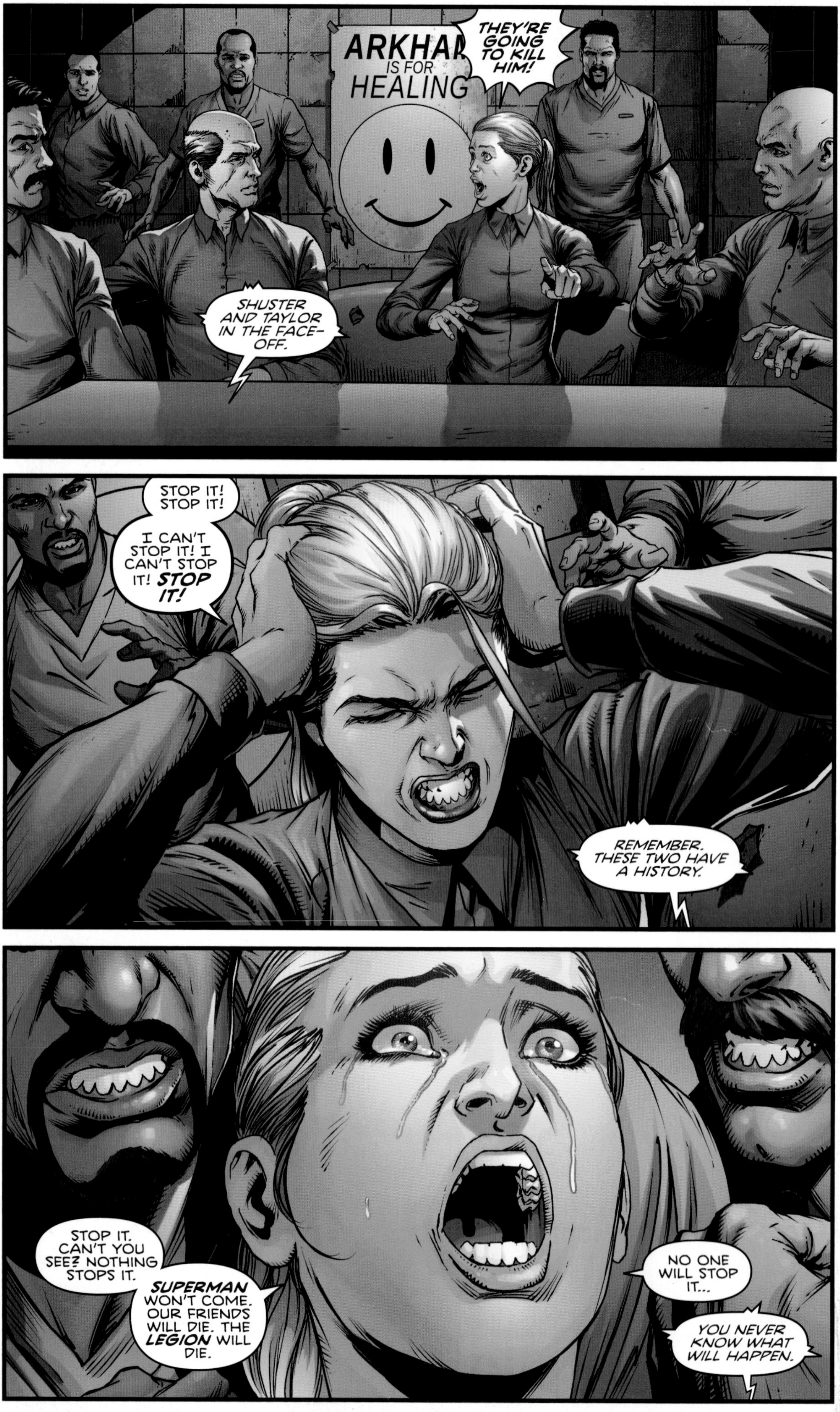
ARKHAM IS FOR HEALING
THEY'RE GOING TO KILL HIM!
SHUSTER AND TAYLOR IN THE FACE-OFF.
STOP IT! STOP IT!
I CAN'T STOP IT! I CAN'T STOP IT! STOP IT!
REMEMBER. THESE TWO HAVE A HISTORY.
STOP IT. CAN'T YOU SEE? NOTHING STOPS IT.
SUPERMAN WON'T COME. OUR FRIENDS WILL DIE. THE LEGION WILL DIE.
NO ONE WILL STOP IT...
YOU NEVER KNOW WHAT WILL HAPPEN.

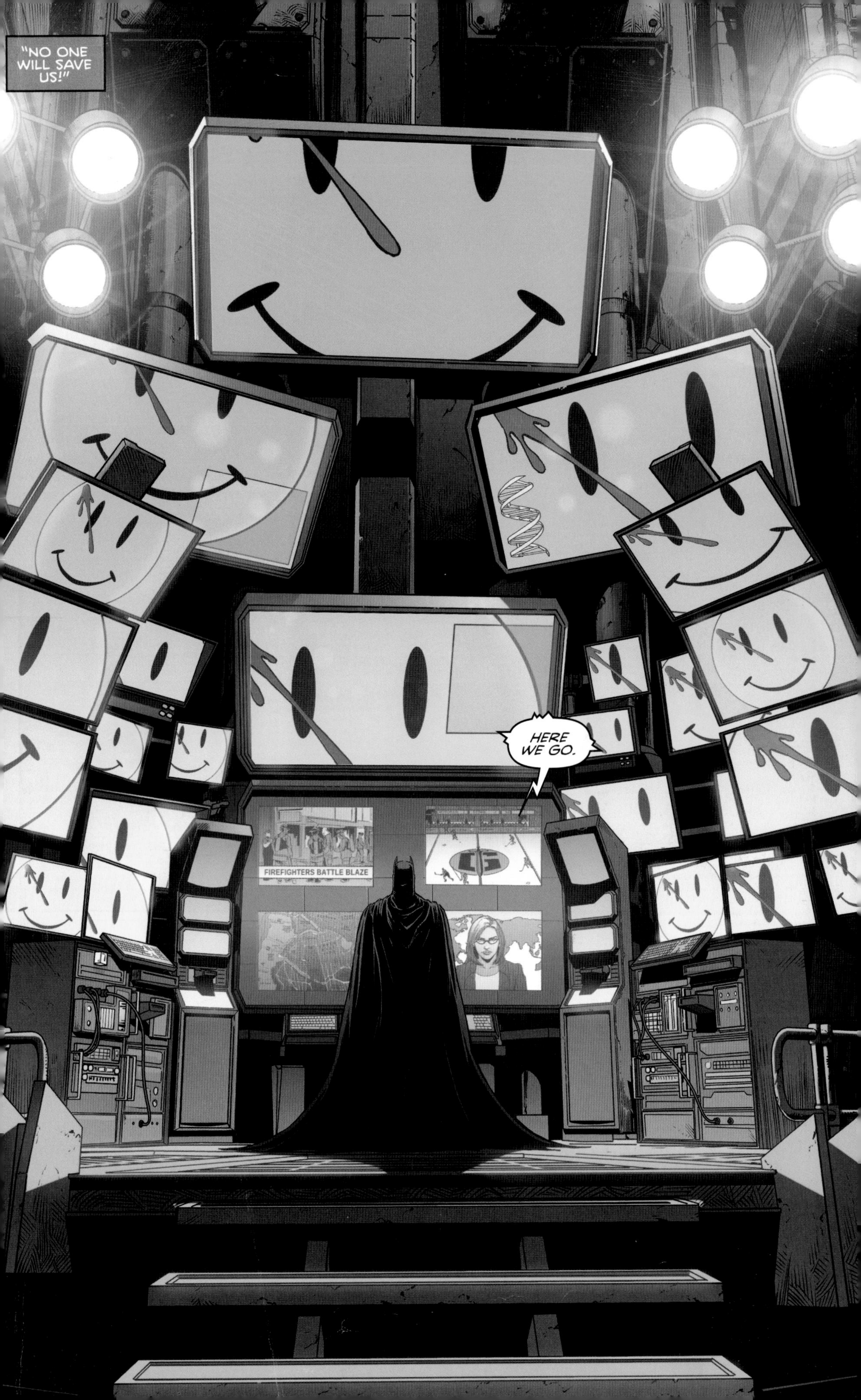
"NO ONE WILL SAVE US!"
FIREFIGHTERS BATTLE BLAZE
HERE WE GO.

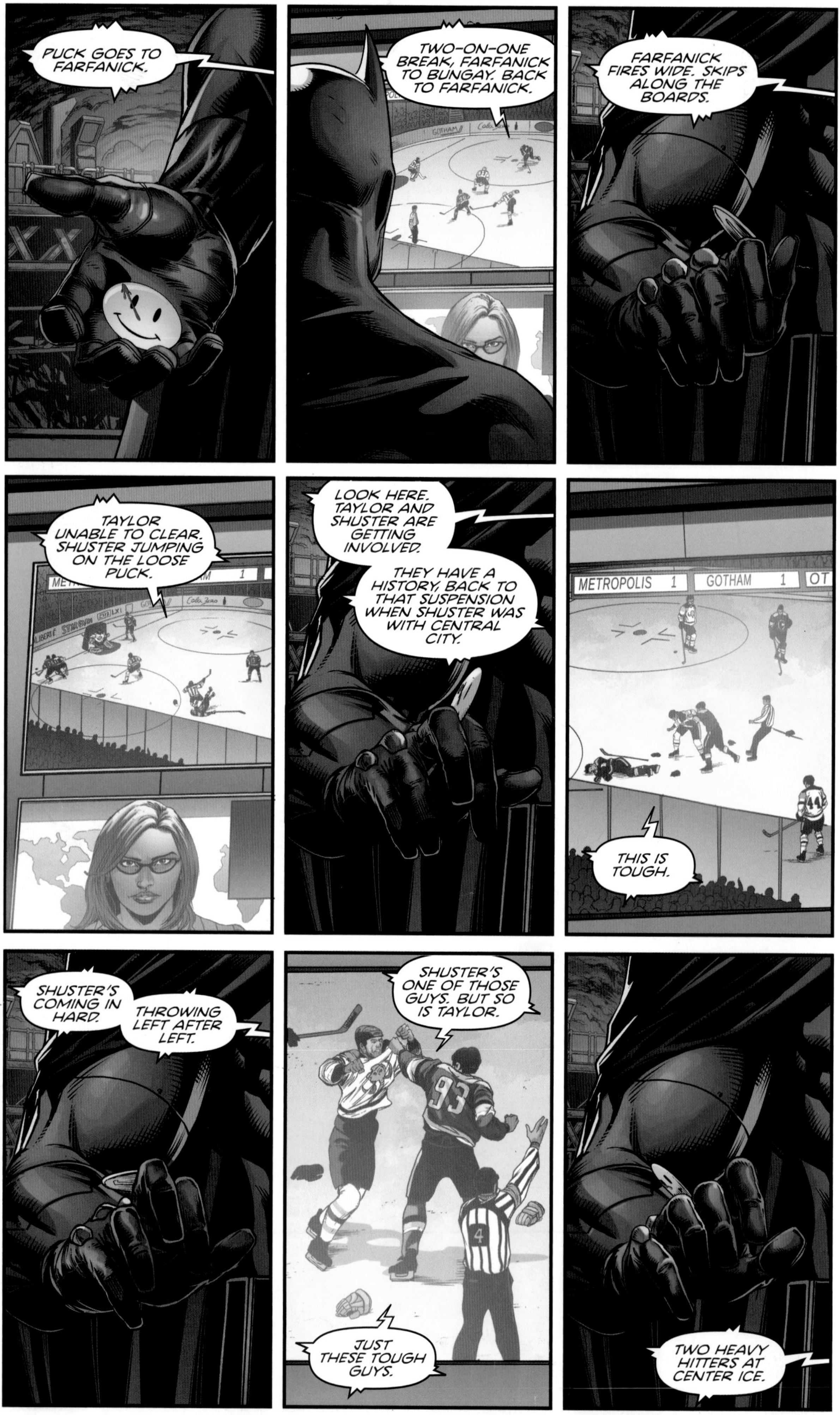
PUCK GOES TO FARFANICK.
TWO-ON-ONE BREAK, FARFANICK TO BUNGAY. BACK TO FARFANICK.
GOTHAM
FARFANICK FIRES WIDE. SKIPS ALONG THE BOARDS.
TAYLOR UNABLE TO CLEAR. SHUSTER JUMPING ON THE LOOSE PUCK.
LOOK HERE. TAYLOR AND SHUSTER ARE GETTING INVOLVED.
THEY HAVE A HISTORY, BACK TO THAT SUSPENSION WHEN SHUSTER WAS WITH CENTRAL CITY.
METROPOLIS 1
GOTHAM 1
OT
THIS IS TOUGH.
SHUSTER'S COMING IN HARD.
THROWING LEFT AFTER LEFT.
SHUSTER'S ONE OF THOSE GUYS. BUT SO IS TAYLOR.
93
JUST THESE TOUGH GUYS.
TWO HEAVY HITTERS AT CENTER ICE.

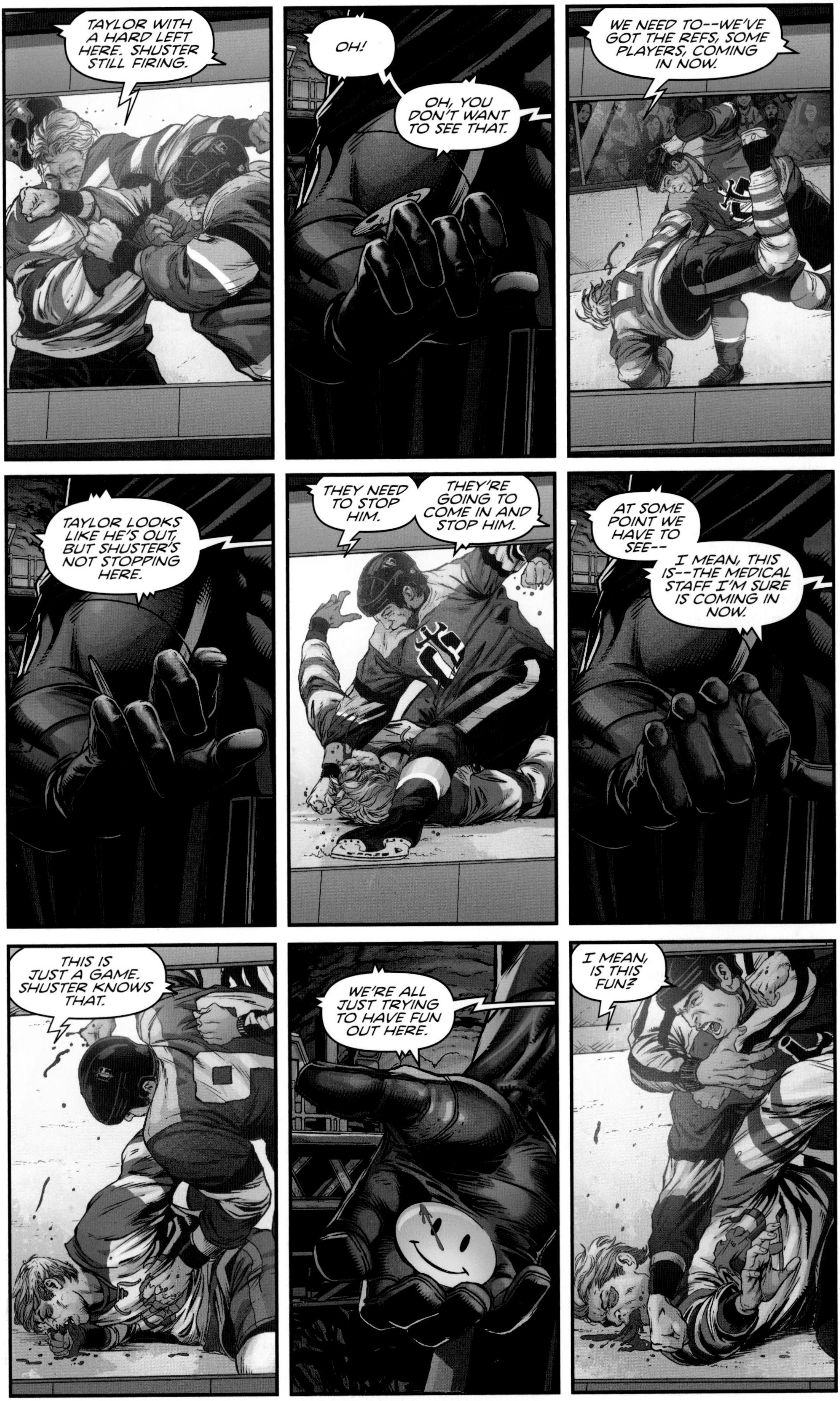
TAYLOR WITH A HARD LEFT HERE. SHUSTER STILL FIRING.
OH!
OH, YOU DON'T WANT TO SEE THAT.
WE NEED TO--WE'VE GOT THE REFS, SOME PLAYERS, COMING IN NOW.
TAYLOR LOOKS LIKE HE'S OUT, BUT SHUSTER'S NOT STOPPING HERE.
THEY NEED TO STOP HIM.
THEY'RE GOING TO COME IN AND STOP HIM.
AT SOME POINT WE HAVE TO SEE--
I MEAN, THIS IS--THE MEDICAL STAFF I'M SURE IS COMING IN NOW.
THIS IS JUST A GAME. SHUSTER KNOWS THAT.
WE'RE ALL JUST TRYING TO HAVE FUN OUT HERE.
I MEAN, IS THIS FUN?

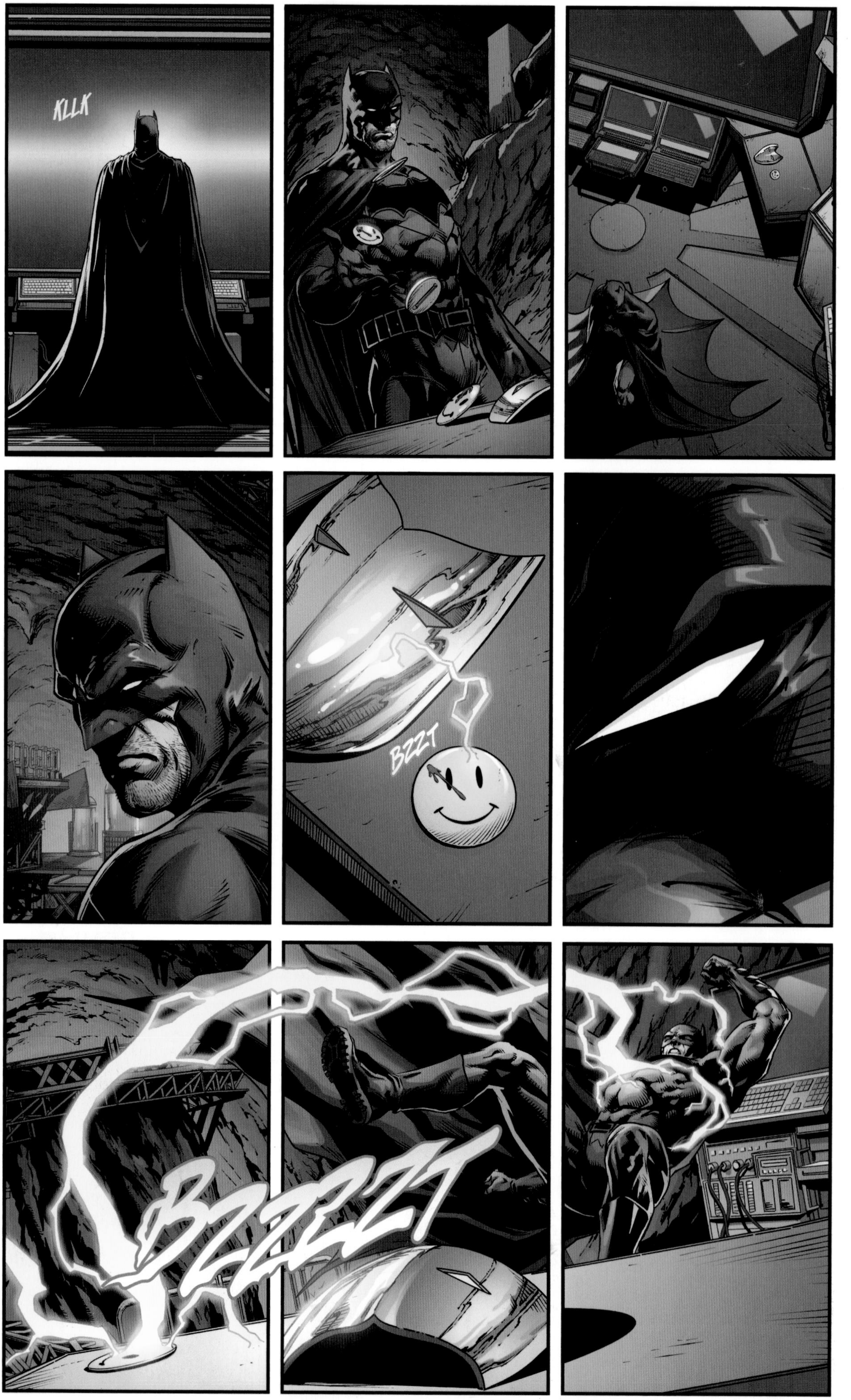
KLLK
BZZT
BZZZT

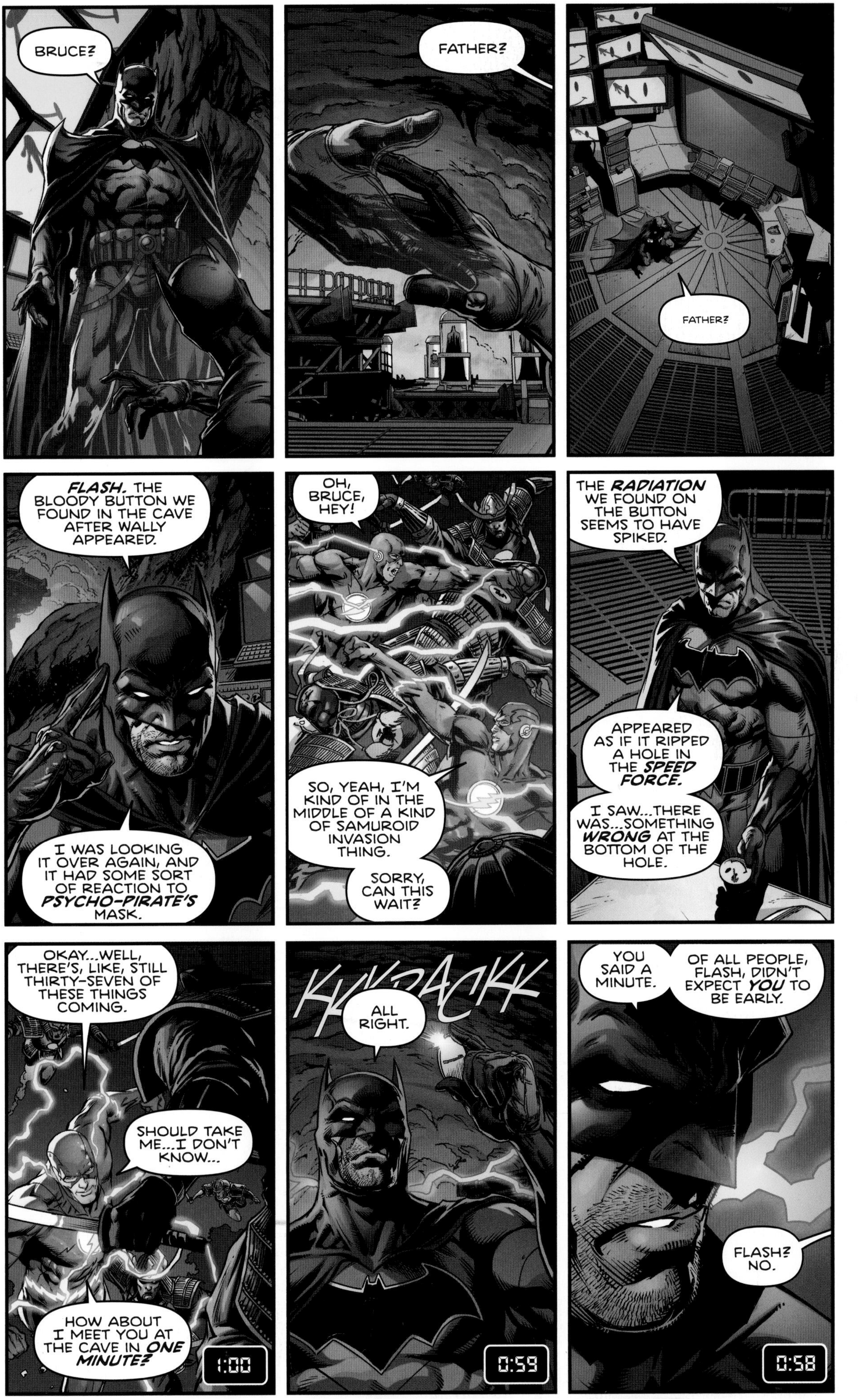
BRUCE?
FATHER?
FATHER?
FLASH. THE BLOODY BUTTON WE FOUND IN THE CAVE AFTER WALLY APPEARED.
I WAS LOOKING IT OVER AGAIN, AND IT HAD SOME SORT OF REACTION TO PSYCHO-PIRATE'S MASK.
OH, BRUCE, HEY!
SO, YEAH, I'M KIND OF IN THE MIDDLE OF A KIND OF SAMUROID INVASION THING.
SORRY, CAN THIS WAIT?
THE RADIATION WE FOUND ON THE BUTTON SEEMS TO HAVE SPIKED.
APPEARED AS IF IT RIPPED A HOLE IN THE SPEED FORCE.
I SAW...THERE WAS...SOMETHING WRONG AT THE BOTTOM OF THE HOLE.
OKAY...WELL, THERE'S, LIKE, STILL THIRTY-SEVEN OF THESE THINGS COMING.
SHOULD TAKE ME...I DON'T KNOW...
HOW ABOUT I MEET YOU AT THE CAVE IN ONE MINUTE?
1:00
KKKRACKK
ALL RIGHT.
0:59
YOU SAID A MINUTE.
OF ALL PEOPLE, FLASH, DIDN'T EXPECT YOU TO BE EARLY.
FLASH? NO.
0:58

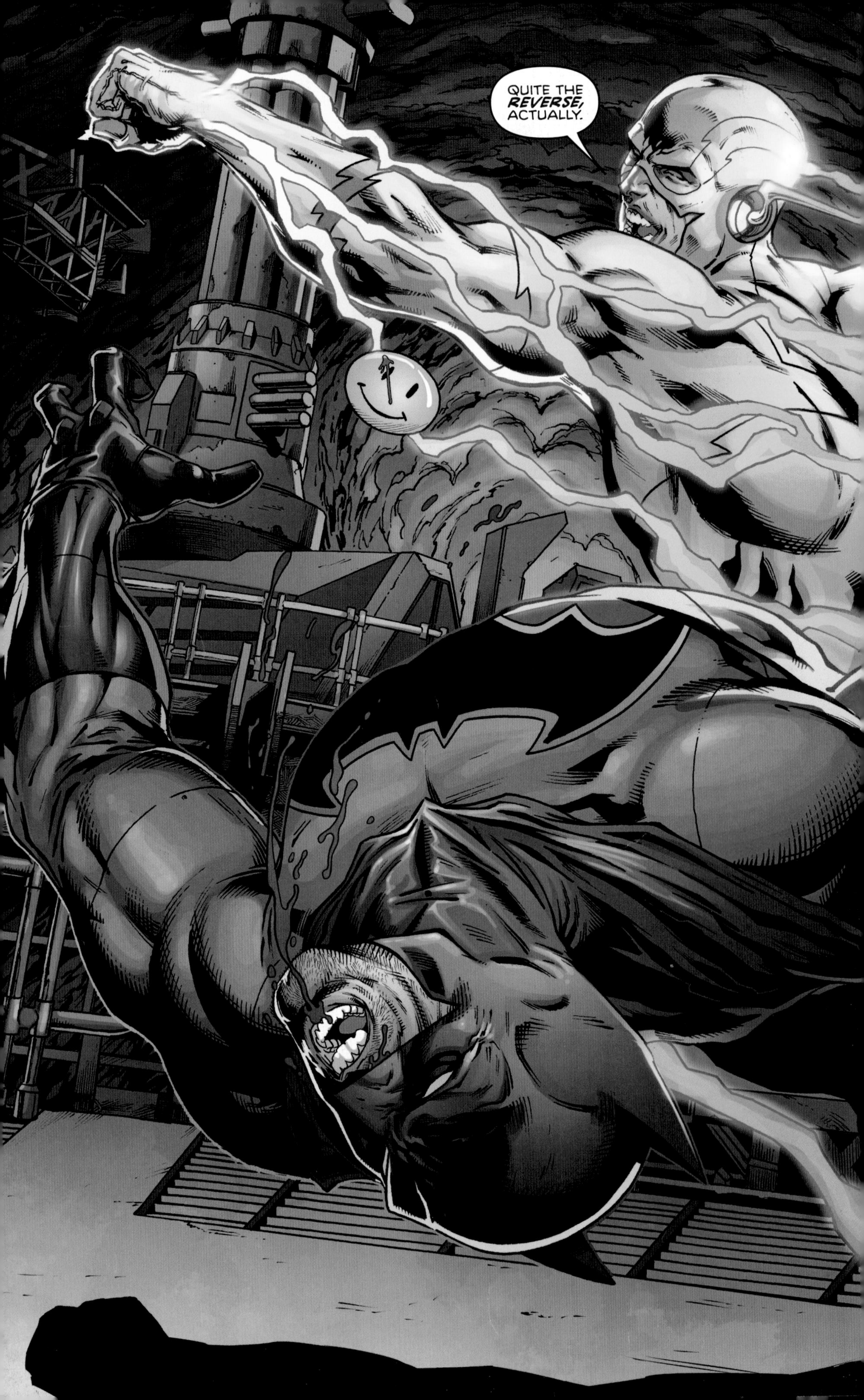
QUITE THE *REVERSE,* ACTUALLY.

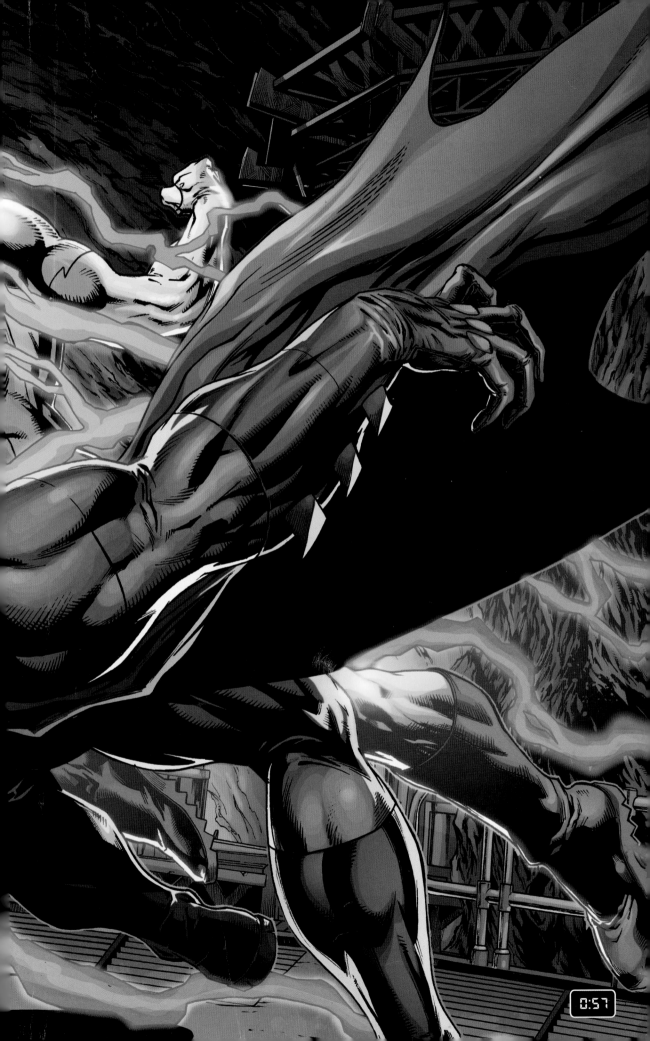

0:57

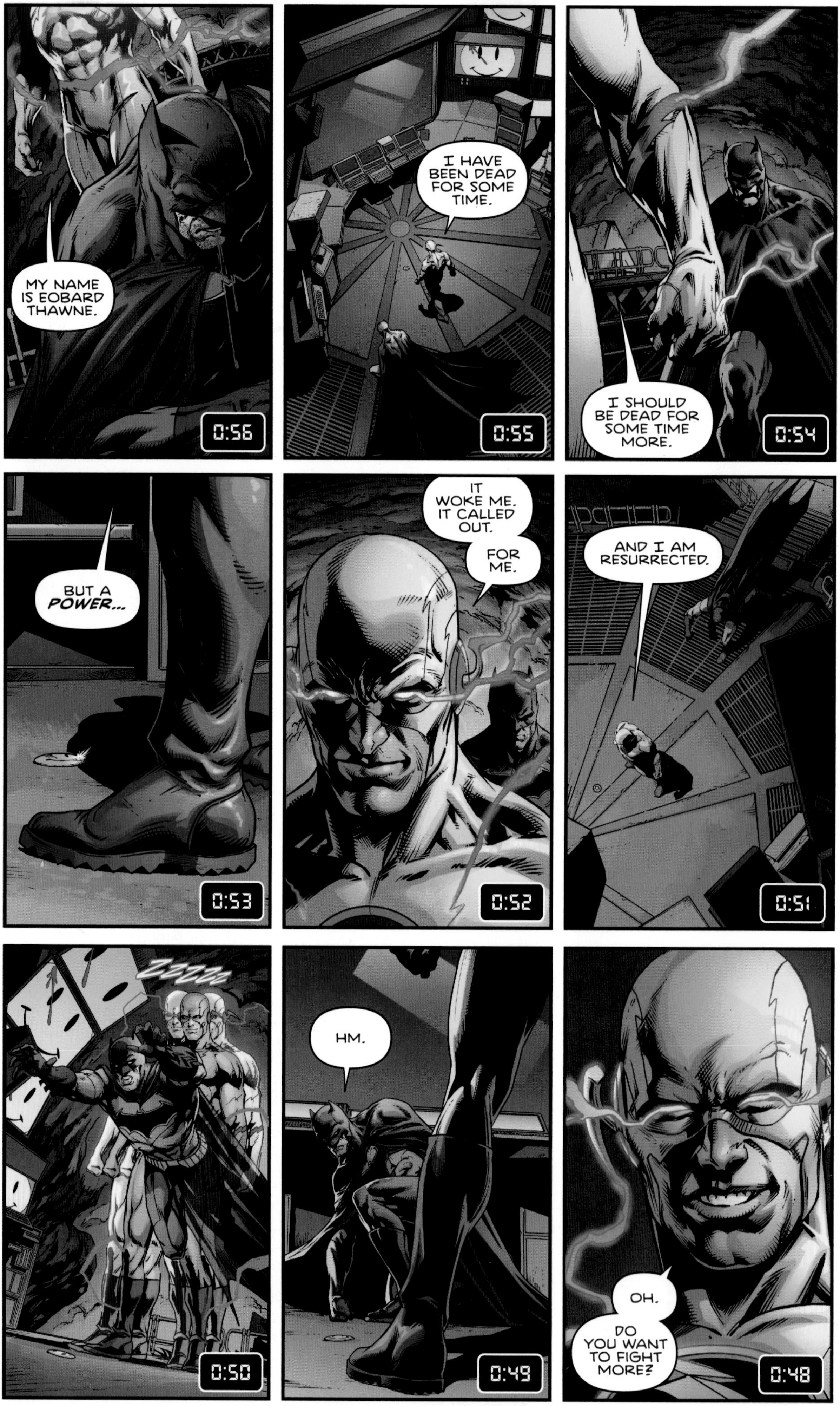
MY NAME IS EOBARD THAWNE.
0:56
I HAVE BEEN DEAD FOR SOME TIME.
0:55
I SHOULD BE DEAD FOR SOME TIME MORE.
0:54
BUT A *POWER...*
0:53
IT WOKE ME. IT CALLED OUT.
FOR ME.
0:52
AND I AM RESURRECTED.
0:51
ZZZZZ
0:50
HM.
0:49
OH.
DO YOU WANT TO FIGHT MORE?
0:48

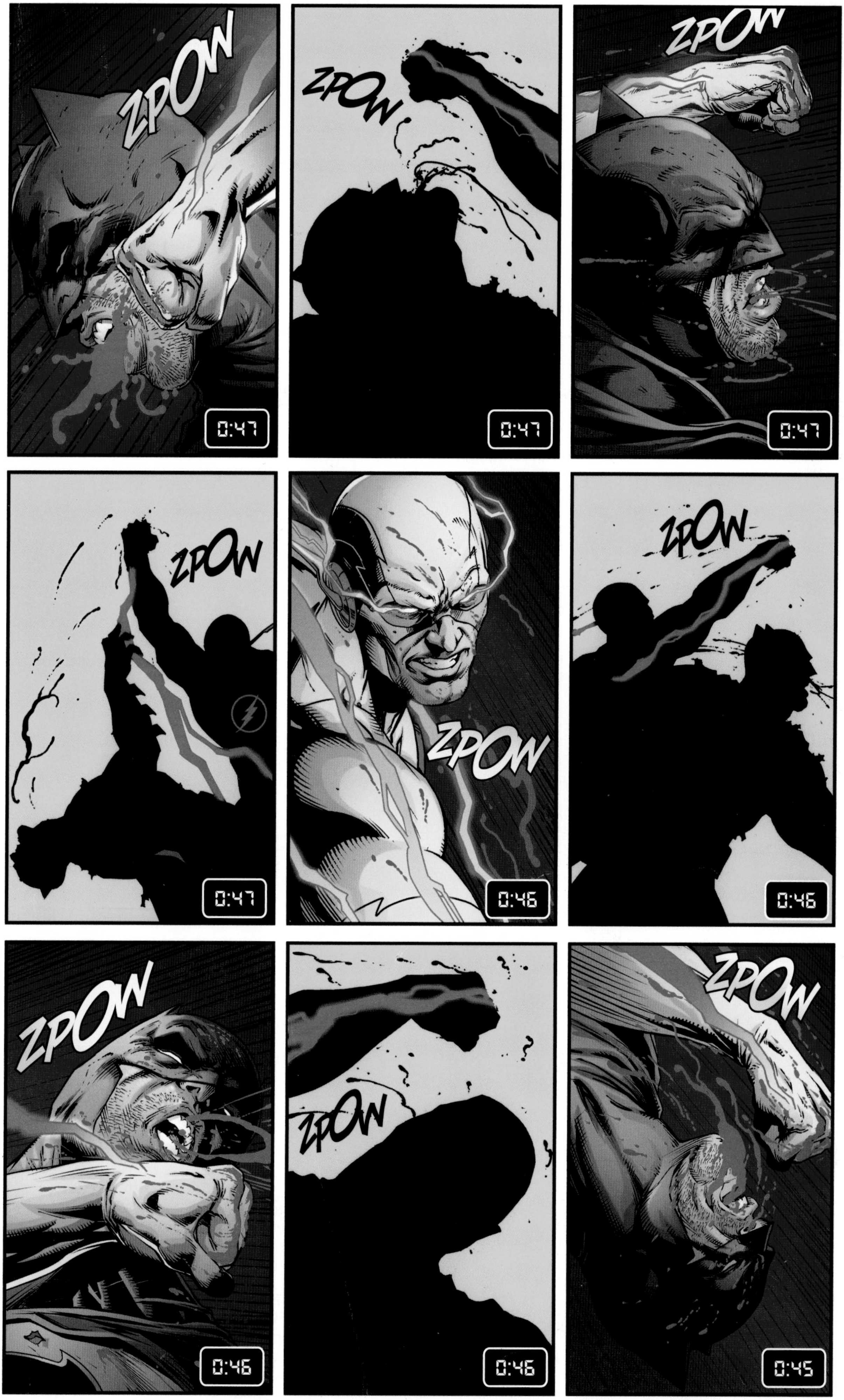
ZPOW
0:47
ZPOW
0:47
ZPOW
0:47
ZPOW
0:47
ZPOW
0:46
ZPOW
0:46
ZPOW
0:46
ZPOW
0:46
ZPOW
0:45

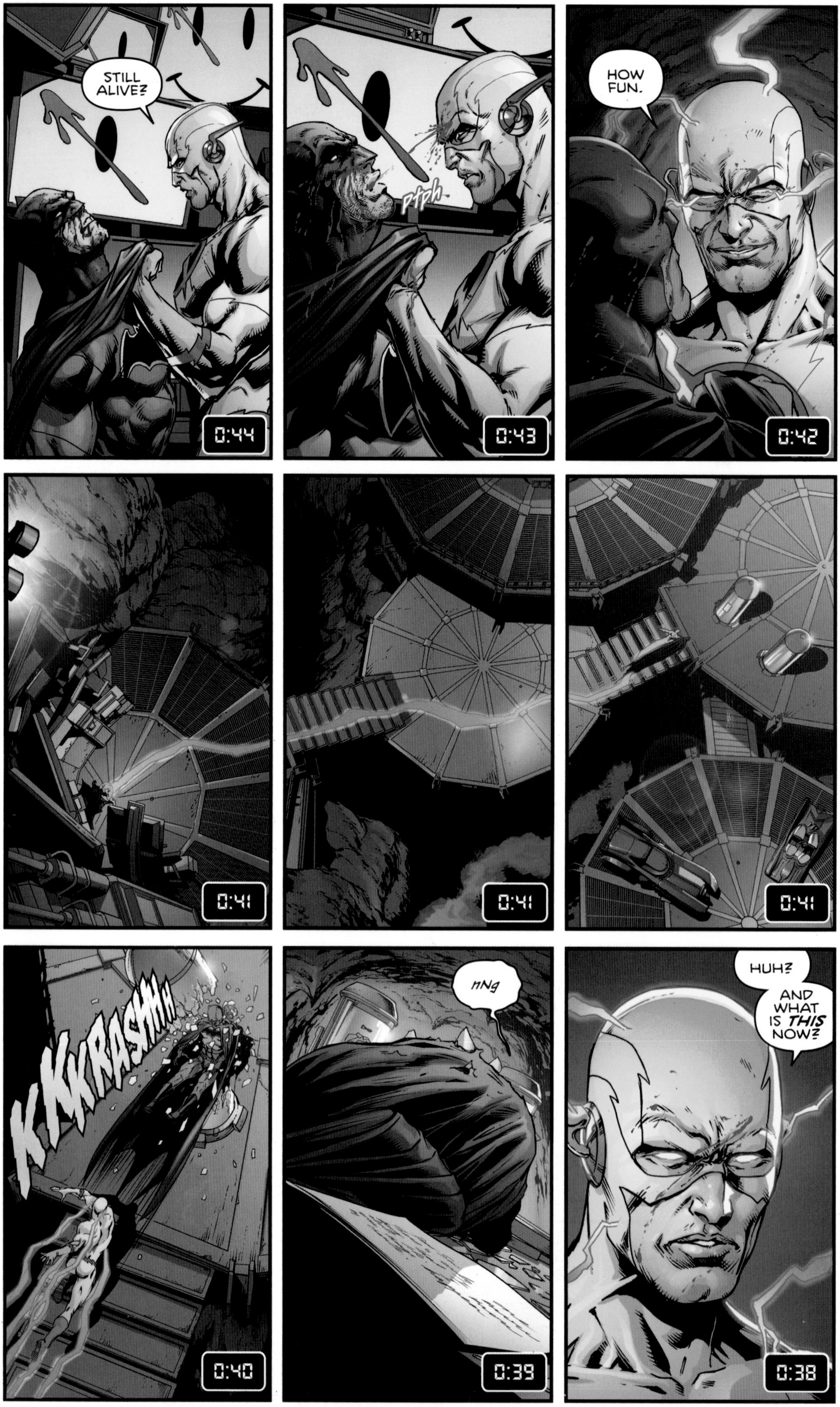
STILL ALIVE?
0:44
ptph
0:43
HOW FUN.
0:42
0:41
0:41
0:41
KKKRASHHH
0:40
nng
0:39
HUH?
AND WHAT IS THIS NOW?
0:38

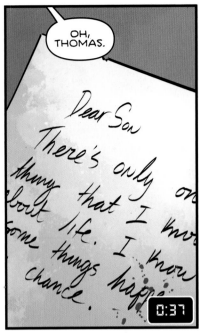

OH, THOMAS.

Dear Son
There's only on
thing that I kno
about life. I know
some things happ
chance.

0:37

IS THIS WHAT YOU DID AFTER YOU KILLED ME?

BEFORE YOU *DIED* WITH YOUR WORLD?

0:36

A MESSAGE SENT ACROSS TIME.

A LETTER TO YOUR DEAD SON.

0:35

"I'M NOT THE HERO OF THIS STORY."

0:34

WAS IT CONSOLING, THOMAS, KNOWING HE WOULD HAVE IT?

THAT THOUGH HE LOST YOU, HE COULD ALWAYS SEE YOU LOVED HIM.

0:33

DID THAT MAKE YOU FEEL BETTER, THOMAS?

AS YOU BURNED?

0:32

I BET IT MADE YOU FEEL JUST *FANTASTIC.*

0:31

NO!

0:30

OH YES.

0:29

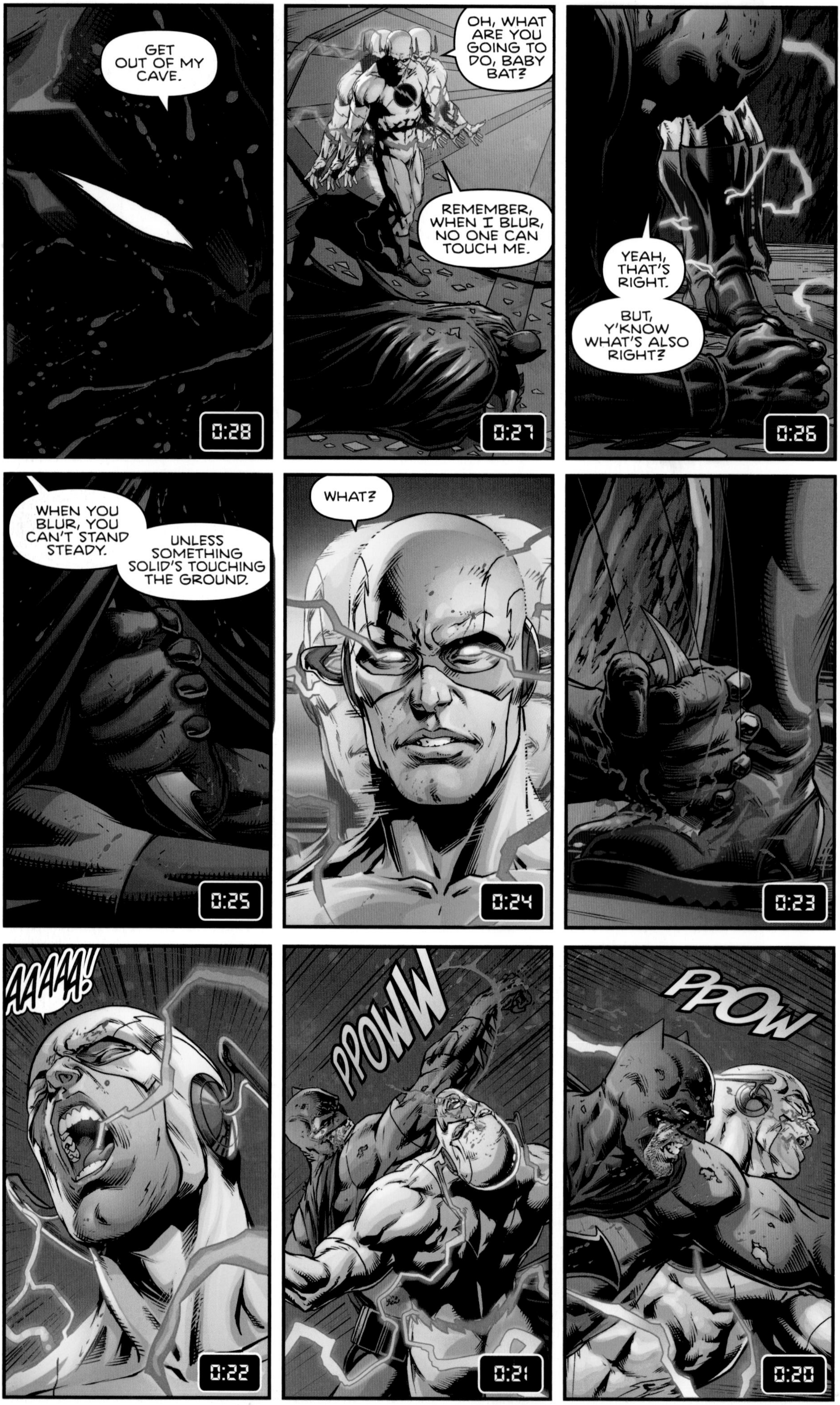
GET OUT OF MY CAVE.
0:28
OH, WHAT ARE YOU GOING TO DO, BABY BAT?
REMEMBER, WHEN I BLUR, NO ONE CAN TOUCH ME.
0:27
YEAH, THAT'S RIGHT.
BUT, Y'KNOW WHAT'S ALSO RIGHT?
0:26
WHEN YOU BLUR, YOU CAN'T STAND STEADY.
UNLESS SOMETHING SOLID'S TOUCHING THE GROUND.
0:25
WHAT?
0:24
0:23
AAAAA!
0:22
PPOWW
0:21
PPOW
0:20

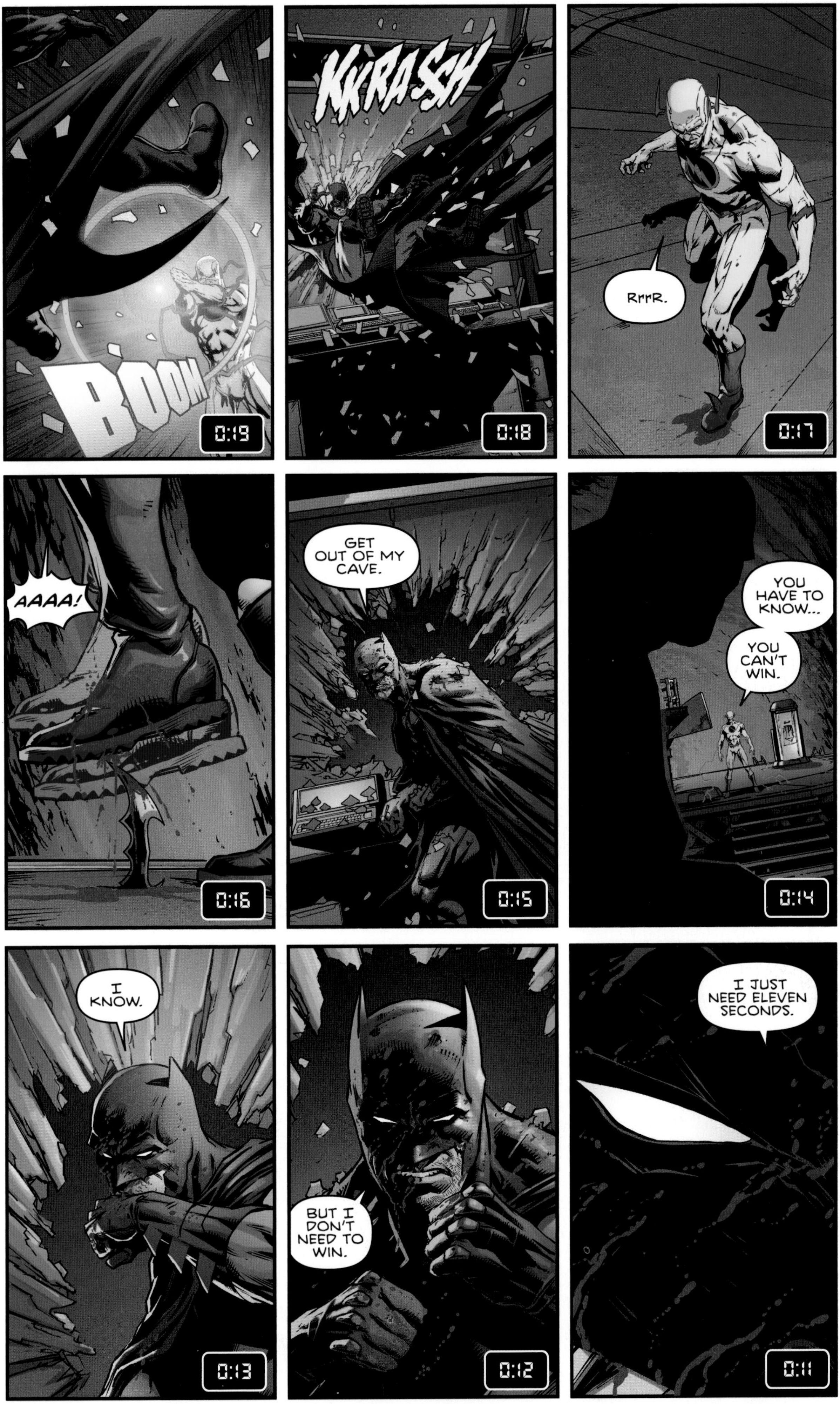

BOOM
0:19
KKRASSH
0:18
RrrR.
0:17
AAAA!
0:16
GET OUT OF MY CAVE.
0:15
YOU HAVE TO KNOW...
YOU CAN'T WIN.
0:14
I KNOW.
0:13
BUT I DON'T NEED TO WIN.
0:12
I JUST NEED ELEVEN SECONDS.
0:11

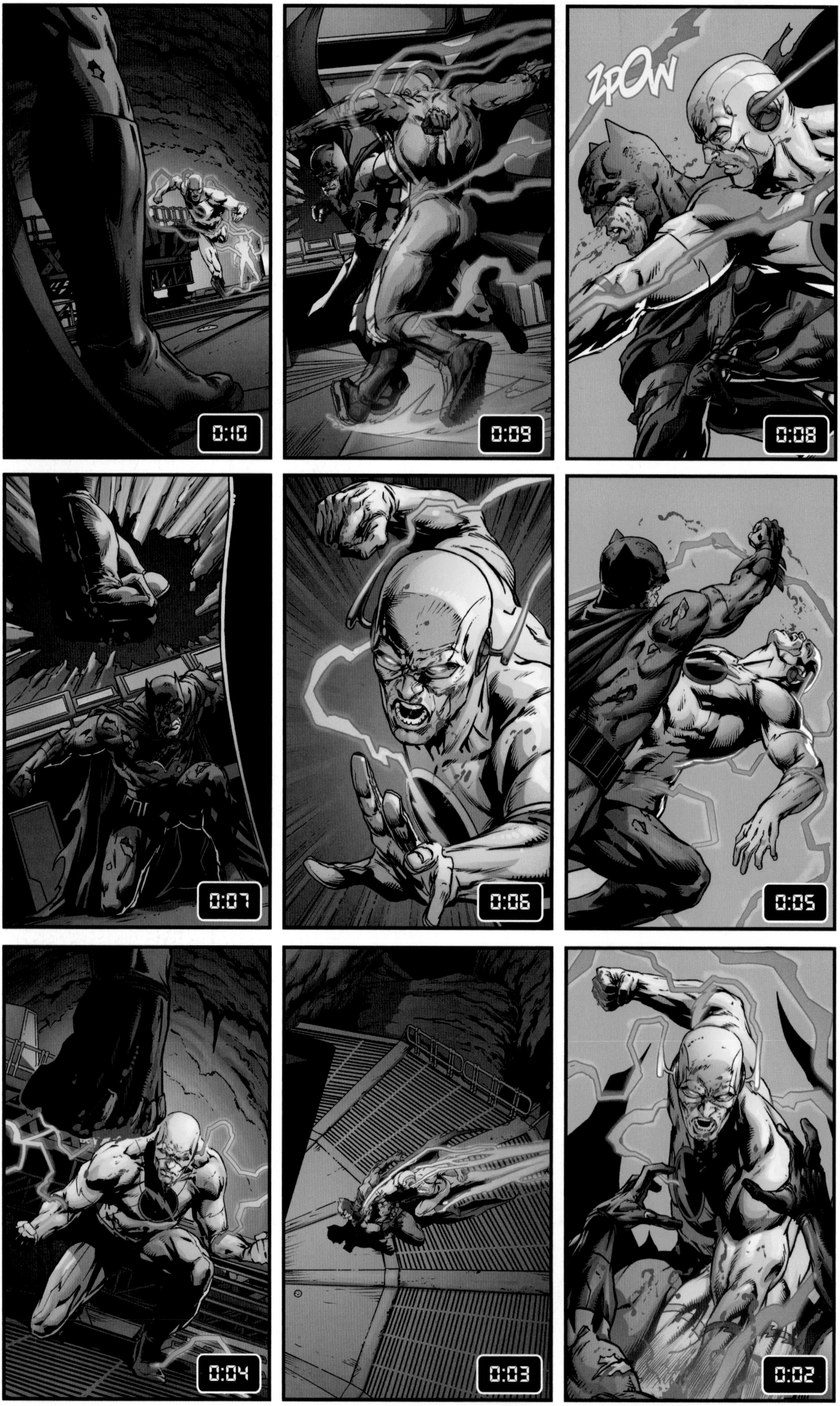
0:10
0:09
ZPOW
0:08
0:07
0:06
0:05
0:04
0:03
0:02

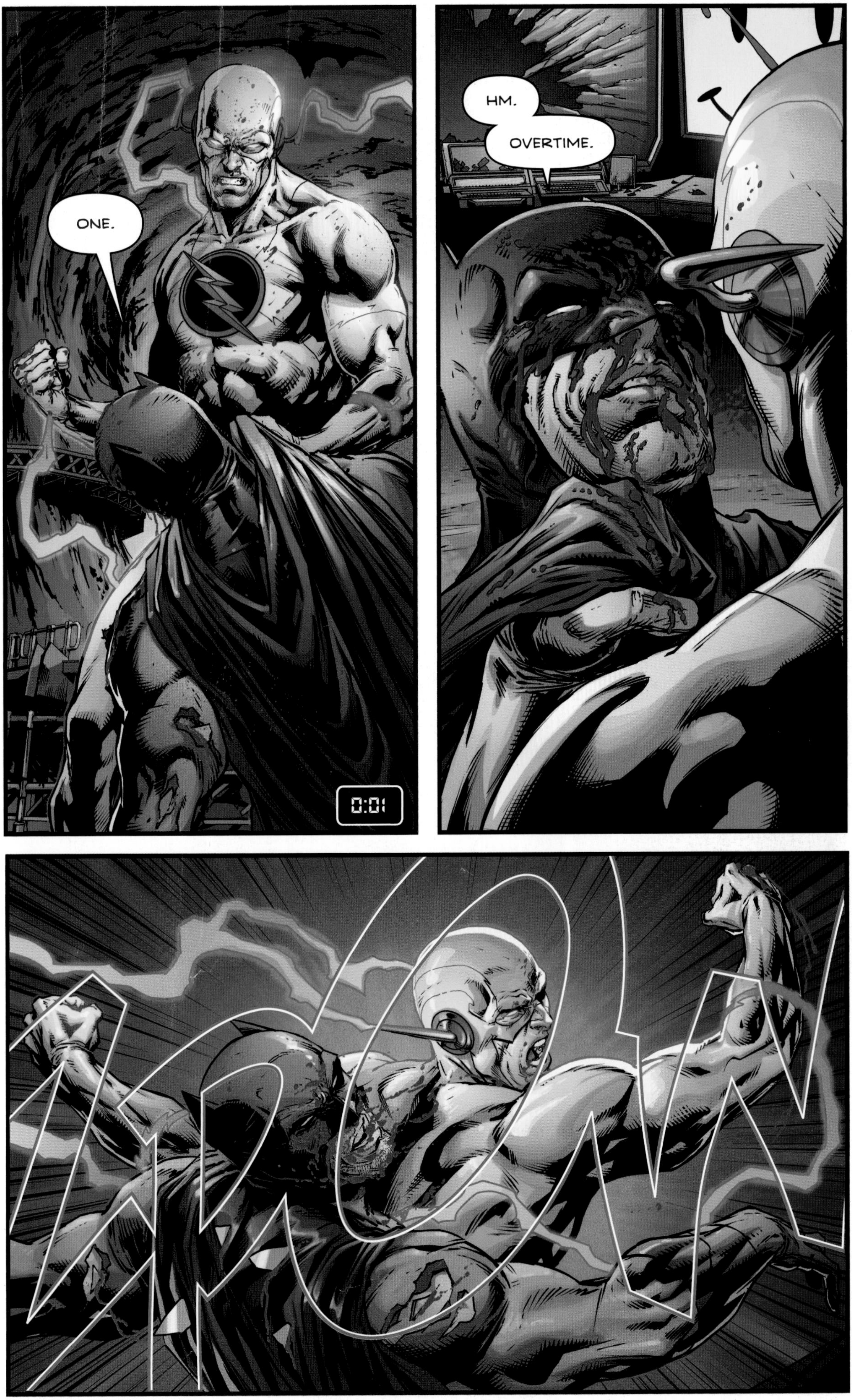
ONE.
0:01
HM.
OVERTIME.

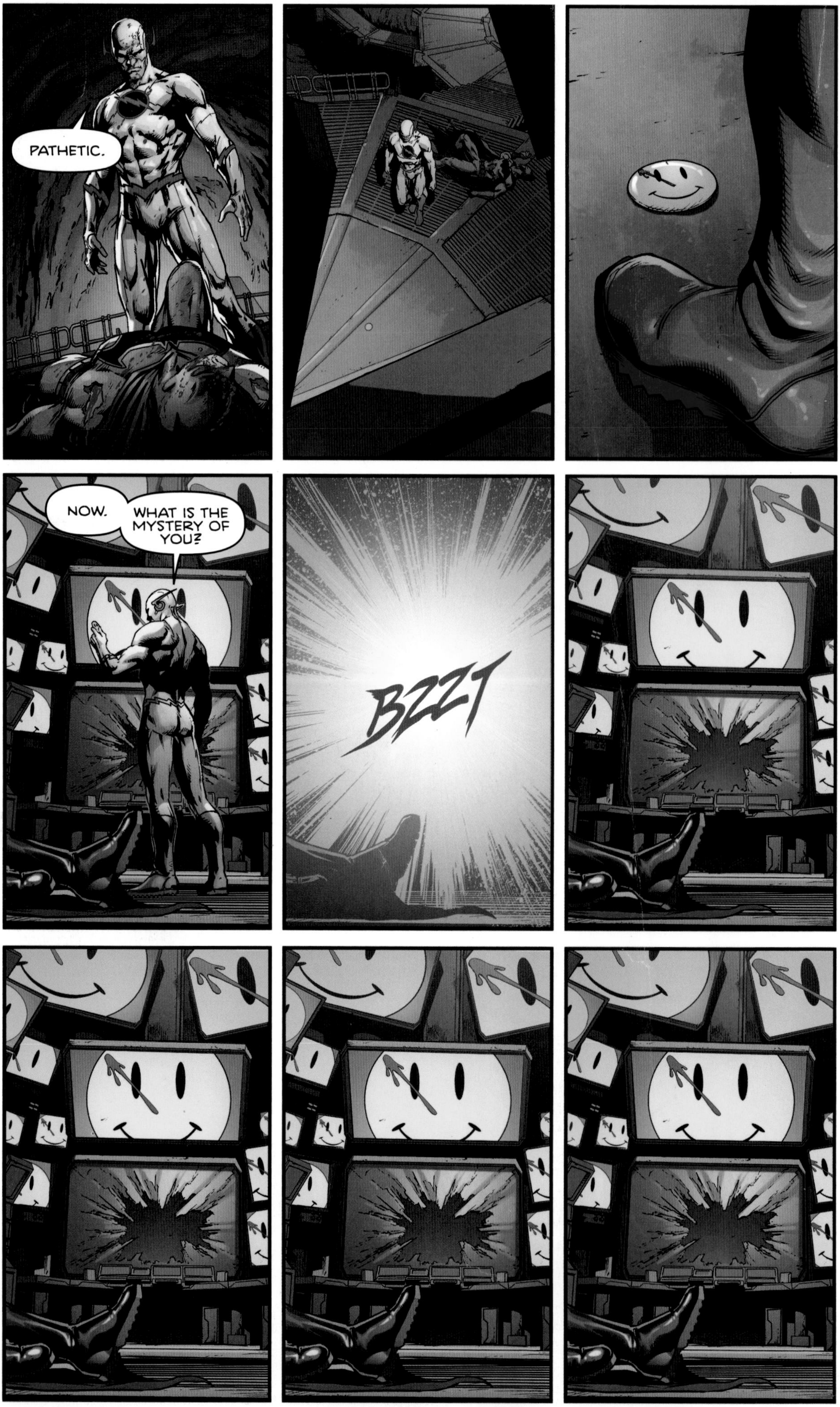
PATHETIC.
NOW.
WHAT IS THE MYSTERY OF YOU?
BZZT

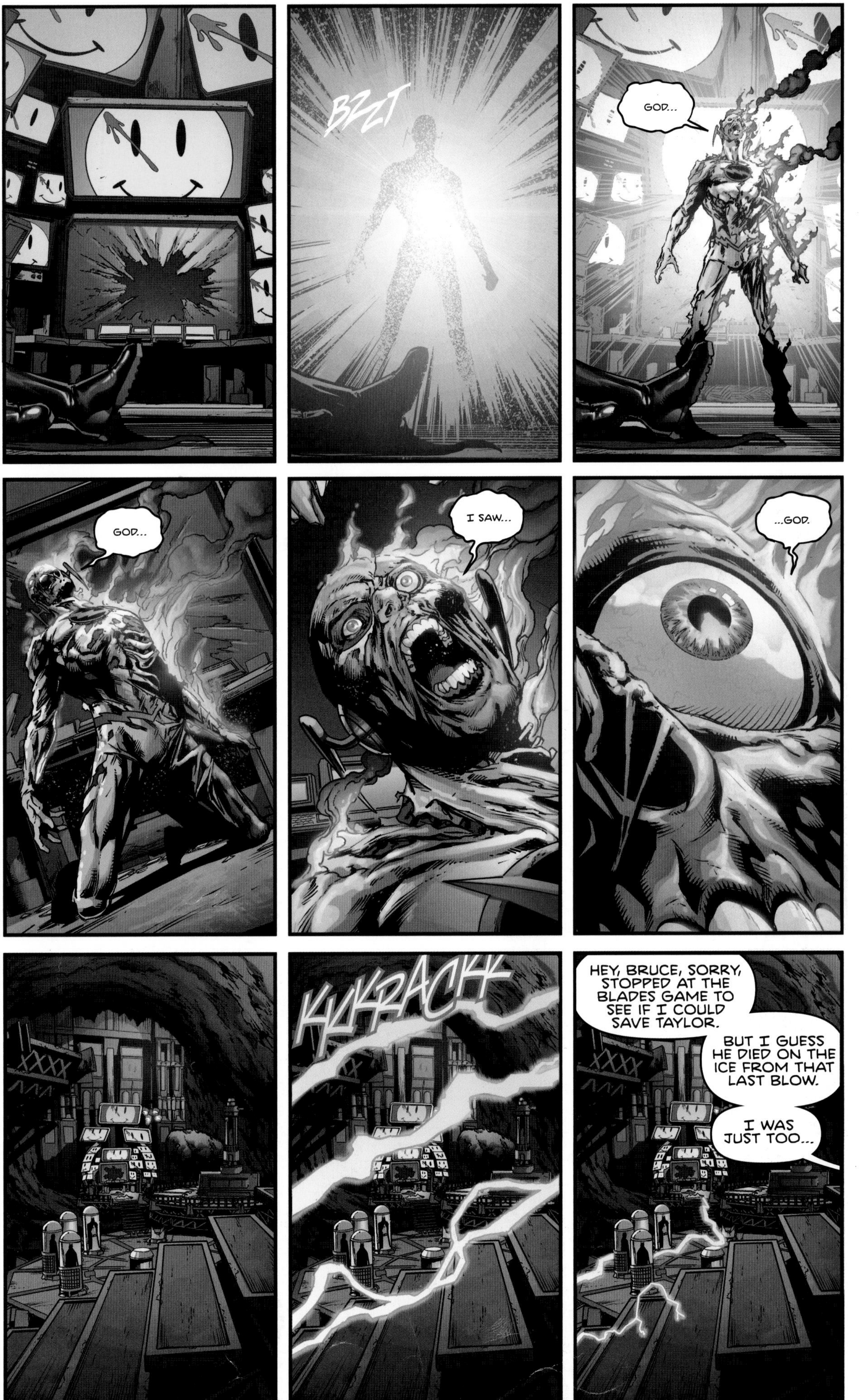
BZZT
GOD...
GOD...
I SAW...
...GOD.
KKKRACKK
HEY, BRUCE, SORRY, STOPPED AT THE BLADES GAME TO SEE IF I COULD SAVE TAYLOR.
BUT I GUESS HE DIED ON THE ICE FROM THAT LAST BLOW.
I WAS JUST TOO...

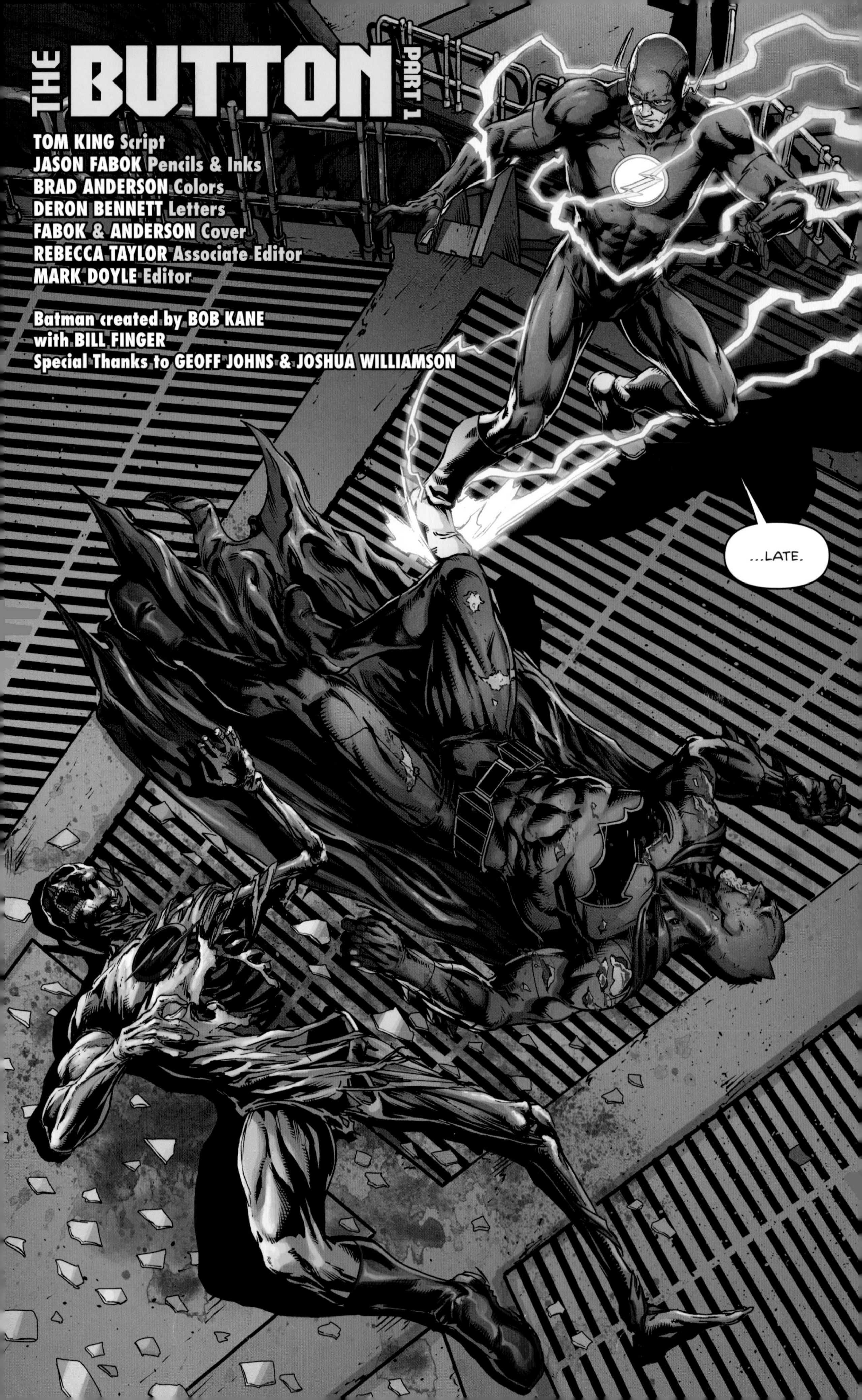
THE BUTTON PART 1
TOM KING Script
JASON FABOK Pencils & Inks
BRAD ANDERSON Colors
DERON BENNETT Letters
FABOK & ANDERSON Cover
REBECCA TAYLOR Associate Editor
MARK DOYLE Editor
Batman created by BOB KANE
with BILL FINGER
Special Thanks to GEOFF JOHNS & JOSHUA WILLIAMSON
...LATE.

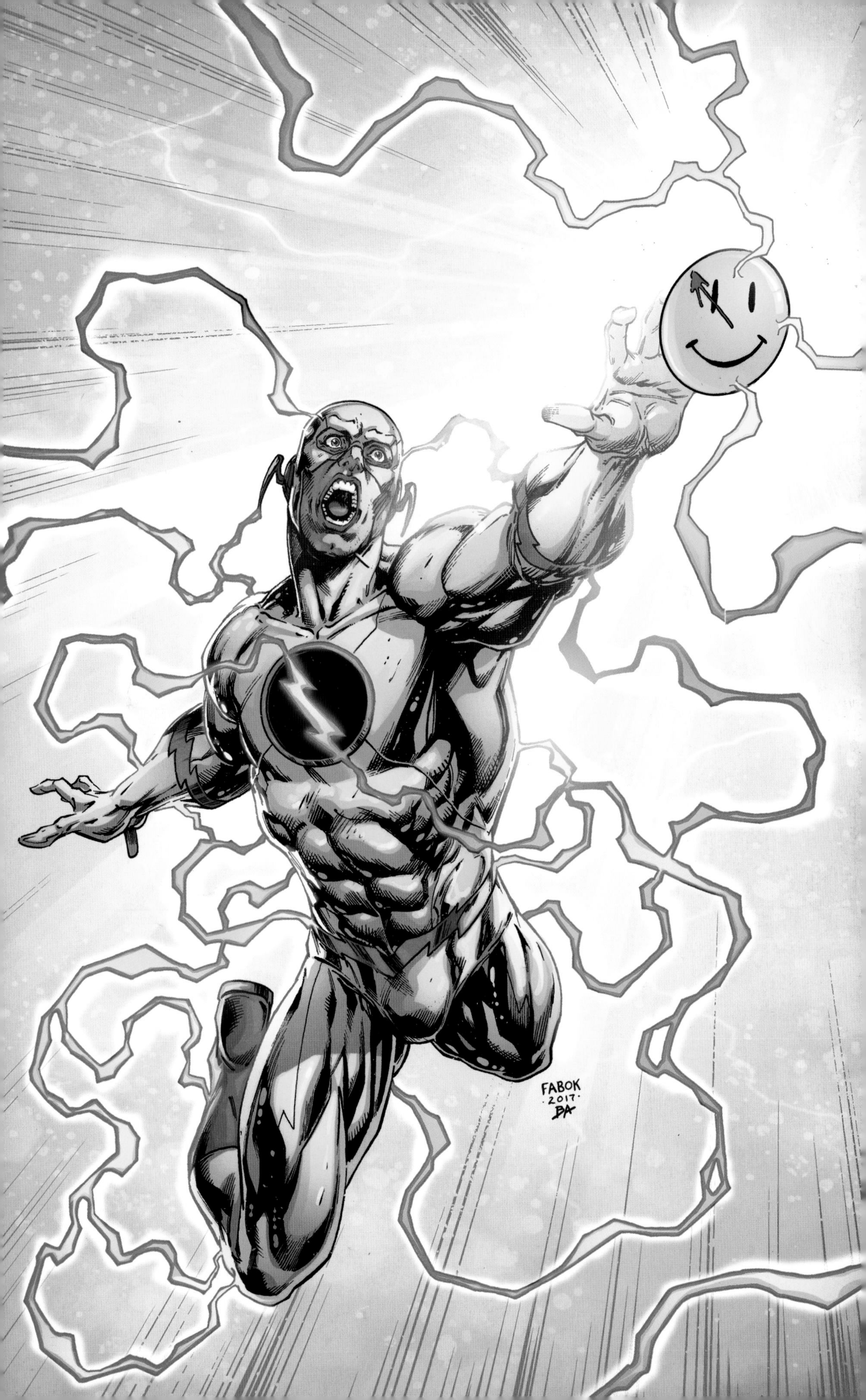
FABOK
·2017·
BA

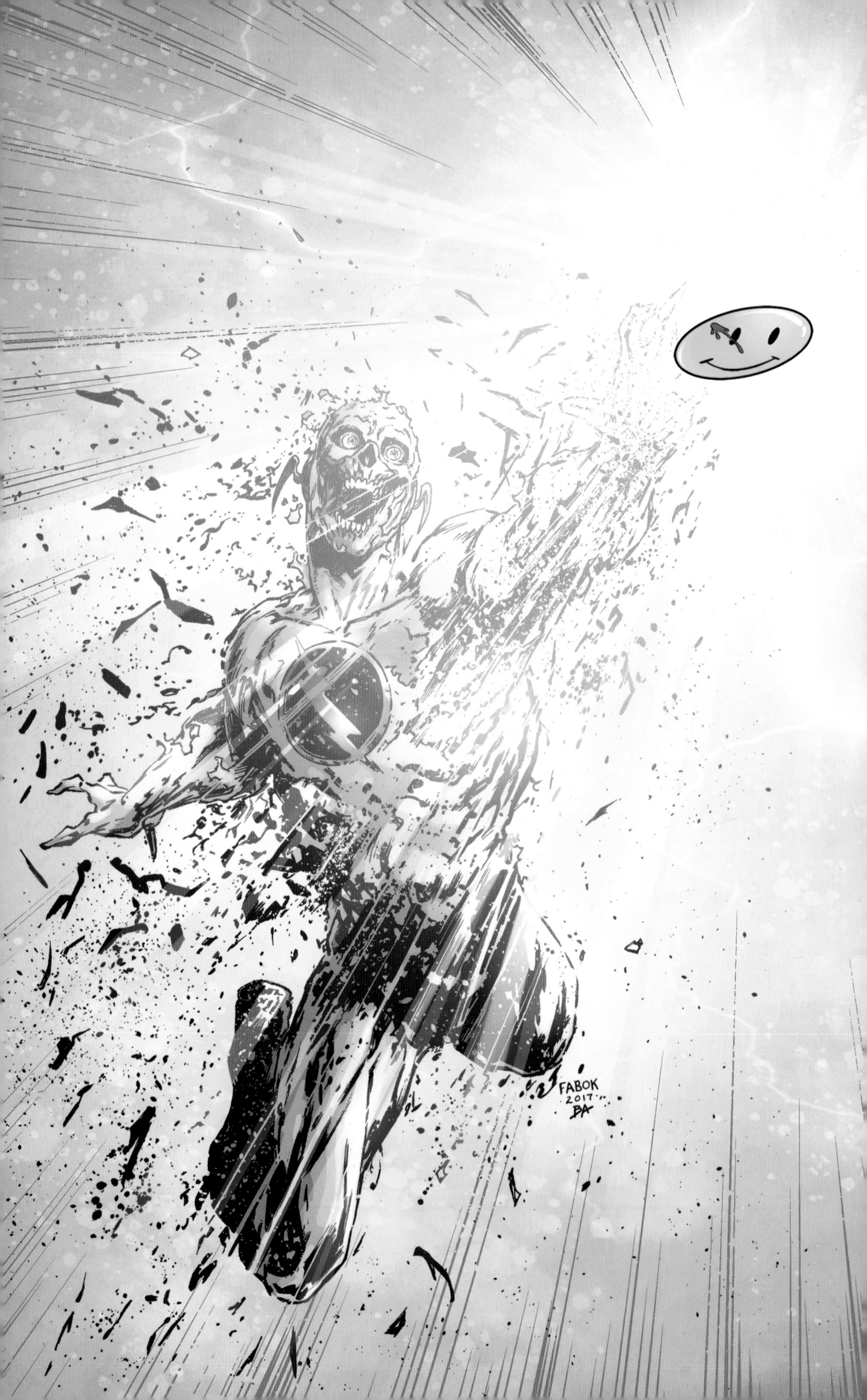
FABOK
2017
BA

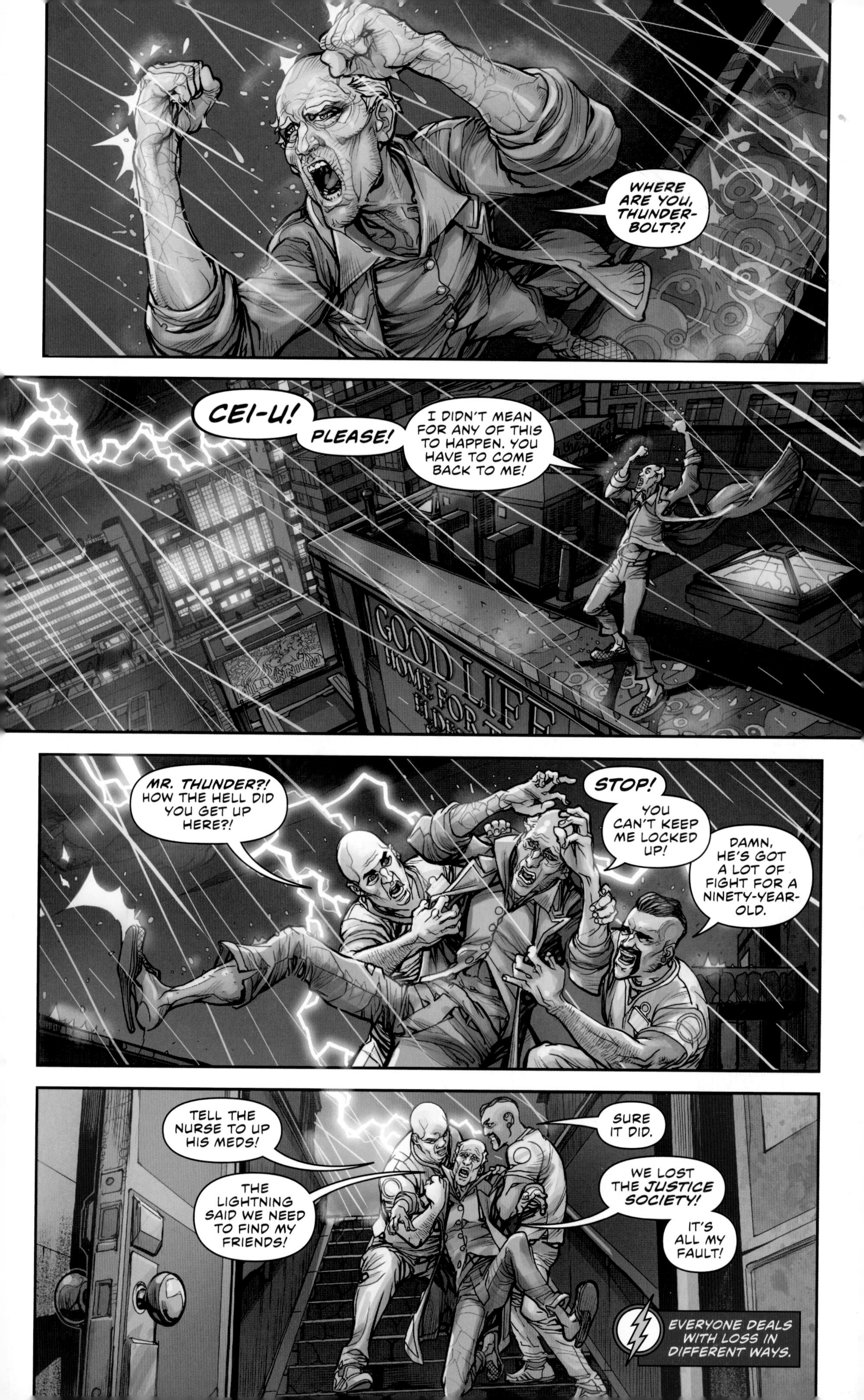
WHERE ARE YOU, THUNDER-BOLT?!
CEI-U!
PLEASE!
I DIDN'T MEAN FOR ANY OF THIS TO HAPPEN. YOU HAVE TO COME BACK TO ME!
GOOD LIFE HOME FOR
MR. THUNDER?! HOW THE HELL DID YOU GET UP HERE?!
STOP!
YOU CAN'T KEEP ME LOCKED UP!
DAMN, HE'S GOT A LOT OF FIGHT FOR A NINETY-YEAR-OLD.
TELL THE NURSE TO UP HIS MEDS!
THE LIGHTNING SAID WE NEED TO FIND MY FRIENDS!
SURE IT DID.
WE LOST THE *JUSTICE SOCIETY*!
IT'S ALL MY FAULT!
EVERYONE DEALS WITH LOSS IN DIFFERENT WAYS.

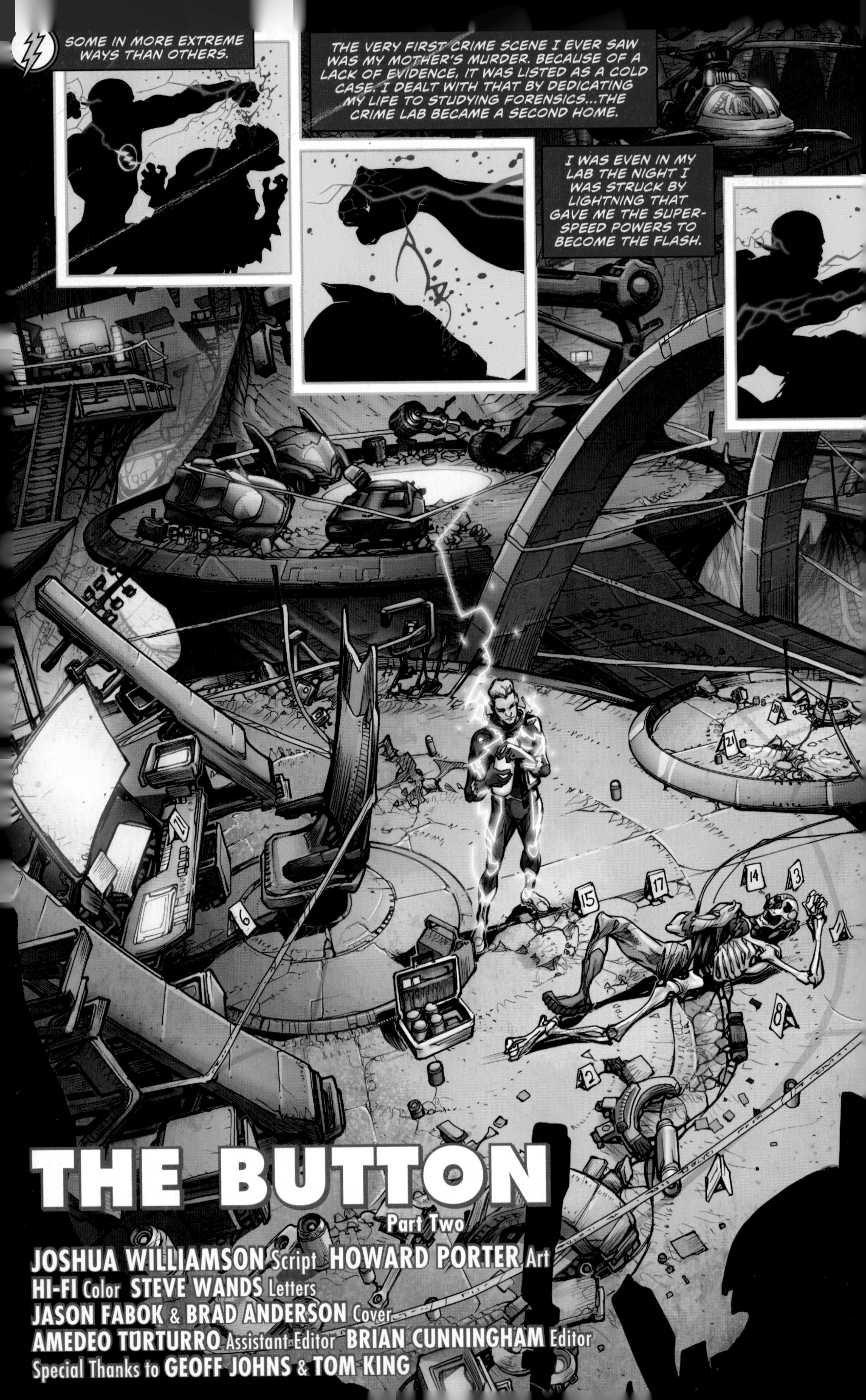
SOME IN MORE EXTREME WAYS THAN OTHERS.
THE VERY FIRST CRIME SCENE I EVER SAW WAS MY MOTHER'S MURDER. BECAUSE OF A LACK OF EVIDENCE, IT WAS LISTED AS A COLD CASE. I DEALT WITH THAT BY DEDICATING MY LIFE TO STUDYING FORENSICS...THE CRIME LAB BECAME A SECOND HOME.
I WAS EVEN IN MY LAB THE NIGHT I WAS STRUCK BY LIGHTNING THAT GAVE ME THE SUPER-SPEED POWERS TO BECOME THE FLASH.
THE BUTTON
Part Two
JOSHUA WILLIAMSON Script HOWARD PORTER Art
HI-FI Color STEVE WANDS Letters
JASON FABOK & BRAD ANDERSON Cover
AMEDEO TURTURRO Assistant Editor BRIAN CUNNINGHAM Editor
Special Thanks to GEOFF JOHNS & TOM KING

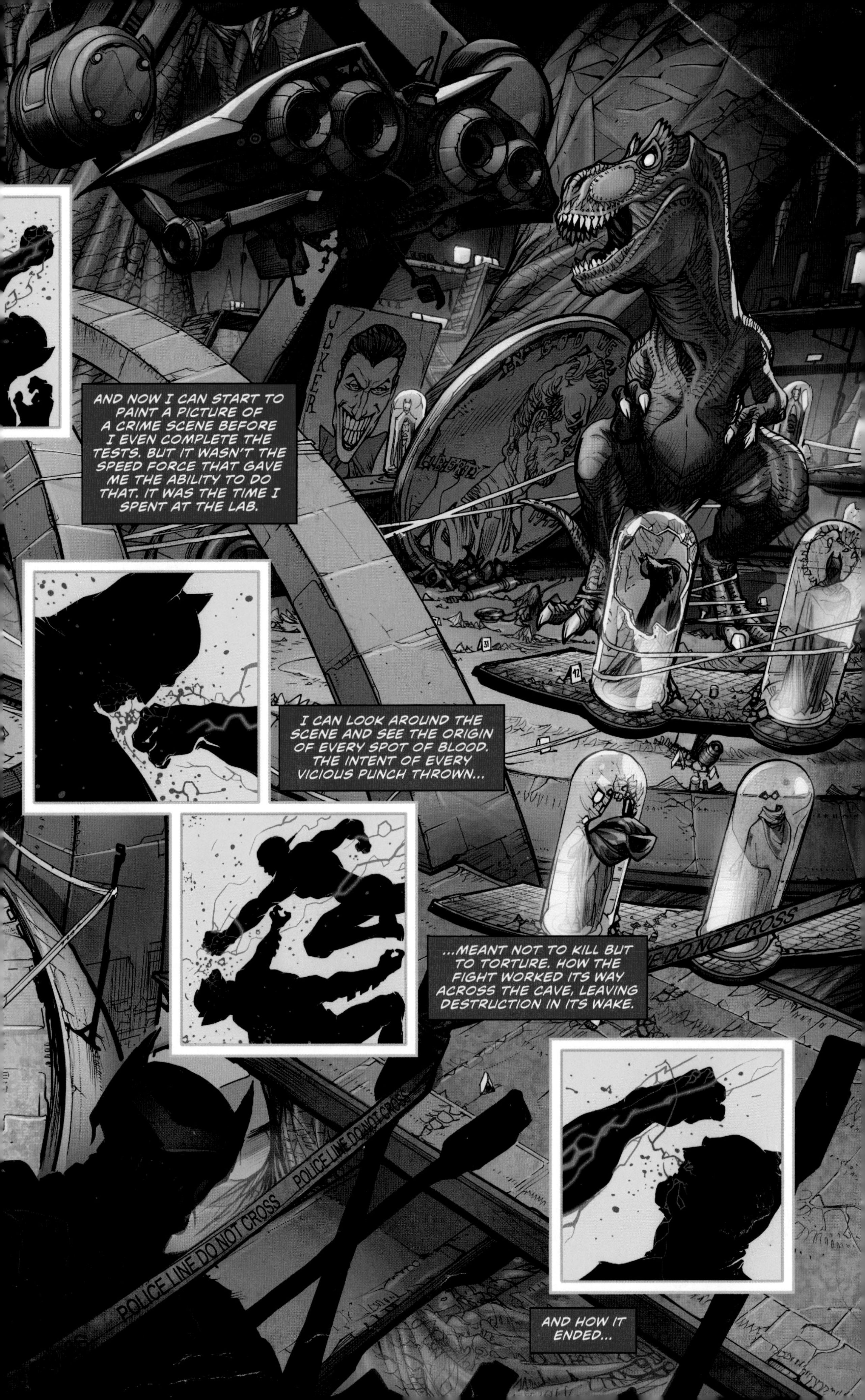
AND NOW I CAN START TO PAINT A PICTURE OF A CRIME SCENE BEFORE I EVEN COMPLETE THE TESTS. BUT IT WASN'T THE SPEED FORCE THAT GAVE ME THE ABILITY TO DO THAT. IT WAS THE TIME I SPENT AT THE LAB.
JOKER
I CAN LOOK AROUND THE SCENE AND SEE THE ORIGIN OF EVERY SPOT OF BLOOD. THE INTENT OF EVERY VICIOUS PUNCH THROWN...
...MEANT NOT TO KILL BUT TO TORTURE. HOW THE FIGHT WORKED ITS WAY ACROSS THE CAVE, LEAVING DESTRUCTION IN ITS WAKE.
DO NOT CROSS
POLICE LINE DO NOT CROSS
POLICE LINE DO NOT CROSS
AND HOW IT ENDED...

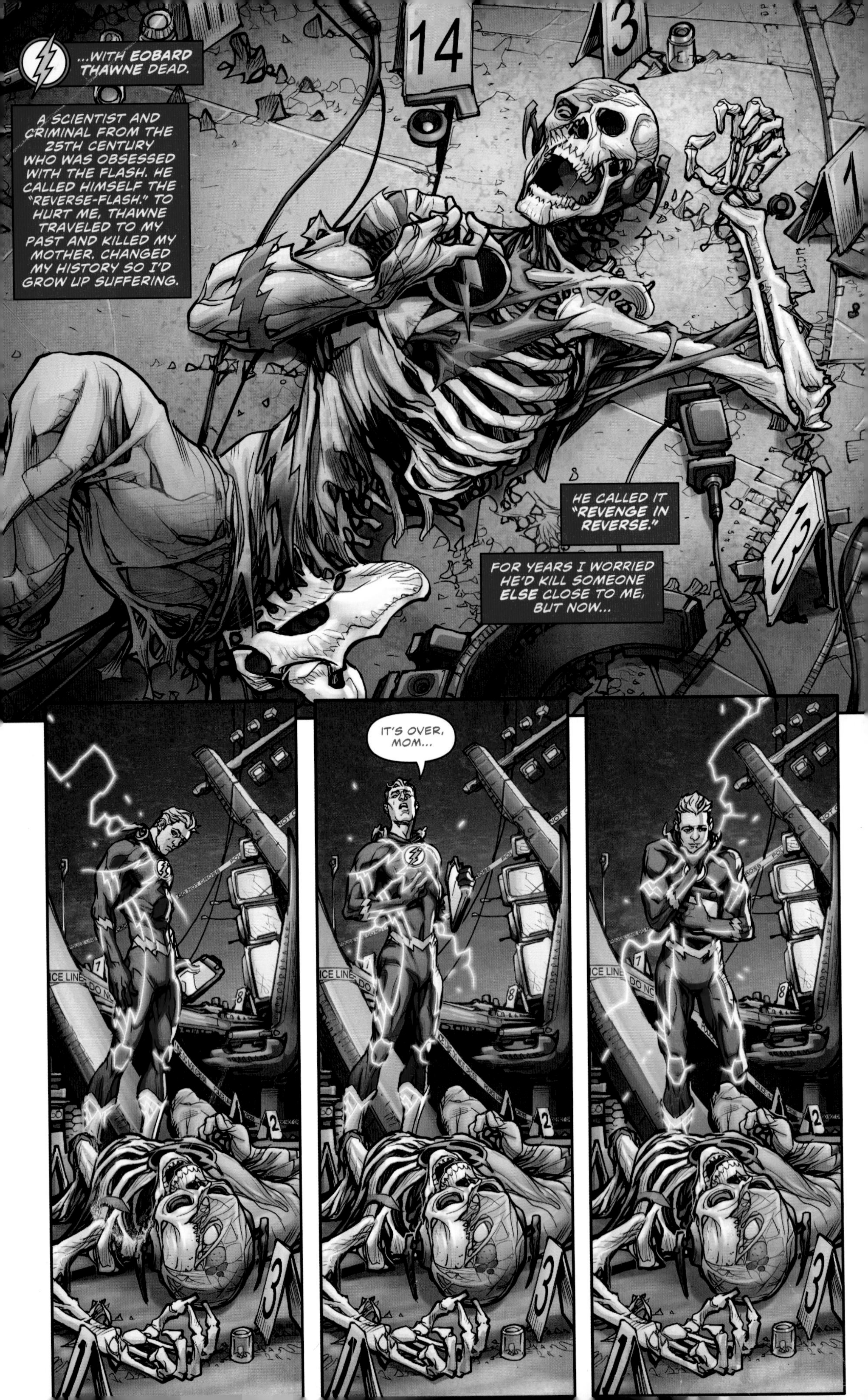
...WITH EOBARD THAWNE DEAD.
A SCIENTIST AND CRIMINAL FROM THE 25TH CENTURY WHO WAS OBSESSED WITH THE FLASH. HE CALLED HIMSELF THE "REVERSE-FLASH." TO HURT ME, THAWNE TRAVELED TO MY PAST AND KILLED MY MOTHER. CHANGED MY HISTORY SO I'D GROW UP SUFFERING.
HE CALLED IT "REVENGE IN REVERSE."
FOR YEARS I WORRIED HE'D KILL SOMEONE ELSE CLOSE TO ME, BUT NOW...
IT'S OVER, MOM...

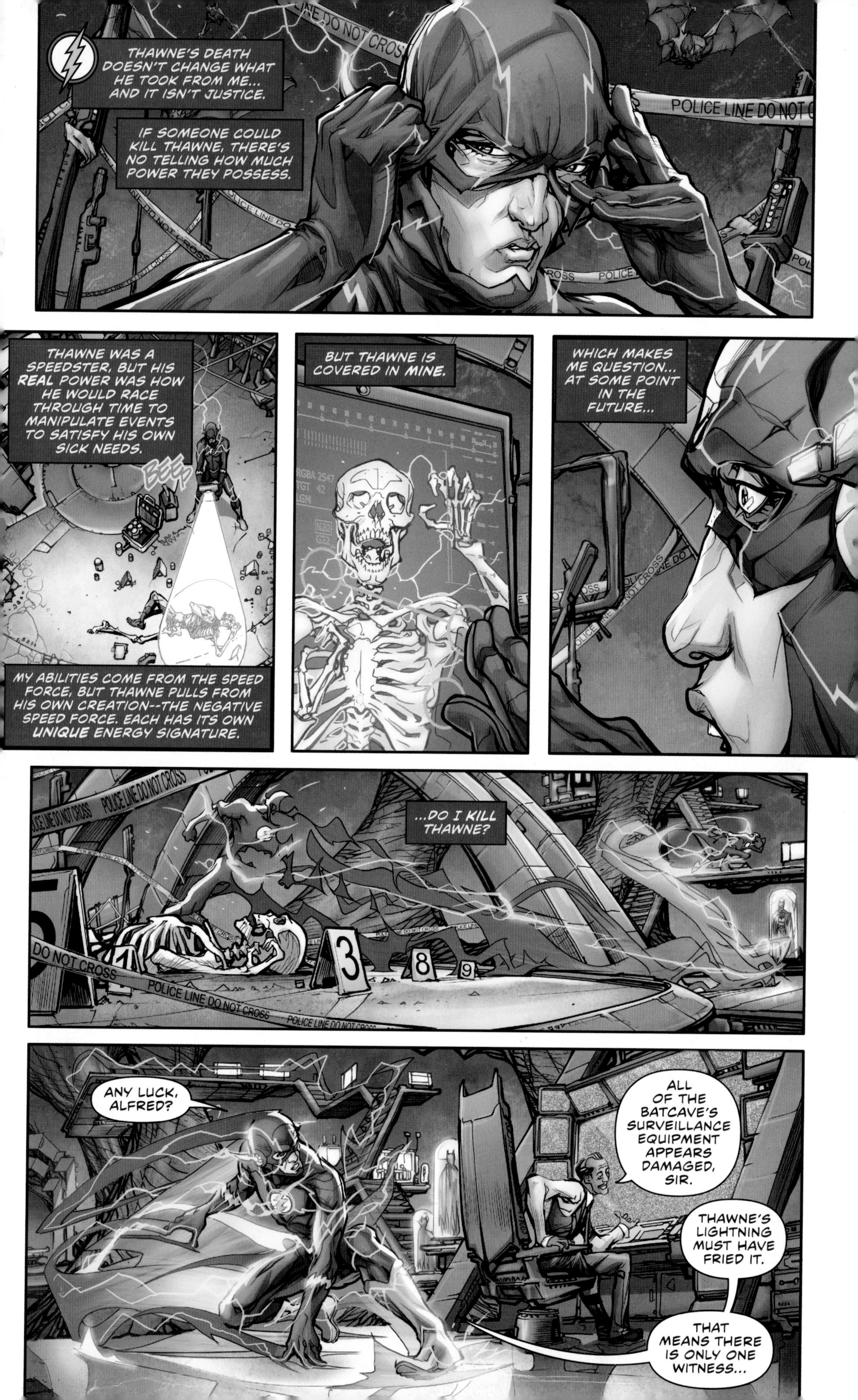

THAWNE'S DEATH DOESN'T CHANGE WHAT HE TOOK FROM ME... AND IT ISN'T JUSTICE.
IF SOMEONE COULD KILL THAWNE, THERE'S NO TELLING HOW MUCH POWER THEY POSSESS.
THAWNE WAS A SPEEDSTER, BUT HIS **REAL** POWER WAS HOW HE WOULD RACE THROUGH TIME TO MANIPULATE EVENTS TO SATISFY HIS OWN SICK NEEDS.
MY ABILITIES COME FROM THE SPEED FORCE, BUT THAWNE PULLS FROM HIS OWN CREATION--THE NEGATIVE SPEED FORCE. EACH HAS ITS OWN **UNIQUE** ENERGY SIGNATURE.
BUT THAWNE IS COVERED IN **MINE.**
WHICH MAKES ME QUESTION... AT SOME POINT IN THE FUTURE...
...DO I **KILL** THAWNE?
ANY LUCK, ALFRED?
ALL OF THE BATCAVE'S SURVEILLANCE EQUIPMENT APPEARS DAMAGED, SIR.
THAWNE'S LIGHTNING MUST HAVE FRIED IT.
THAT MEANS THERE IS ONLY ONE WITNESS...

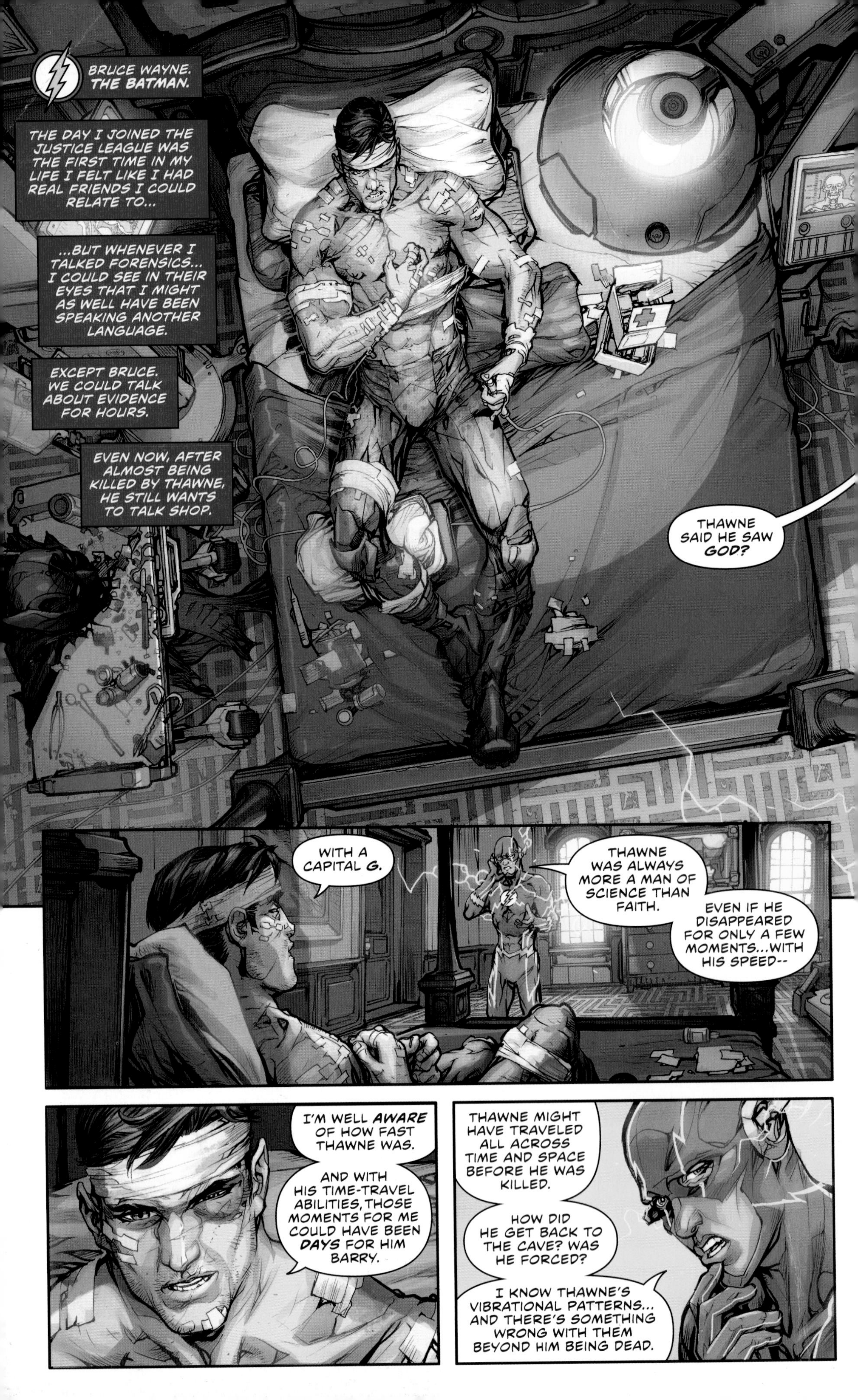
BRUCE WAYNE. THE BATMAN.
THE DAY I JOINED THE JUSTICE LEAGUE WAS THE FIRST TIME IN MY LIFE I FELT LIKE I HAD REAL FRIENDS I COULD RELATE TO...
...BUT WHENEVER I TALKED FORENSICS... I COULD SEE IN THEIR EYES THAT I MIGHT AS WELL HAVE BEEN SPEAKING ANOTHER LANGUAGE.
EXCEPT BRUCE. WE COULD TALK ABOUT EVIDENCE FOR HOURS.
EVEN NOW, AFTER ALMOST BEING KILLED BY THAWNE, HE STILL WANTS TO TALK SHOP.
THAWNE SAID HE SAW GOD?
WITH A CAPITAL G.
THAWNE WAS ALWAYS MORE A MAN OF SCIENCE THAN FAITH.
EVEN IF HE DISAPPEARED FOR ONLY A FEW MOMENTS...WITH HIS SPEED--
I'M WELL AWARE OF HOW FAST THAWNE WAS.
AND WITH HIS TIME-TRAVEL ABILITIES, THOSE MOMENTS FOR ME COULD HAVE BEEN DAYS FOR HIM BARRY.
THAWNE MIGHT HAVE TRAVELED ALL ACROSS TIME AND SPACE BEFORE HE WAS KILLED.
HOW DID HE GET BACK TO THE CAVE? WAS HE FORCED?
I KNOW THAWNE'S VIBRATIONAL PATTERNS... AND THERE'S SOMETHING WRONG WITH THEM BEYOND HIM BEING DEAD.

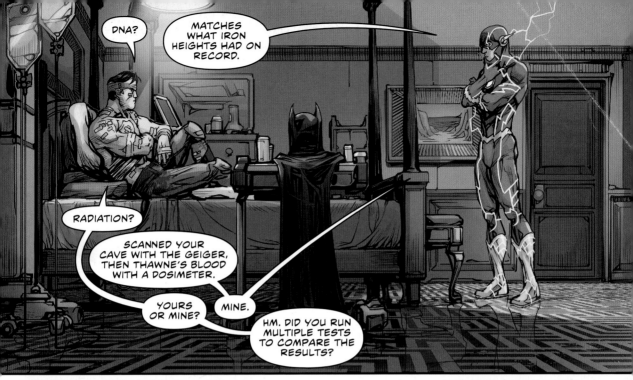

DNA?

MATCHES WHAT IRON HEIGHTS HAD ON RECORD.

RADIATION?

SCANNED YOUR CAVE WITH THE GEIGER, THEN THAWNE'S BLOOD WITH A DOSIMETER.

YOURS OR MINE?

MINE.

HM. DID YOU RUN MULTIPLE TESTS TO COMPARE THE RESULTS?

BRUCE, COME ON...

SORRY.

WE RESEARCHED THAT BUTTON FOR MONTHS AND FOUND *NOTHING*. THE BLOOD ON IT DIDN'T MATCH ANY SAMPLES FOUND IN A.R.G.U.S., THE D.E.O. OR S.T.A.R. LABS.

BUT WHEN YOU CALLED ME YOU SAID THE BUTTON REACTED TO CONTACT WITH PSYCHO-PIRATE'S MASK...

...THAT YOU *SAW* SOMETHING.

THERE WAS...A GHOST.

WHAT...?

I...

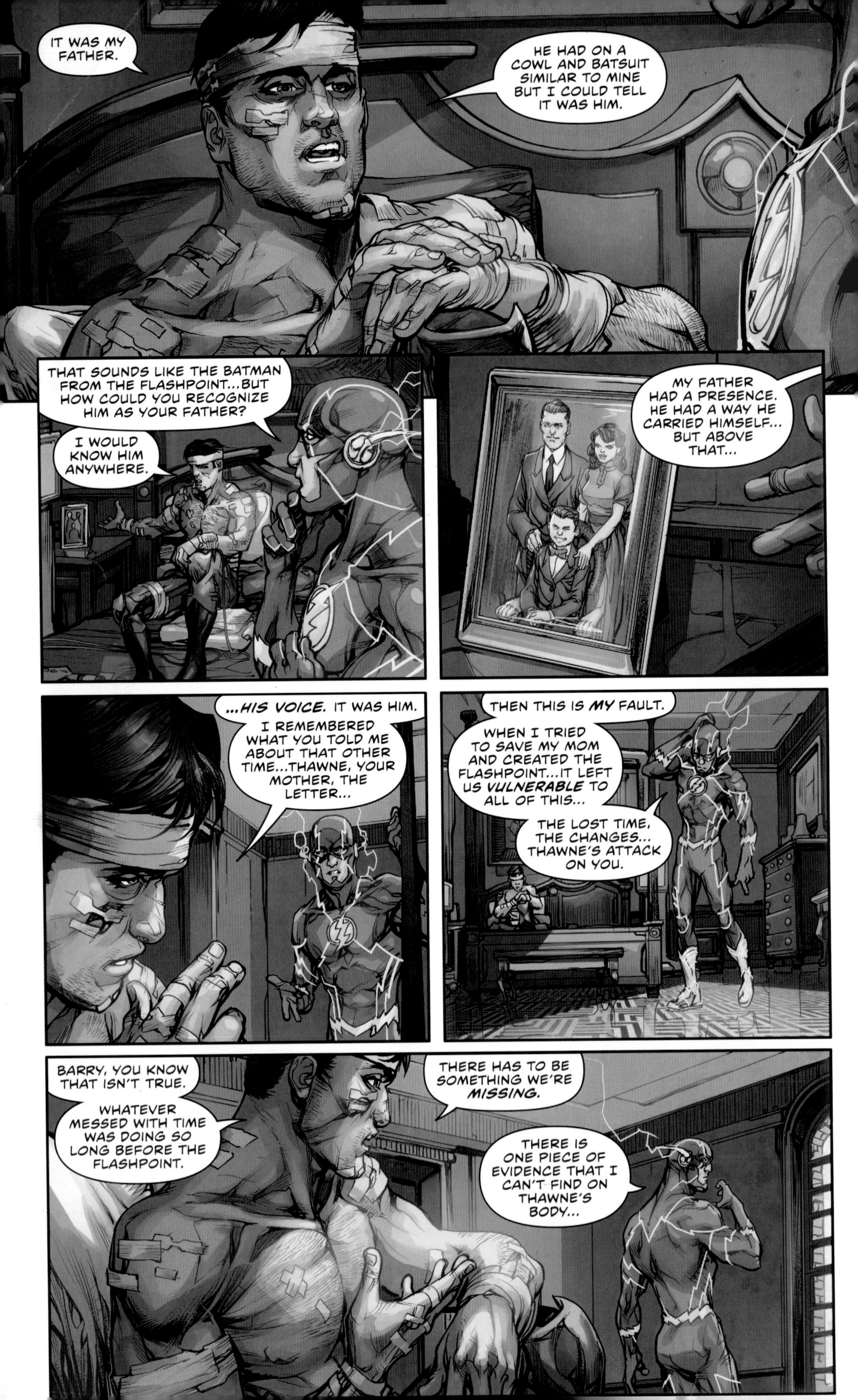
IT WAS MY FATHER.
HE HAD ON A COWL AND BATSUIT SIMILAR TO MINE BUT I COULD TELL IT WAS HIM.
THAT SOUNDS LIKE THE BATMAN FROM THE FLASHPOINT...BUT HOW COULD YOU RECOGNIZE HIM AS YOUR FATHER?
I WOULD KNOW HIM ANYWHERE.
MY FATHER HAD A PRESENCE. HE HAD A WAY HE CARRIED HIMSELF... BUT ABOVE THAT...
...HIS VOICE. IT WAS HIM.
I REMEMBERED WHAT YOU TOLD ME ABOUT THAT OTHER TIME...THAWNE, YOUR MOTHER, THE LETTER...
THEN THIS IS MY FAULT.
WHEN I TRIED TO SAVE MY MOM AND CREATED THE FLASHPOINT...IT LEFT US VULNERABLE TO ALL OF THIS...
THE LOST TIME, THE CHANGES... THAWNE'S ATTACK ON YOU.
BARRY, YOU KNOW THAT ISN'T TRUE.
WHATEVER MESSED WITH TIME WAS DOING SO LONG BEFORE THE FLASHPOINT.
THERE HAS TO BE SOMETHING WE'RE MISSING.
THERE IS ONE PIECE OF EVIDENCE THAT I CAN'T FIND ON THAWNE'S BODY...

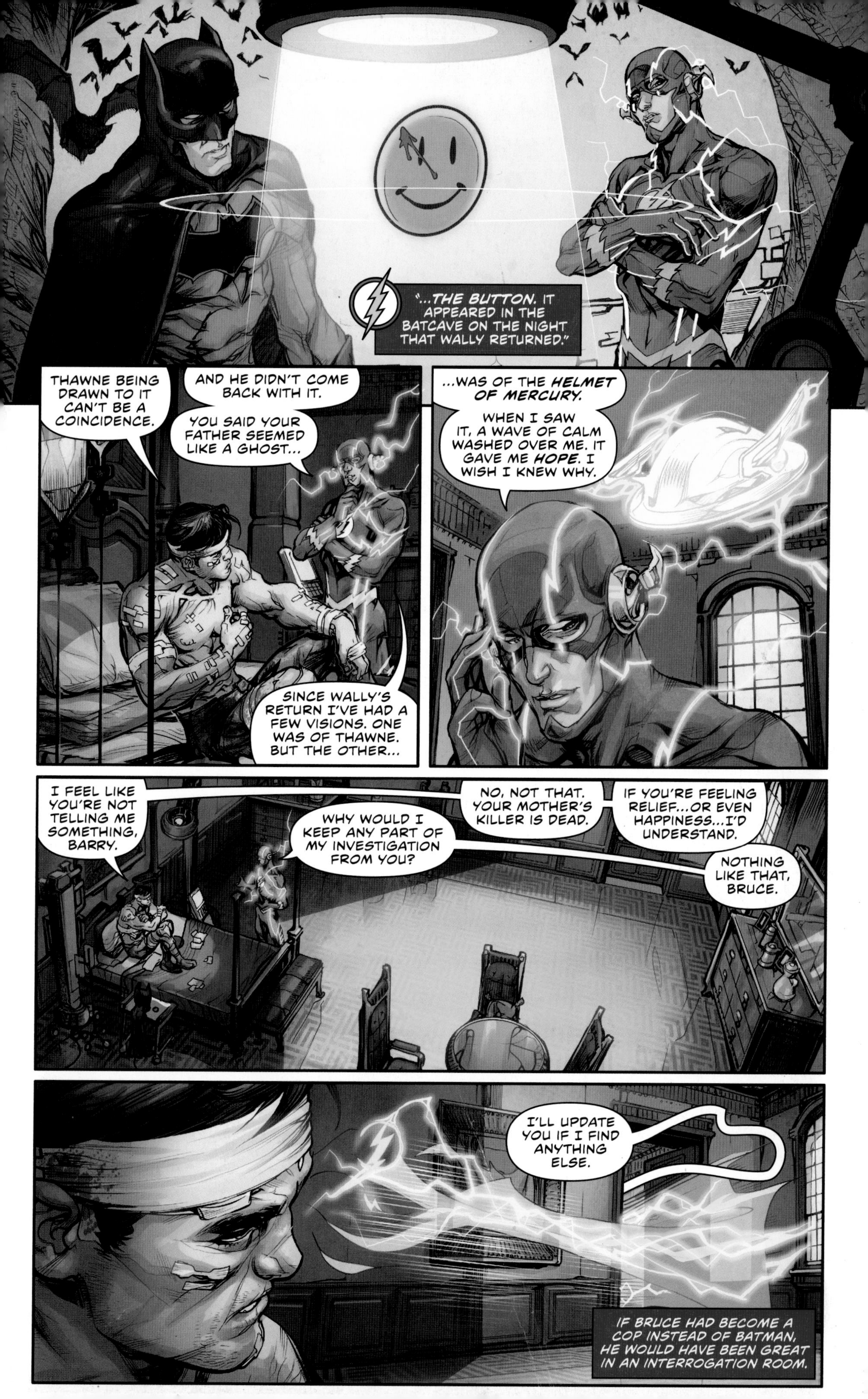
"...THE BUTTON. IT APPEARED IN THE BATCAVE ON THE NIGHT THAT WALLY RETURNED."
THAWNE BEING DRAWN TO IT CAN'T BE A COINCIDENCE.
AND HE DIDN'T COME BACK WITH IT.
YOU SAID YOUR FATHER SEEMED LIKE A GHOST...
SINCE WALLY'S RETURN I'VE HAD A FEW VISIONS. ONE WAS OF THAWNE. BUT THE OTHER...
...WAS OF THE HELMET OF MERCURY.
WHEN I SAW IT, A WAVE OF CALM WASHED OVER ME. IT GAVE ME HOPE. I WISH I KNEW WHY.
I FEEL LIKE YOU'RE NOT TELLING ME SOMETHING, BARRY.
WHY WOULD I KEEP ANY PART OF MY INVESTIGATION FROM YOU?
NO, NOT THAT. YOUR MOTHER'S KILLER IS DEAD.
IF YOU'RE FEELING RELIEF...OR EVEN HAPPINESS...I'D UNDERSTAND.
NOTHING LIKE THAT, BRUCE.
I'LL UPDATE YOU IF I FIND ANYTHING ELSE.
IF BRUCE HAD BECOME A COP INSTEAD OF BATMAN, HE WOULD HAVE BEEN GREAT IN AN INTERROGATION ROOM.

THE TRACES OF MY SPEED FORCE ON THAWNE'S BODY WASN'T ALL I DIDN'T TELL BRUCE ABOUT... THERE WAS SOMETHING ELSE, TOO. MASSIVE AMOUNTS OF THE SAME RADIATION WE FOUND ON THE BUTTON. MUCH MORE THAN COULD HAVE COME FROM *JUST* THE BUTTON.

JUSTICE LEAGUE Watchtower.

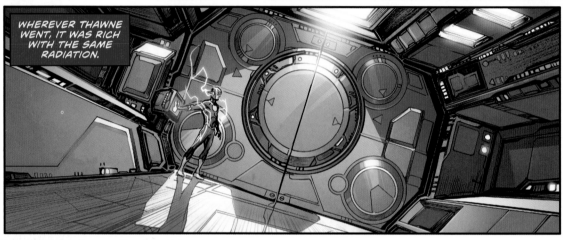

WHEREVER THAWNE WENT, IT WAS RICH WITH THE SAME RADIATION.

HAL NICKNAMED THIS "THE HALL OF LOST AND FOUND."

AFTER THE JUSTICE LEAGUE'S MISSIONS, WE SECURE THE STRAY ARTIFACTS HERE.

I WISH BATMAN AND I HAD PLACED THE BUTTON HERE THE NIGHT IT SHOWED UP IN THE BATCAVE...THE NIGHT WALLY RETURNED...

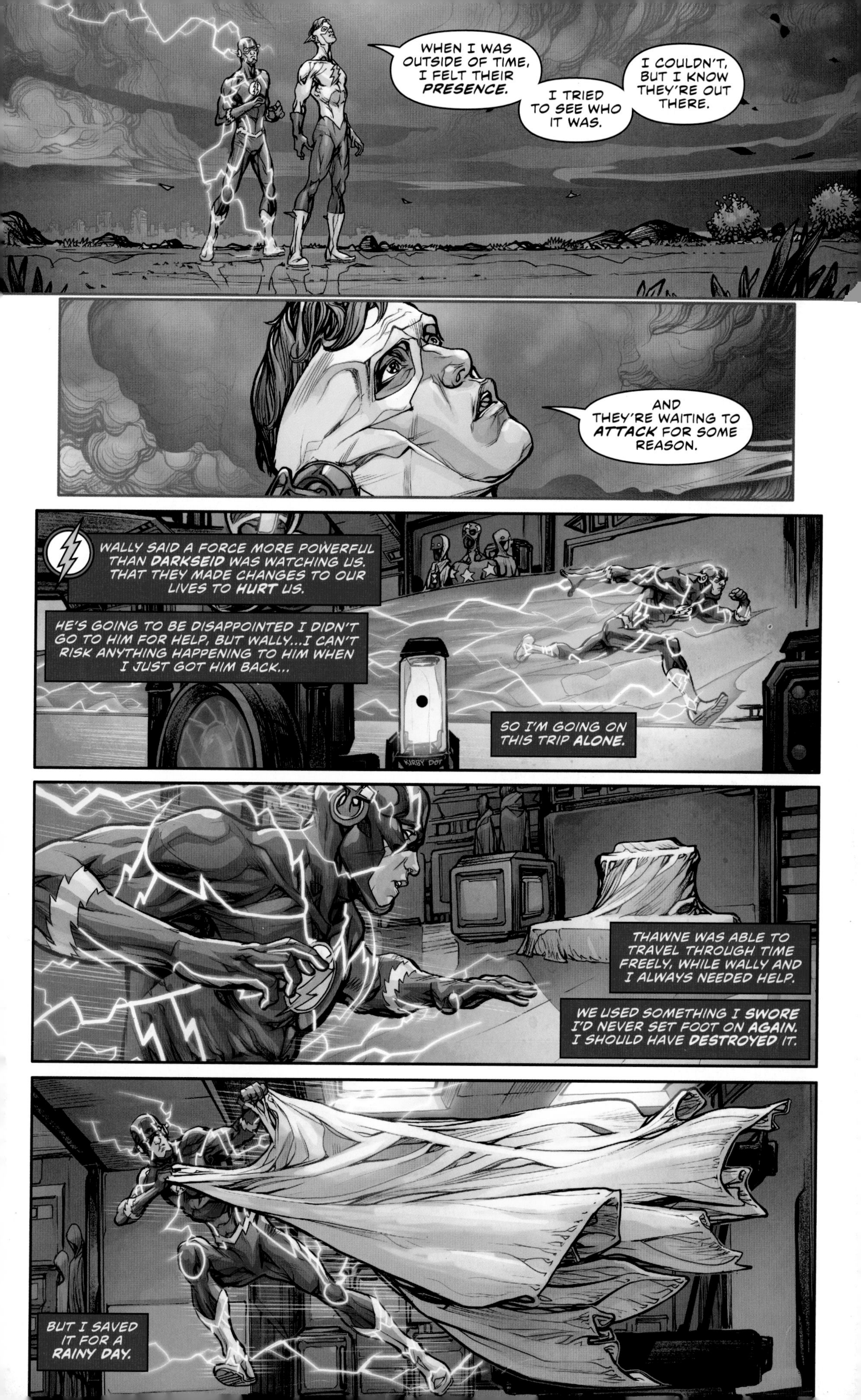
WHEN I WAS OUTSIDE OF TIME, I FELT THEIR PRESENCE.
I TRIED TO SEE WHO IT WAS.
I COULDN'T, BUT I KNOW THEY'RE OUT THERE.
AND THEY'RE WAITING TO ATTACK FOR SOME REASON.
WALLY SAID A FORCE MORE POWERFUL THAN DARKSEID WAS WATCHING US. THAT THEY MADE CHANGES TO OUR LIVES TO HURT US.
HE'S GOING TO BE DISAPPOINTED I DIDN'T GO TO HIM FOR HELP, BUT WALLY...I CAN'T RISK ANYTHING HAPPENING TO HIM WHEN I JUST GOT HIM BACK...
SO I'M GOING ON THIS TRIP ALONE.
KIRBY DOT
THAWNE WAS ABLE TO TRAVEL THROUGH TIME FREELY, WHILE WALLY AND I ALWAYS NEEDED HELP.
WE USED SOMETHING I SWORE I'D NEVER SET FOOT ON AGAIN. I SHOULD HAVE DESTROYED IT.
BUT I SAVED IT FOR A RAINY DAY.

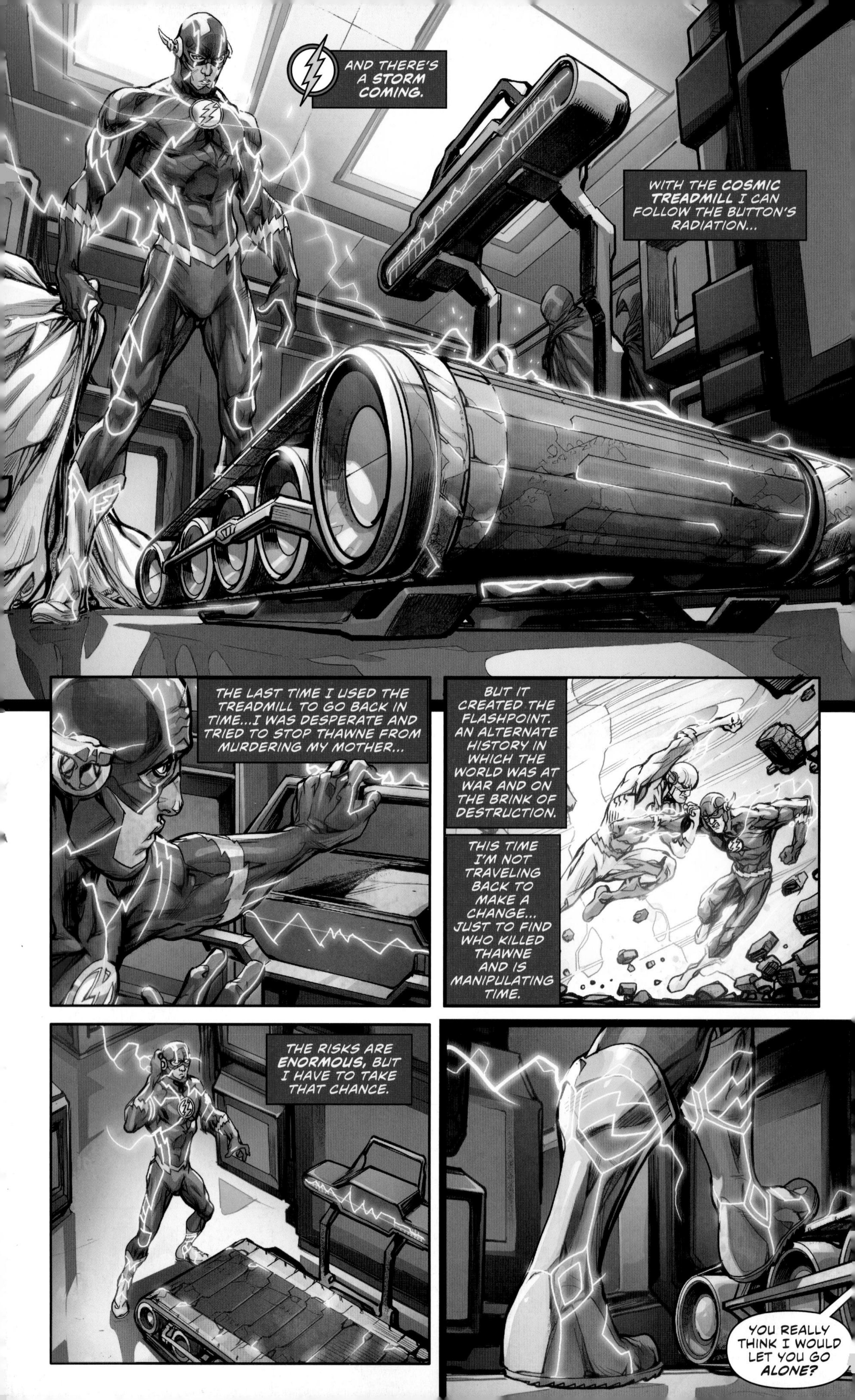
AND THERE'S A STORM COMING.
WITH THE COSMIC TREADMILL I CAN FOLLOW THE BUTTON'S RADIATION...
THE LAST TIME I USED THE TREADMILL TO GO BACK IN TIME...I WAS DESPERATE AND TRIED TO STOP THAWNE FROM MURDERING MY MOTHER...
BUT IT CREATED THE FLASHPOINT. AN ALTERNATE HISTORY IN WHICH THE WORLD WAS AT WAR AND ON THE BRINK OF DESTRUCTION.
THIS TIME I'M NOT TRAVELING BACK TO MAKE A CHANGE... JUST TO FIND WHO KILLED THAWNE AND IS MANIPULATING TIME.
THE RISKS ARE ENORMOUS, BUT I HAVE TO TAKE THAT CHANCE.
YOU REALLY THINK I WOULD LET YOU GO ALONE?

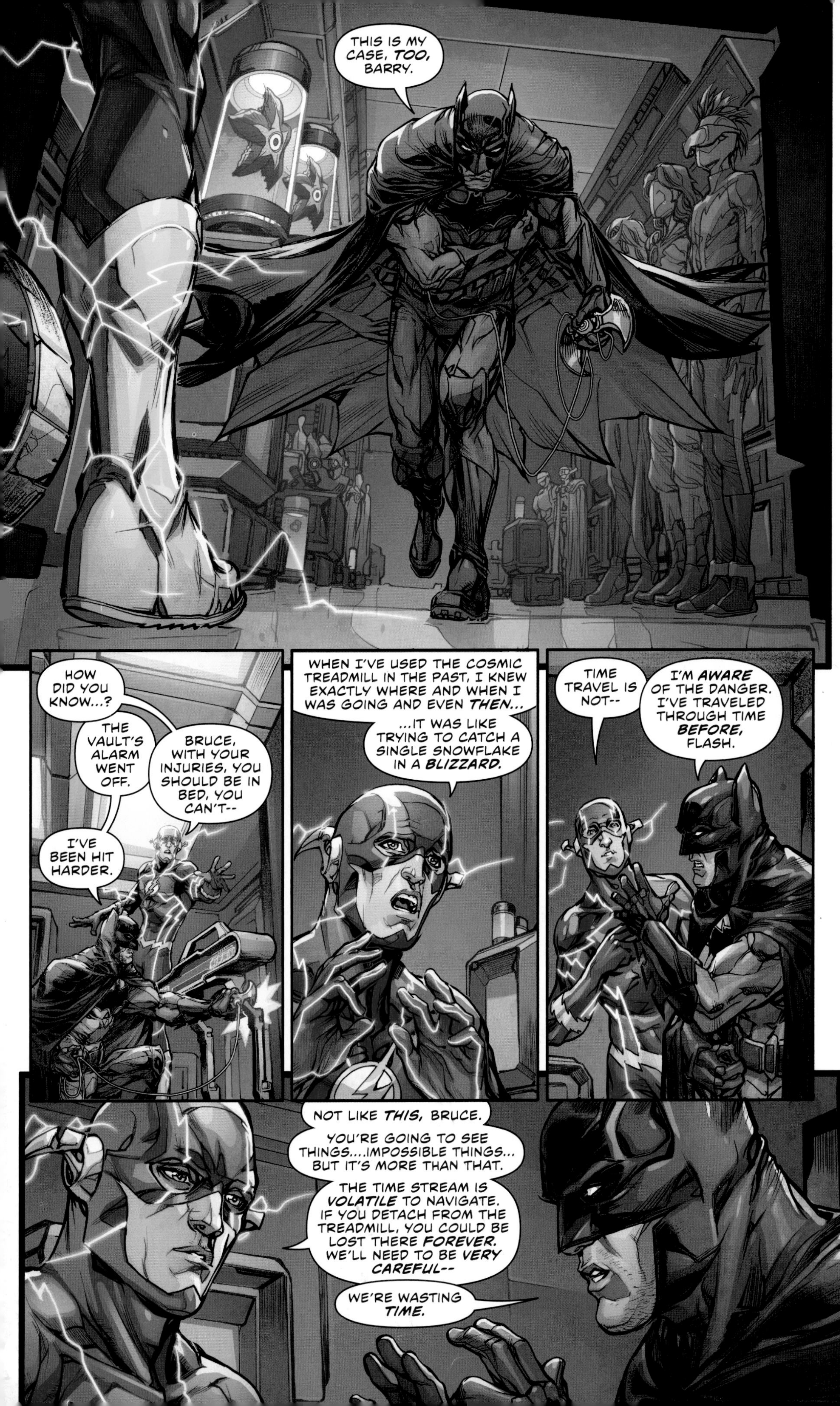
THIS IS MY CASE, *TOO,* BARRY.
HOW DID YOU KNOW...?
THE VAULT'S ALARM WENT OFF.
BRUCE, WITH YOUR INJURIES, YOU SHOULD BE IN BED, YOU CAN'T--
I'VE BEEN HIT HARDER.
WHEN I'VE USED THE COSMIC TREADMILL IN THE PAST, I KNEW EXACTLY WHERE AND WHEN I WAS GOING AND EVEN *THEN...*
...IT WAS LIKE TRYING TO CATCH A SINGLE SNOWFLAKE IN A *BLIZZARD.*
TIME TRAVEL IS NOT--
I'M *AWARE* OF THE DANGER. I'VE TRAVELED THROUGH TIME *BEFORE,* FLASH.
NOT LIKE *THIS,* BRUCE.
YOU'RE GOING TO SEE THINGS....IMPOSSIBLE THINGS... BUT IT'S MORE THAN THAT.
THE TIME STREAM IS *VOLATILE* TO NAVIGATE. IF YOU DETACH FROM THE TREADMILL, YOU COULD BE LOST THERE *FOREVER.* WE'LL NEED TO BE *VERY CAREFUL--*
WE'RE WASTING *TIME.*

SHOULD'VE KNOWN IT WAS POINTLESS ARGUING WITH YOU.

HOLD ON!

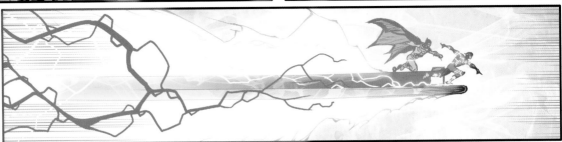

KRAKKATHOOOM

I'VE *NEVER* SEEN ANYTHING LIKE THIS BEFORE.

THIS TURBULENCE IS MAKING IT HARD TO KEEP THE TREADMILL STEADY--!

LOOK!

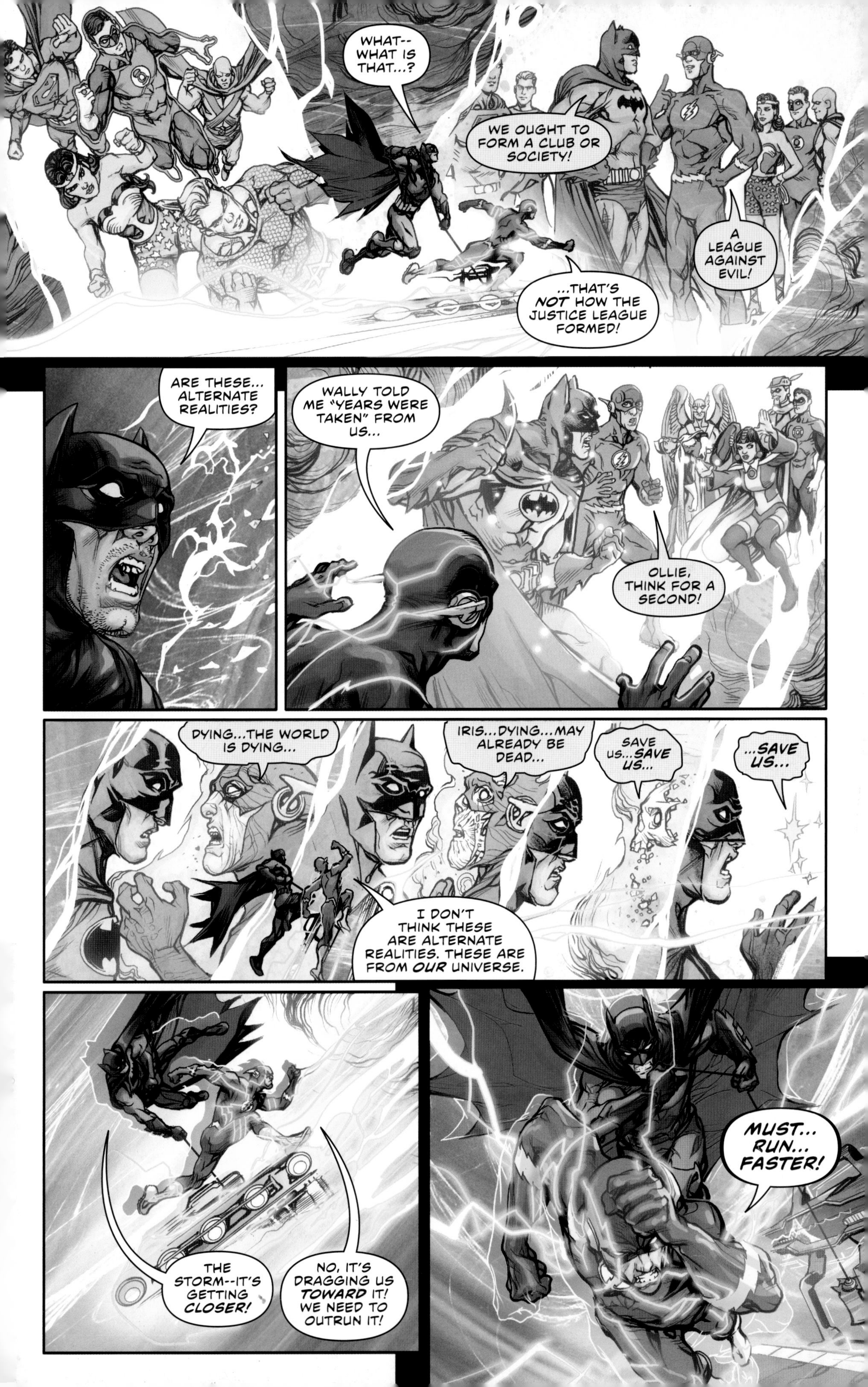
WHAT-- WHAT IS THAT...?
WE OUGHT TO FORM A CLUB OR SOCIETY!
A LEAGUE AGAINST EVIL!
...THAT'S NOT HOW THE JUSTICE LEAGUE FORMED!
ARE THESE... ALTERNATE REALITIES?
WALLY TOLD ME "YEARS WERE TAKEN" FROM US...
OLLIE, THINK FOR A SECOND!
DYING...THE WORLD IS DYING...
IRIS...DYING...MAY ALREADY BE DEAD...
SAVE US...SAVE US...
...SAVE US...
I DON'T THINK THESE ARE ALTERNATE REALITIES. THESE ARE FROM OUR UNIVERSE.
THE STORM--IT'S GETTING CLOSER!
NO, IT'S DRAGGING US TOWARD IT! WE NEED TO OUTRUN IT!
MUST... RUN... FASTER!

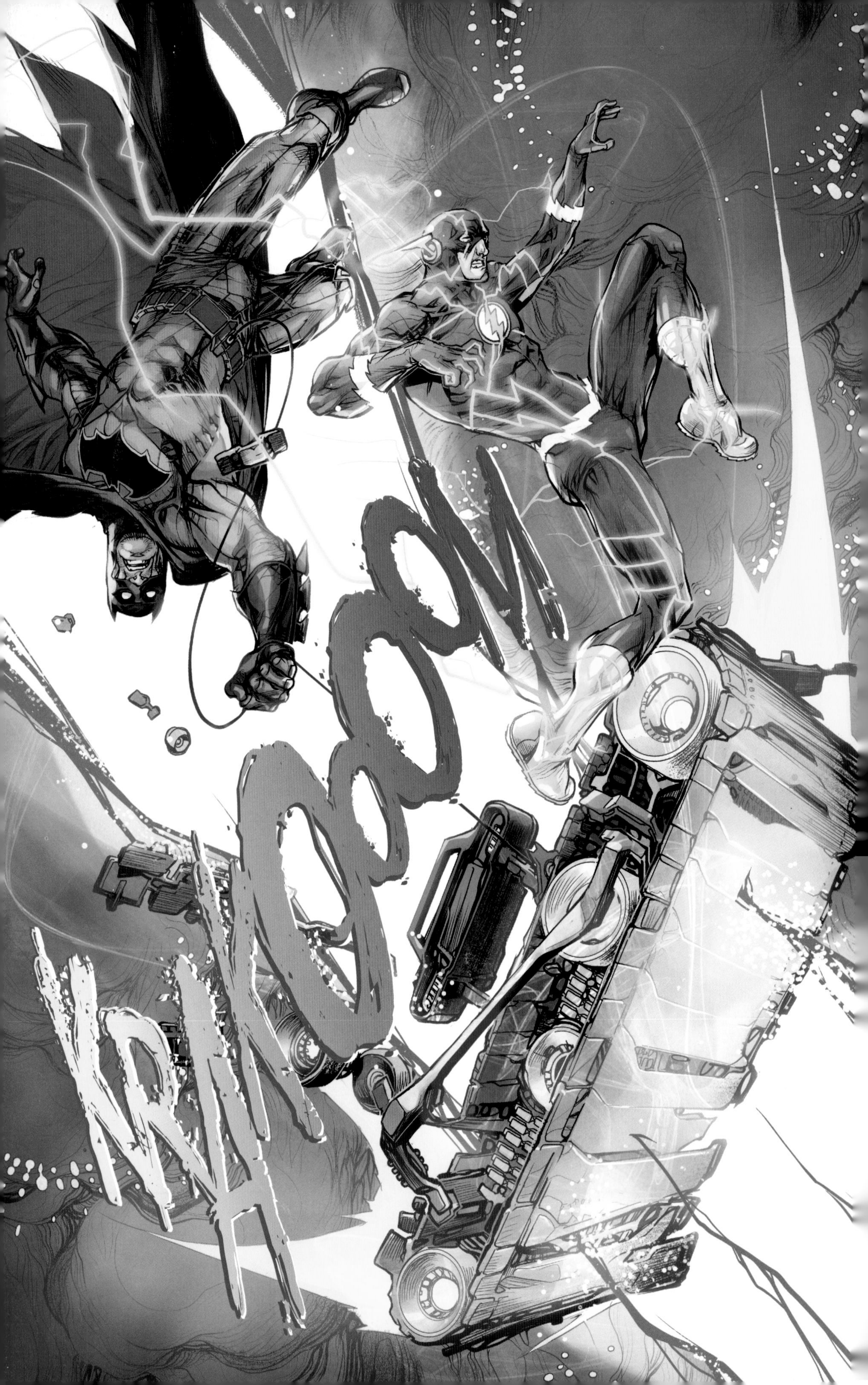
KRAKOOOM

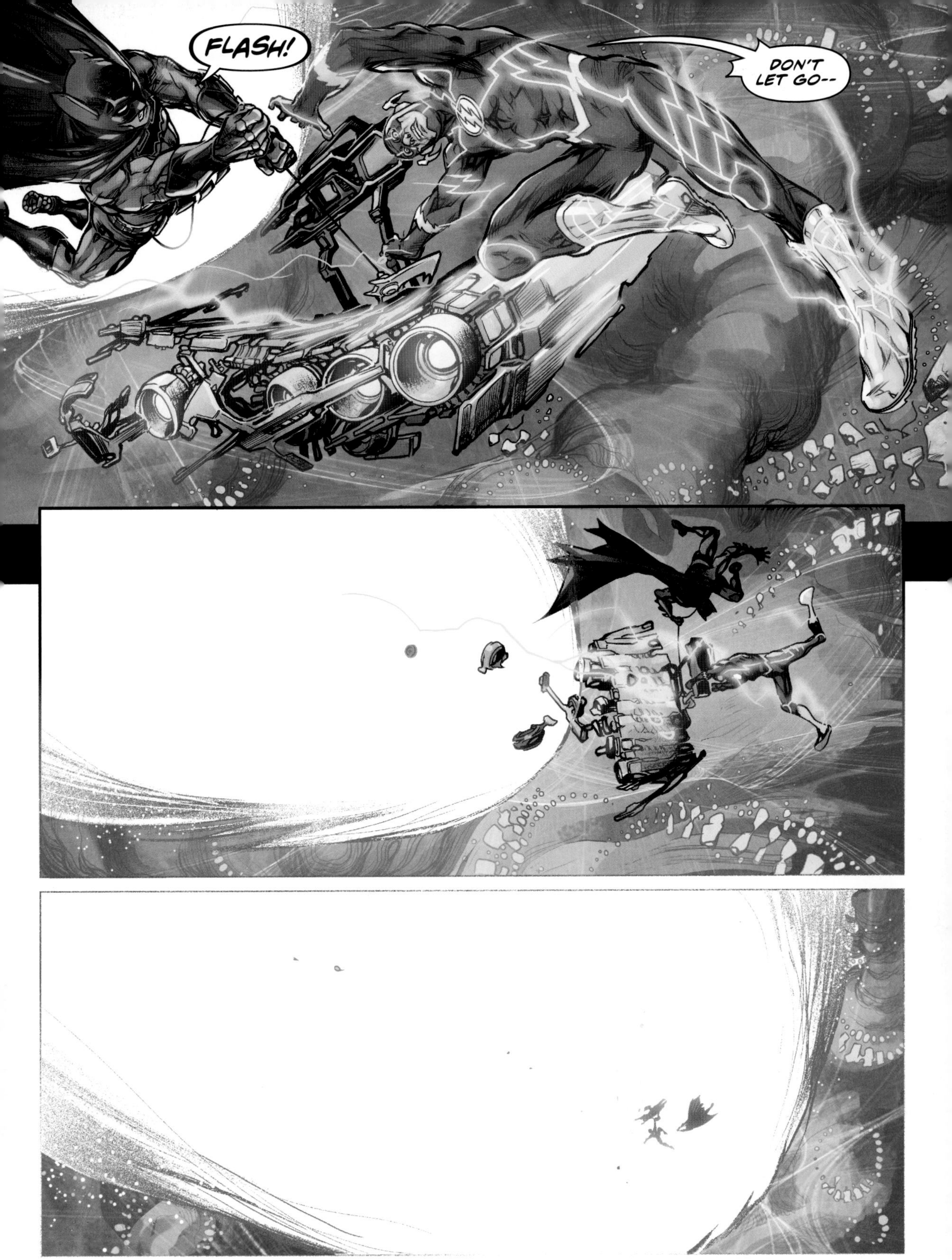
FLASH!
DON'T LET GO--

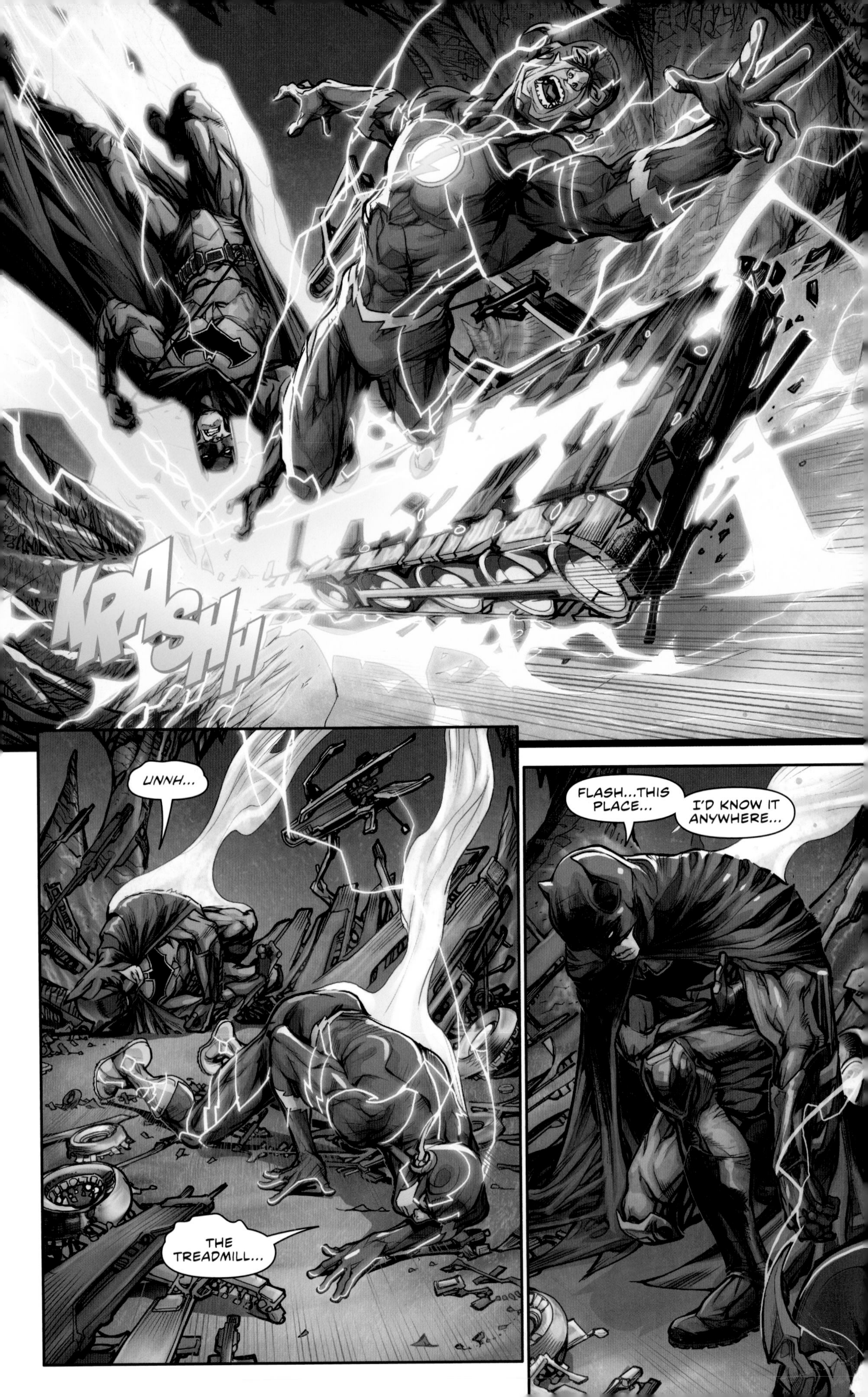
KRASHH
UNNH...
THE TREADMILL...
FLASH...THIS PLACE...
I'D KNOW IT ANYWHERE...

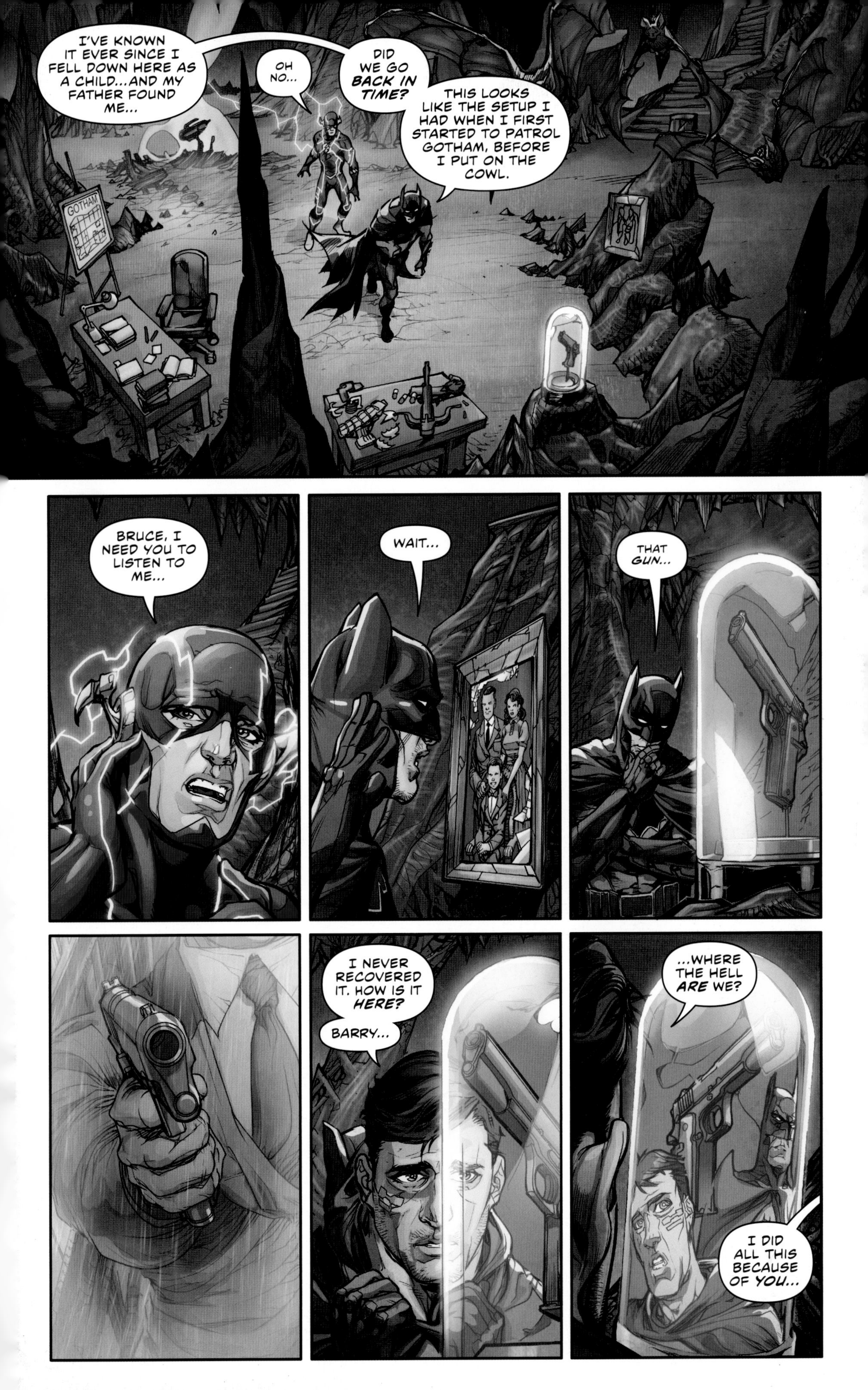
I'VE KNOWN IT EVER SINCE I FELL DOWN HERE AS A CHILD...AND MY FATHER FOUND ME...
OH NO...
DID WE GO BACK IN TIME?
THIS LOOKS LIKE THE SETUP I HAD WHEN I FIRST STARTED TO PATROL GOTHAM, BEFORE I PUT ON THE COWL.
GOTHAM
BRUCE, I NEED YOU TO LISTEN TO ME...
WAIT...
THAT GUN...
I NEVER RECOVERED IT. HOW IS IT HERE?
BARRY...
...WHERE THE HELL ARE WE?
I DID ALL THIS BECAUSE OF YOU...

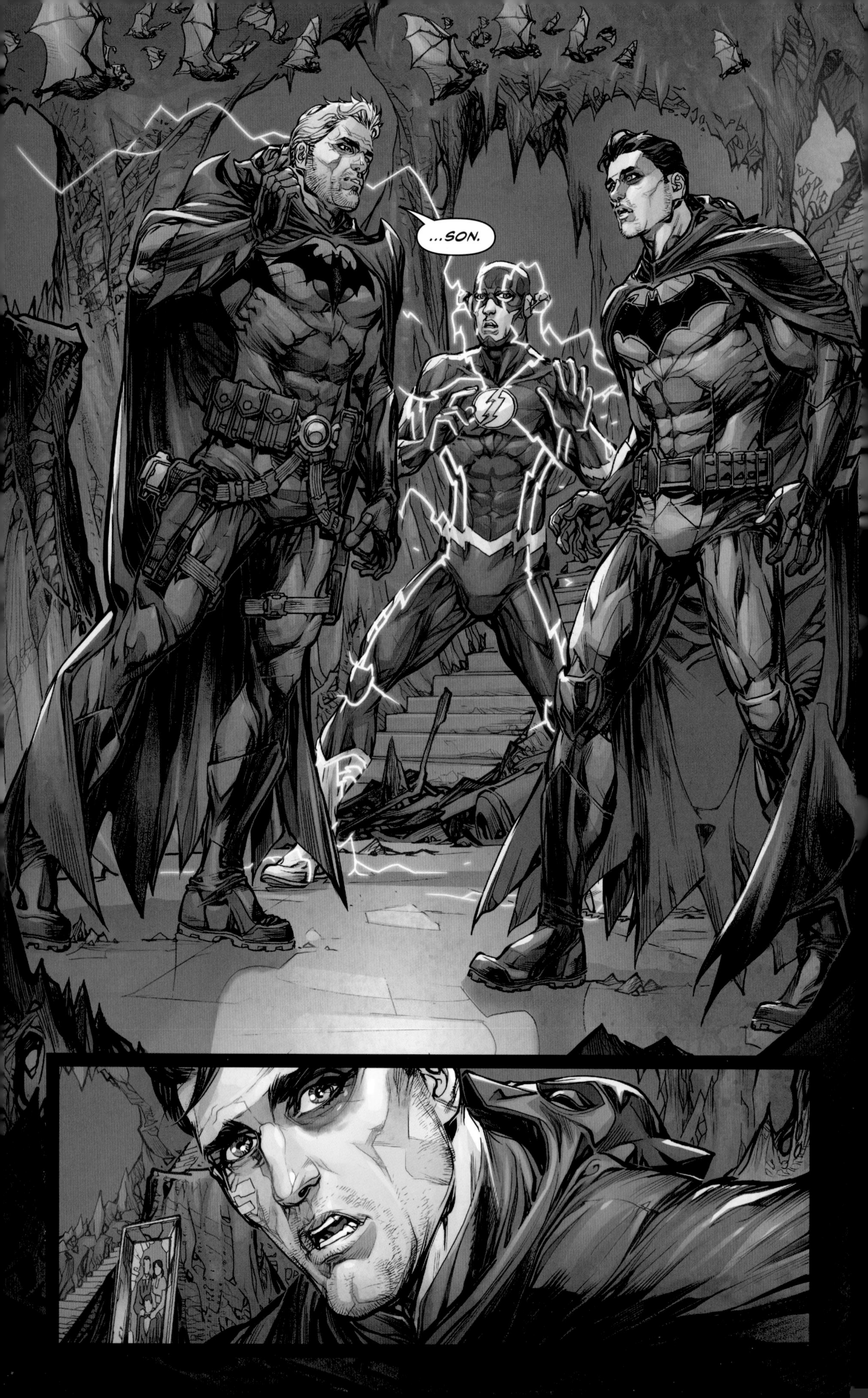
...SON.

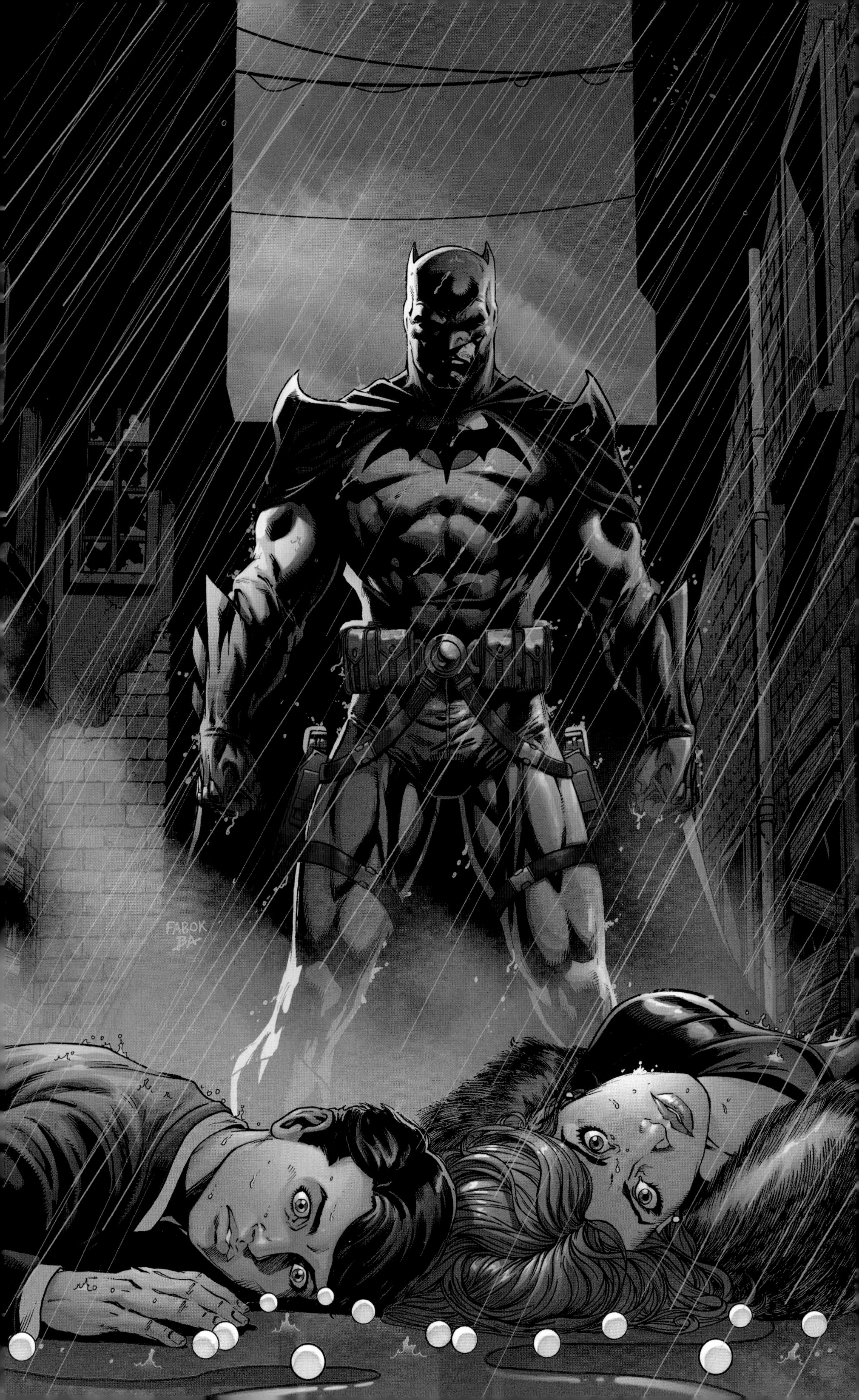
FABOK
BA

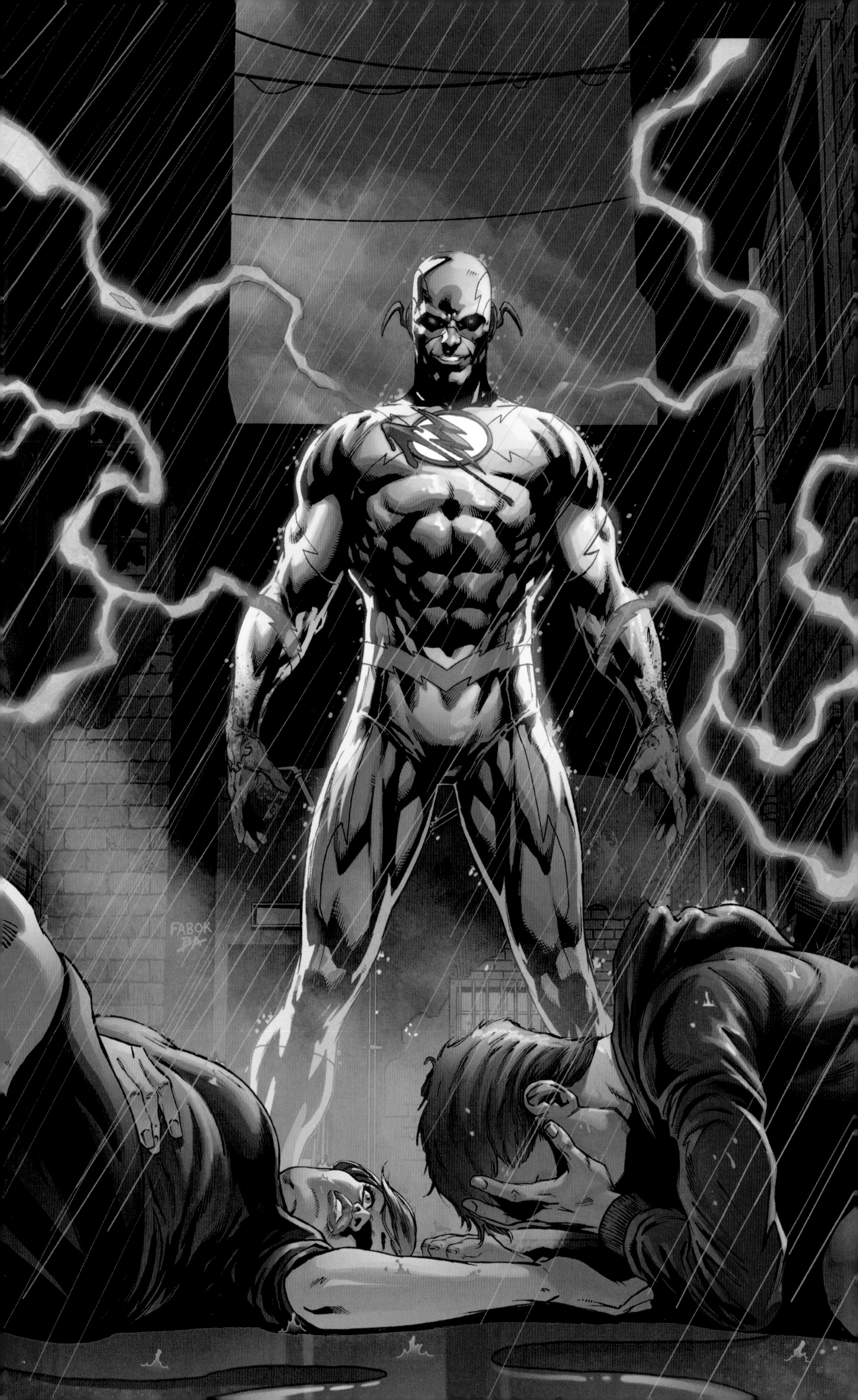
FABOK

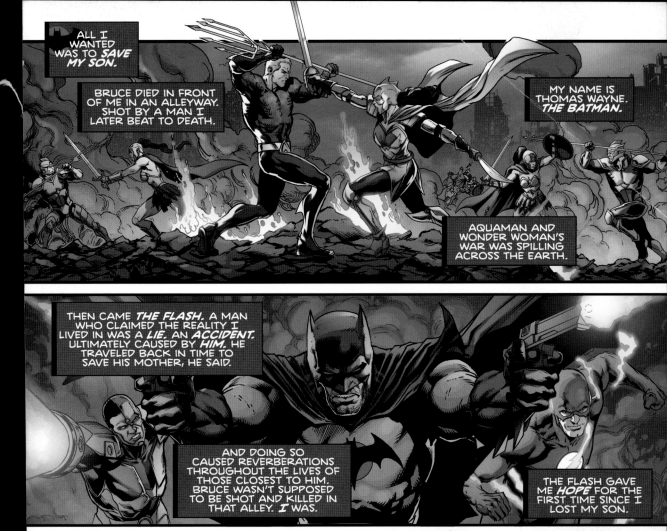

ALL I WANTED WAS TO *SAVE MY SON.*

BRUCE DIED IN FRONT OF ME IN AN ALLEYWAY. SHOT BY A MAN I LATER BEAT TO DEATH.

MY NAME IS THOMAS WAYNE. *THE BATMAN.*

AQUAMAN AND WONDER WOMAN'S WAR WAS SPILLING ACROSS THE EARTH.

THEN CAME *THE FLASH.* A MAN WHO CLAIMED THE REALITY I LIVED IN WAS A *LIE,* AN *ACCIDENT.* ULTIMATELY CAUSED BY *HIM.* HE TRAVELED BACK IN TIME TO SAVE HIS MOTHER, HE SAID.

AND DOING SO CAUSED REVERBERATIONS THROUGHOUT THE LIVES OF THOSE CLOSEST TO HIM. BRUCE WASN'T SUPPOSED TO BE SHOT AND KILLED IN THAT ALLEY. *I* WAS.

THE FLASH GAVE ME *HOPE* FOR THE FIRST TIME SINCE I LOST MY SON.

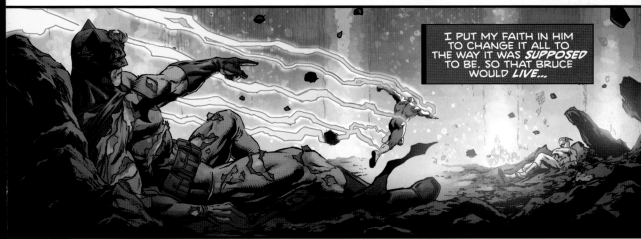

I PUT MY FAITH IN HIM TO CHANGE IT ALL TO THE WAY IT WAS *SUPPOSED* TO BE. SO THAT BRUCE WOULD *LIVE...*

...AND *I* WOULD *DIE.*

AS WOULD THIS *NIGHTMARE* OF A *WORLD.*

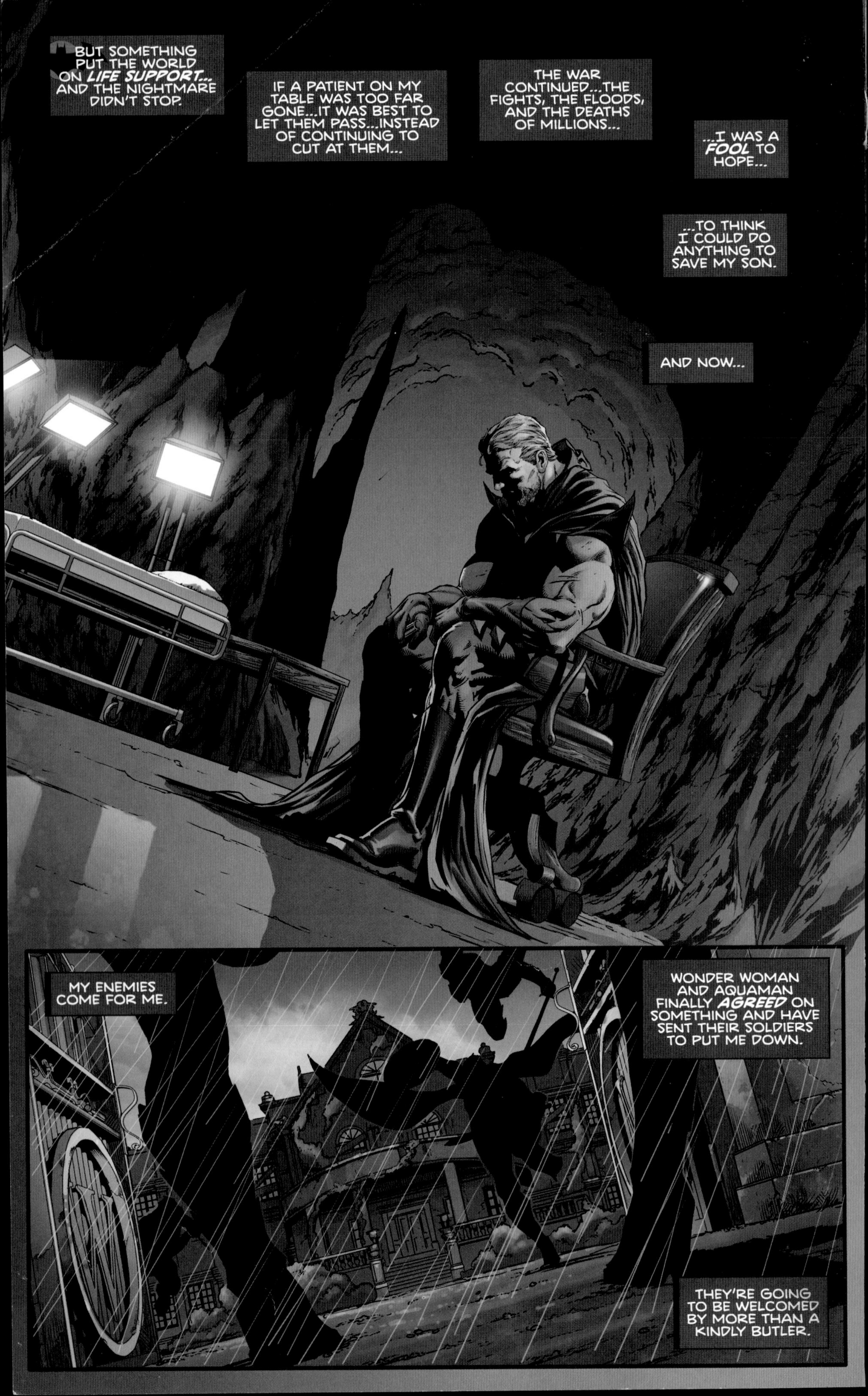
BUT SOMETHING PUT THE WORLD ON LIFE SUPPORT... AND THE NIGHTMARE DIDN'T STOP.
IF A PATIENT ON MY TABLE WAS TOO FAR GONE...IT WAS BEST TO LET THEM PASS...INSTEAD OF CONTINUING TO CUT AT THEM...
THE WAR CONTINUED...THE FIGHTS, THE FLOODS, AND THE DEATHS OF MILLIONS...
...I WAS A FOOL TO HOPE...
...TO THINK I COULD DO ANYTHING TO SAVE MY SON.
AND NOW...
MY ENEMIES COME FOR ME.
WONDER WOMAN AND AQUAMAN FINALLY AGREED ON SOMETHING AND HAVE SENT THEIR SOLDIERS TO PUT ME DOWN.
THEY'RE GOING TO BE WELCOMED BY MORE THAN A KINDLY BUTLER.

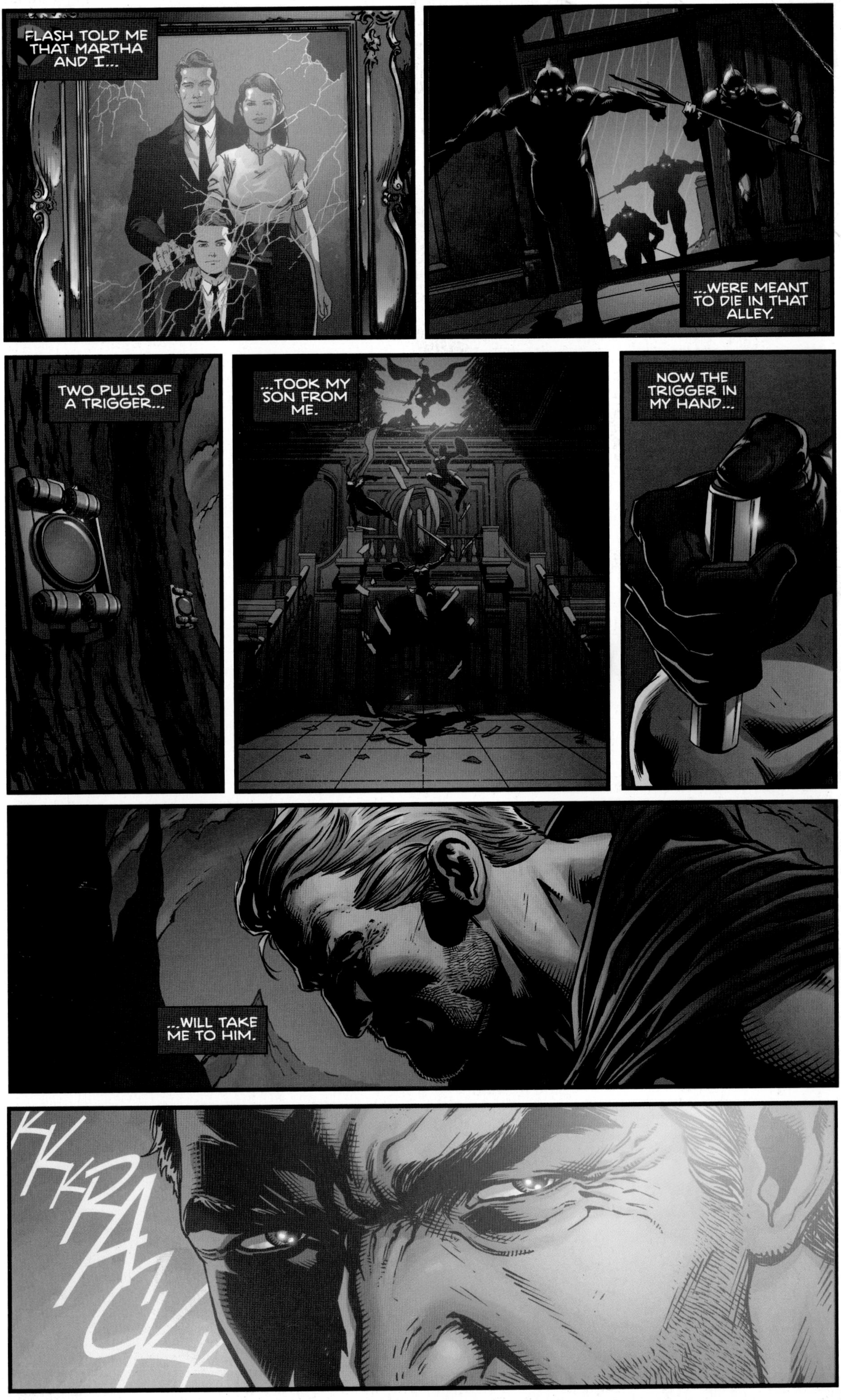
FLASH TOLD ME THAT MARTHA AND I...
...WERE MEANT TO DIE IN THAT ALLEY.
TWO PULLS OF A TRIGGER...
...TOOK MY SON FROM ME.
NOW THE TRIGGER IN MY HAND...
...WILL TAKE ME TO HIM.
KKRACKK

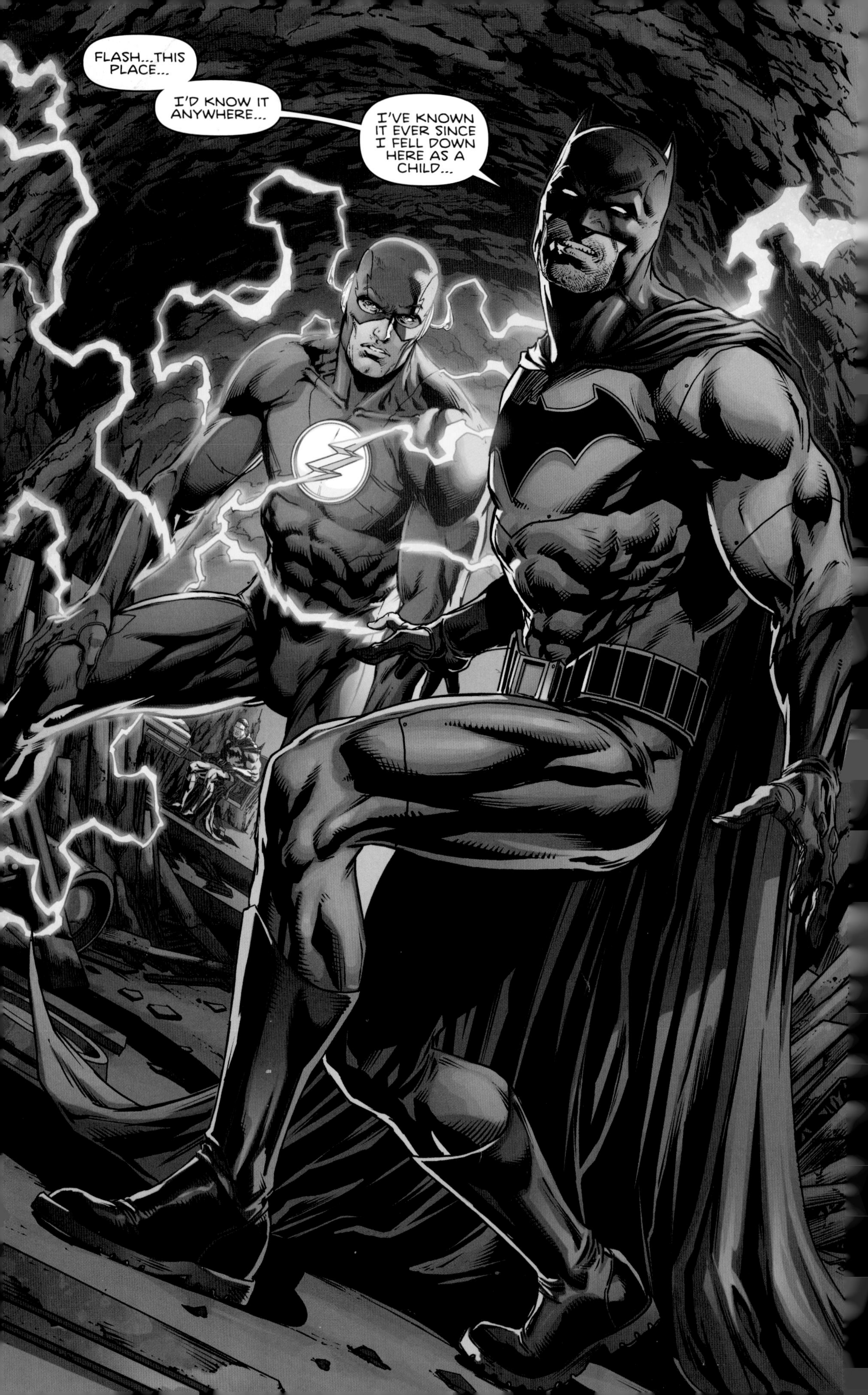
FLASH...THIS PLACE...
I'D KNOW IT ANYWHERE...
I'VE KNOWN IT EVER SINCE I FELL DOWN HERE AS A CHILD...

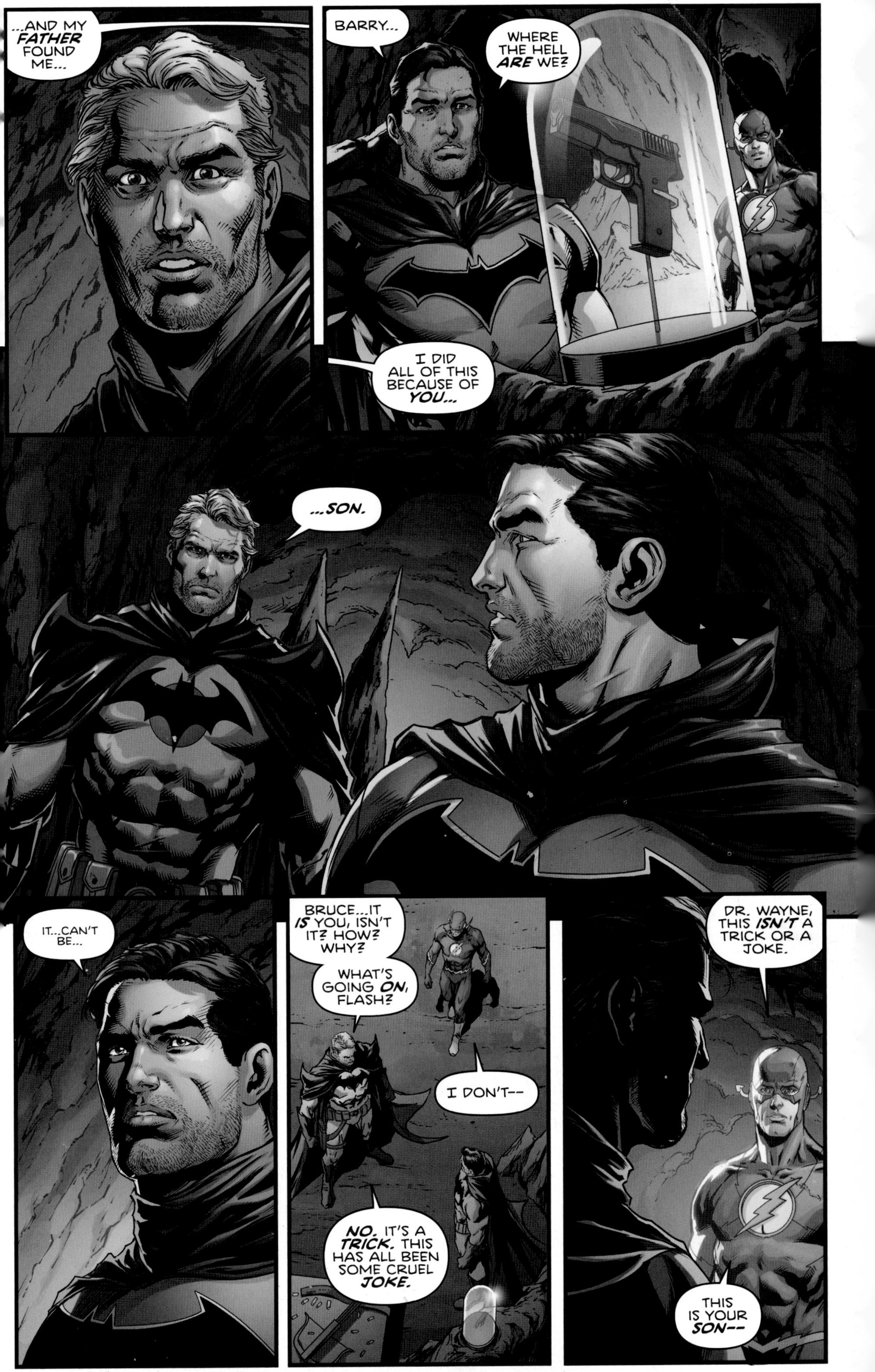
...AND MY FATHER FOUND ME...
BARRY...
WHERE THE HELL ARE WE?
I DID ALL OF THIS BECAUSE OF YOU...
...SON.
IT...CAN'T BE...
BRUCE...IT IS YOU, ISN'T IT? HOW? WHY?
WHAT'S GOING ON, FLASH?
I DON'T--
NO. IT'S A TRICK. THIS HAS ALL BEEN SOME CRUEL JOKE.
DR. WAYNE, THIS ISN'T A TRICK OR A JOKE.
THIS IS YOUR SON--

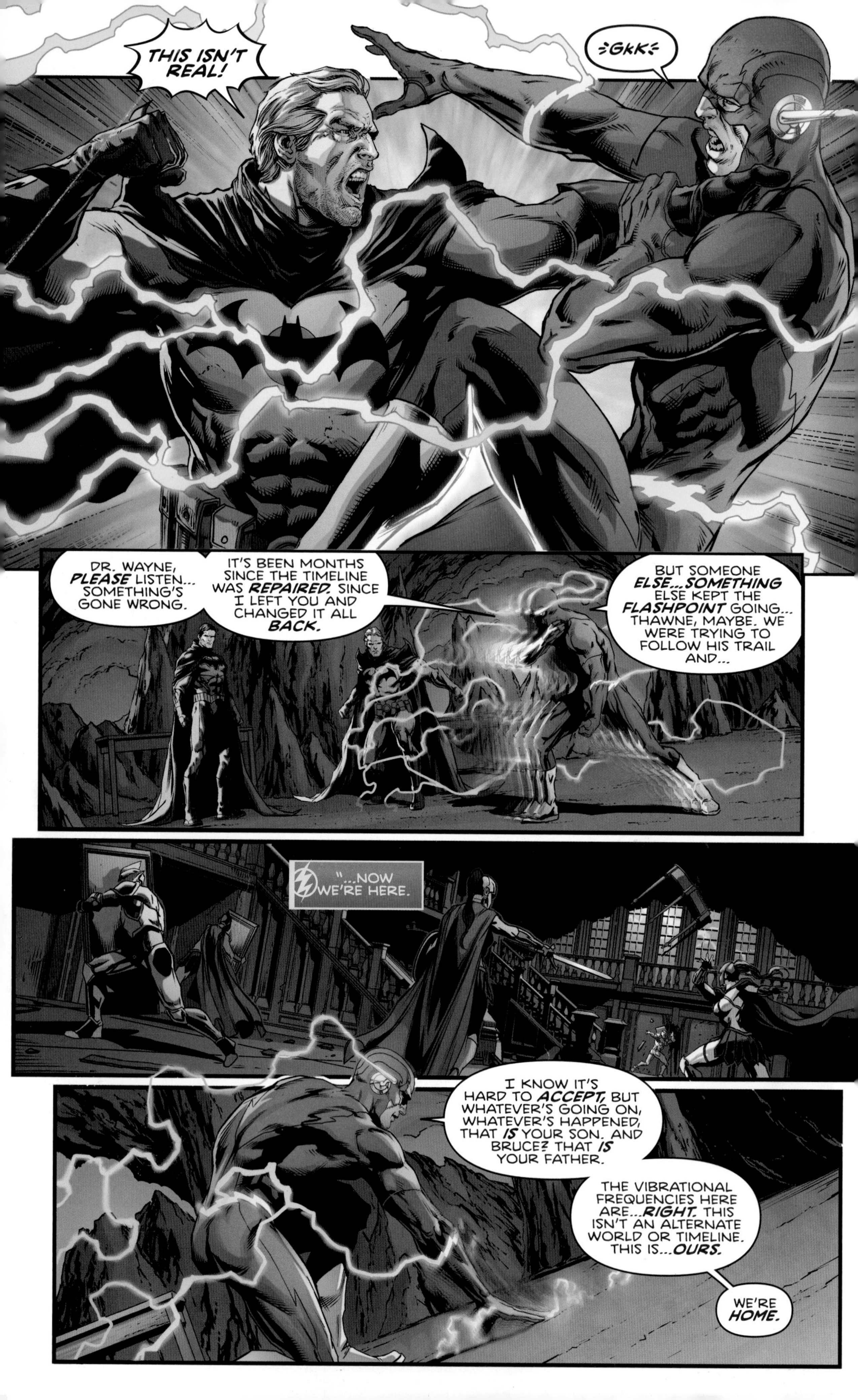
THIS ISN'T REAL!
GKK
DR. WAYNE, PLEASE LISTEN... SOMETHING'S GONE WRONG.
IT'S BEEN MONTHS SINCE THE TIMELINE WAS REPAIRED. SINCE I LEFT YOU AND CHANGED IT ALL BACK.
BUT SOMEONE ELSE...SOMETHING ELSE KEPT THE FLASHPOINT GOING... THAWNE, MAYBE. WE WERE TRYING TO FOLLOW HIS TRAIL AND...
"...NOW WE'RE HERE.
I KNOW IT'S HARD TO ACCEPT, BUT WHATEVER'S GOING ON, WHATEVER'S HAPPENED, THAT IS YOUR SON. AND BRUCE? THAT IS YOUR FATHER.
THE VIBRATIONAL FREQUENCIES HERE ARE...RIGHT. THIS ISN'T AN ALTERNATE WORLD OR TIMELINE. THIS IS...OURS.
WE'RE HOME.

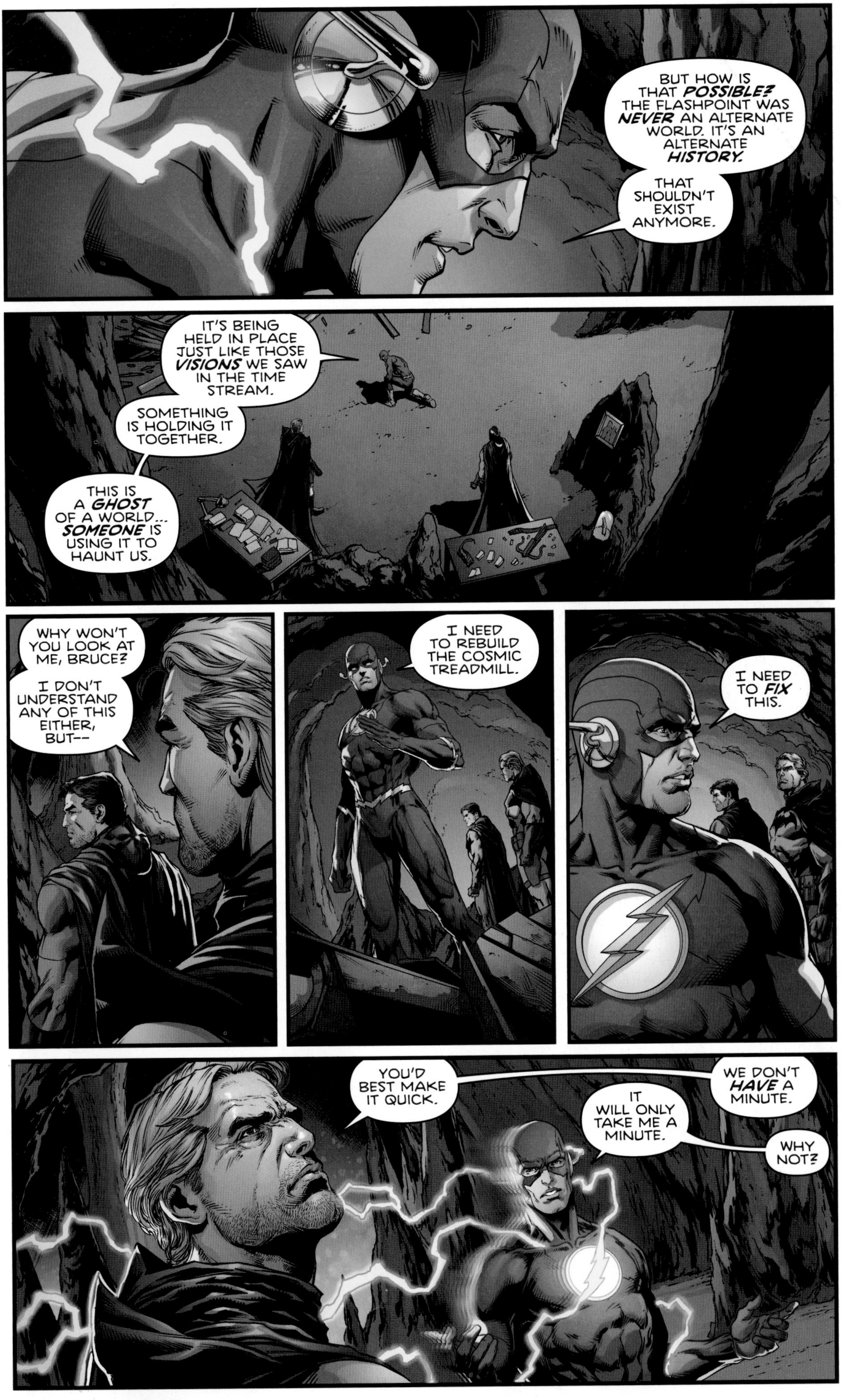
BUT HOW IS THAT *POSSIBLE?* THE FLASHPOINT WAS *NEVER* AN ALTERNATE WORLD. IT'S AN ALTERNATE *HISTORY.*
THAT SHOULDN'T EXIST ANYMORE.
IT'S BEING HELD IN PLACE JUST LIKE THOSE *VISIONS* WE SAW IN THE TIME STREAM.
SOMETHING IS HOLDING IT TOGETHER.
THIS IS A *GHOST* OF A WORLD... *SOMEONE* IS USING IT TO HAUNT US.
WHY WON'T YOU LOOK AT ME, BRUCE?
I DON'T UNDERSTAND ANY OF THIS EITHER, BUT--
I NEED TO REBUILD THE COSMIC TREADMILL.
I NEED TO *FIX* THIS.
YOU'D BEST MAKE IT QUICK.
IT WILL ONLY TAKE ME A MINUTE.
WE DON'T *HAVE* A MINUTE.
WHY NOT?

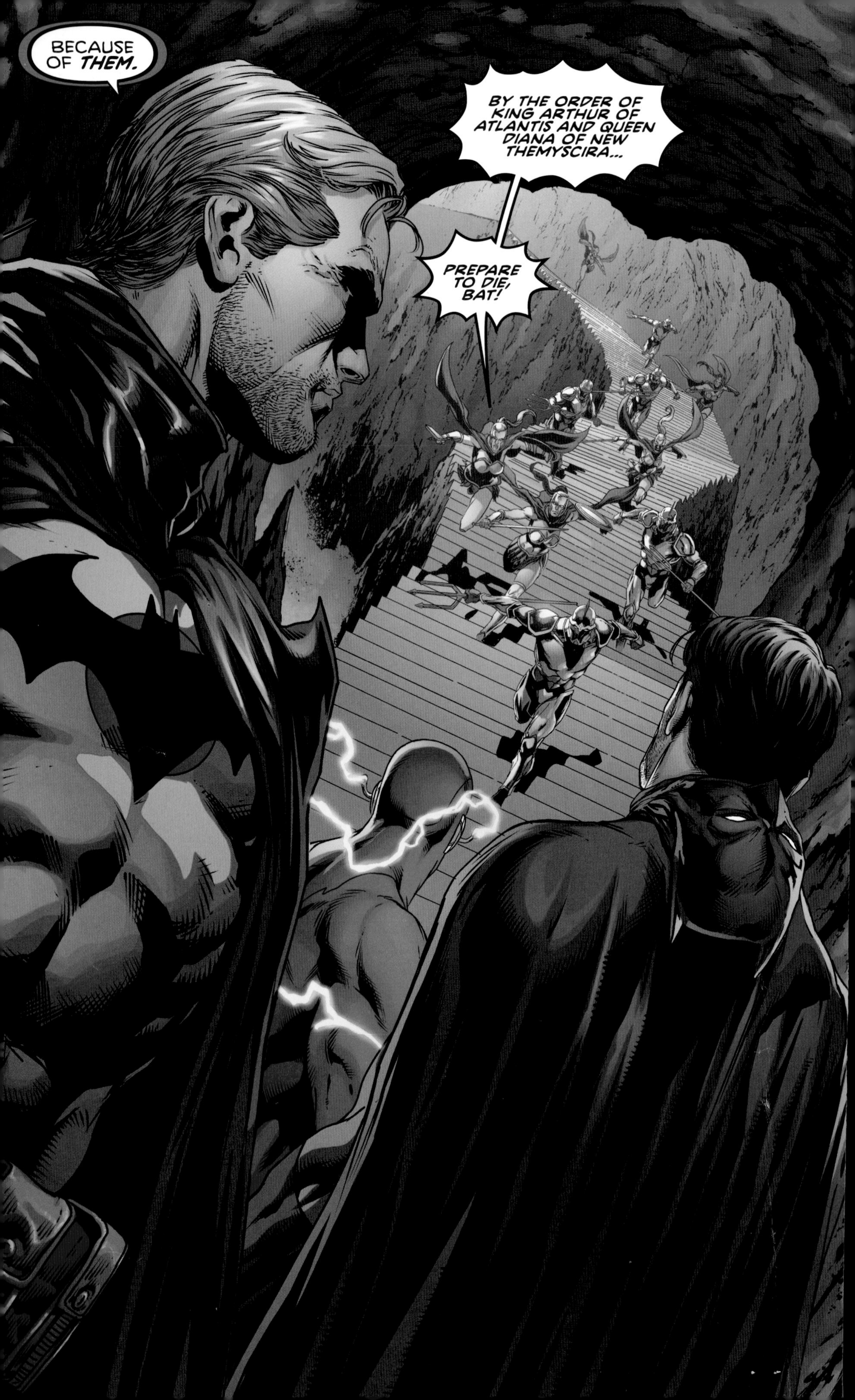
BECAUSE OF *THEM.*
BY THE ORDER OF KING ARTHUR OF ATLANTIS AND QUEEN DIANA OF NEW THEMYSCIRA...
PREPARE TO DIE, BAT!

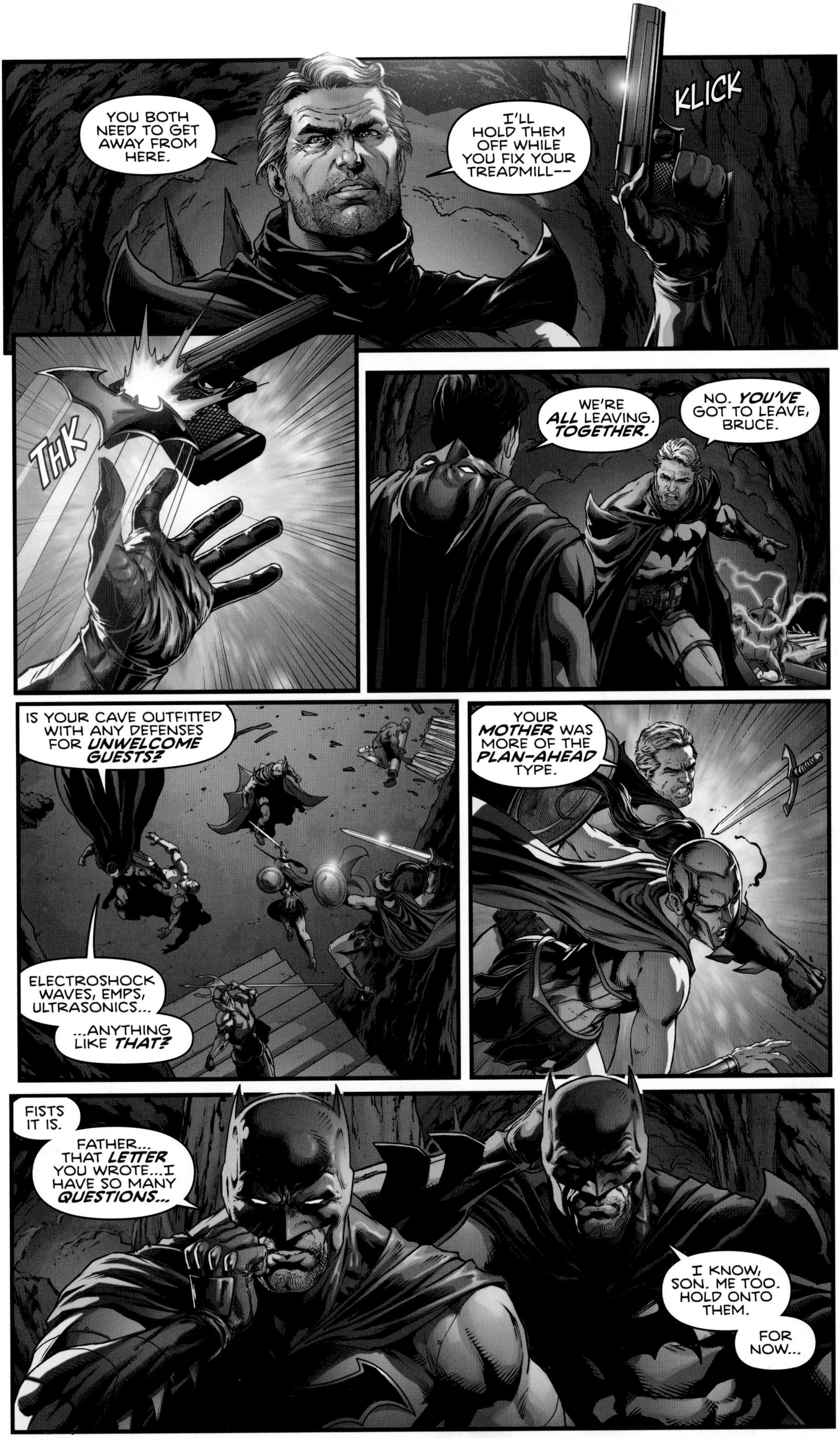

YOU BOTH NEED TO GET AWAY FROM HERE.
I'LL HOLD THEM OFF WHILE YOU FIX YOUR TREADMILL--
KLICK
THK
WE'RE ALL LEAVING. TOGETHER.
NO. YOU'VE GOT TO LEAVE, BRUCE.
IS YOUR CAVE OUTFITTED WITH ANY DEFENSES FOR UNWELCOME GUESTS?
ELECTROSHOCK WAVES, EMPS, ULTRASONICS...
...ANYTHING LIKE THAT?
YOUR MOTHER WAS MORE OF THE PLAN-AHEAD TYPE.
FISTS IT IS.
FATHER... THAT LETTER YOU WROTE...I HAVE SO MANY QUESTIONS...
I KNOW, SON. ME TOO. HOLD ONTO THEM.
FOR NOW...

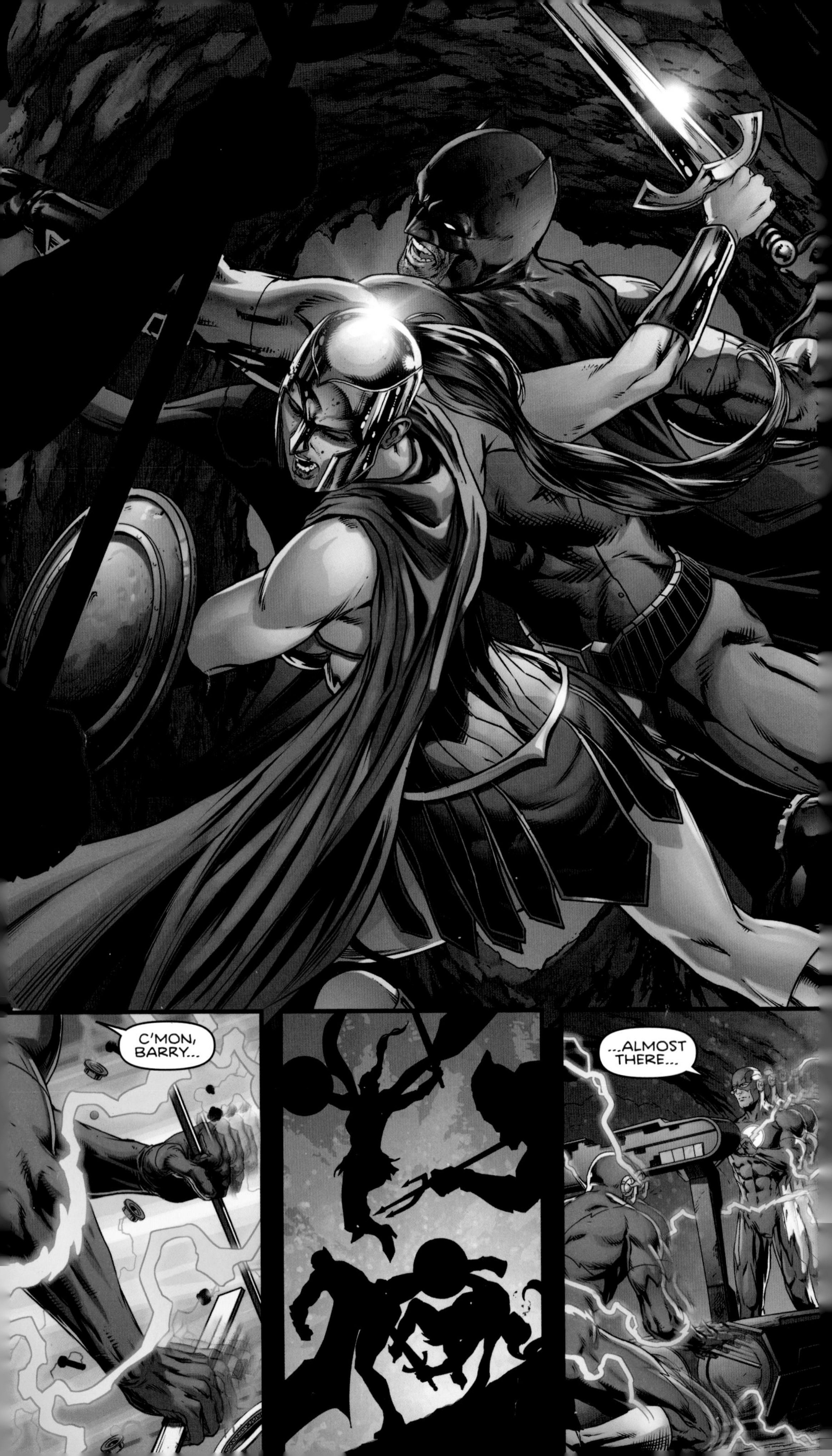
C'MON, BARRY...
...ALMOST THERE...

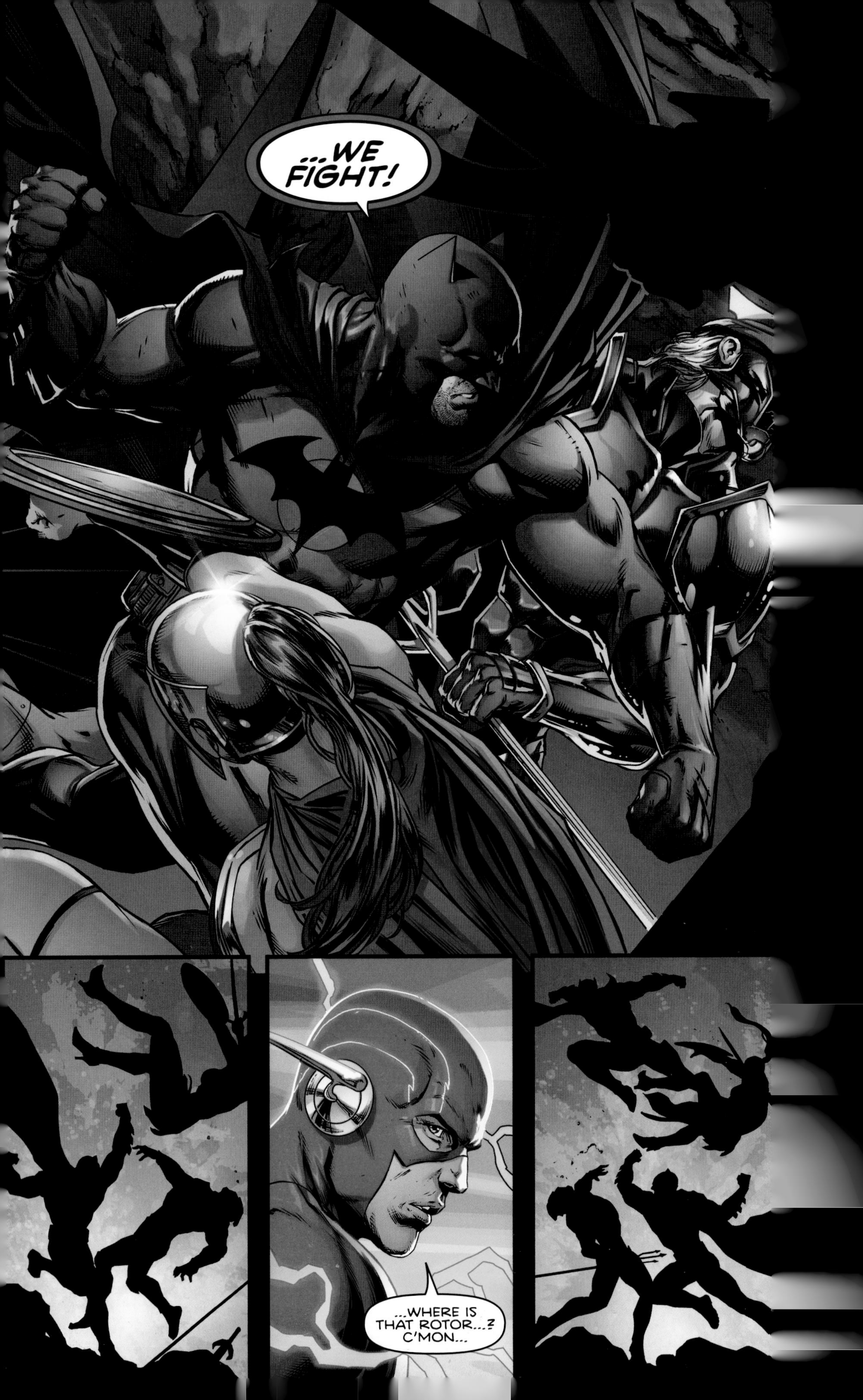
...WE FIGHT!
...WHERE IS THAT ROTOR...? C'MON...

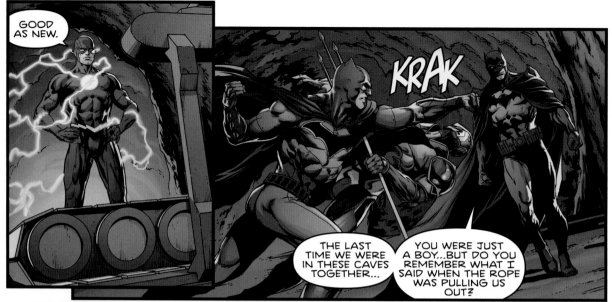

GOOD AS NEW.

KRAK

THE LAST TIME WE WERE IN THESE CAVES TOGETHER...

YOU WERE JUST A BOY...BUT DO YOU REMEMBER WHAT I SAID WHEN THE ROPE WAS PULLING US OUT?

BARELY... YOU WERE WHISPERING BECAUSE YOU DIDN'T...

...WANT TO SCARE THE BATS...

DAD.

OKAY, GUYS, LET'S GO!

KRACKAKRACK

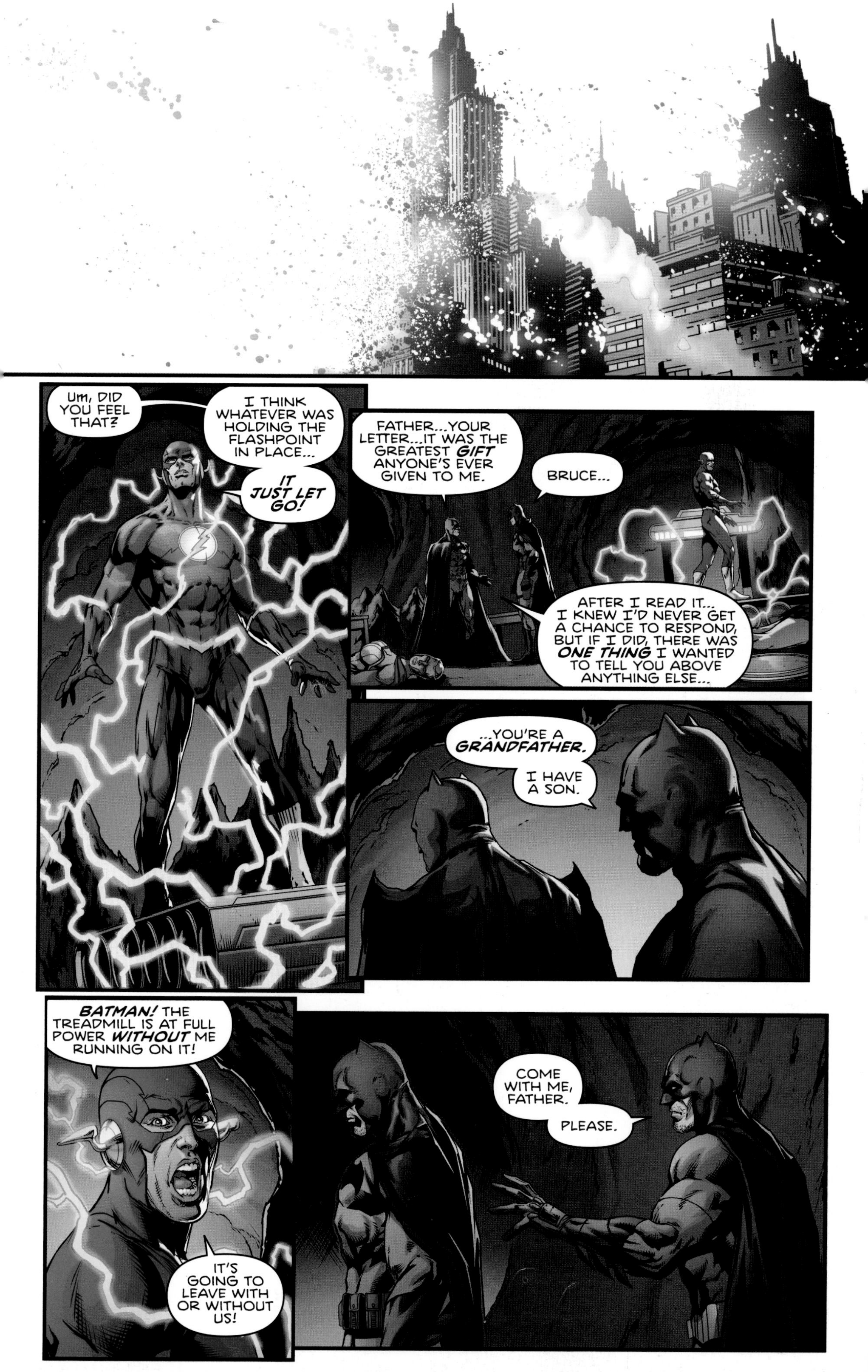
UM, DID YOU FEEL THAT?
I THINK WHATEVER WAS HOLDING THE FLASHPOINT IN PLACE...
IT JUST LET GO!
FATHER...YOUR LETTER...IT WAS THE GREATEST GIFT ANYONE'S EVER GIVEN TO ME.
BRUCE...
AFTER I READ IT... I KNEW I'D NEVER GET A CHANCE TO RESPOND, BUT IF I DID, THERE WAS ONE THING I WANTED TO TELL YOU ABOVE ANYTHING ELSE...
...YOU'RE A GRANDFATHER.
I HAVE A SON.
BATMAN! THE TREADMILL IS AT FULL POWER WITHOUT ME RUNNING ON IT!
IT'S GOING TO LEAVE WITH OR WITHOUT US!
COME WITH ME, FATHER.
PLEASE.

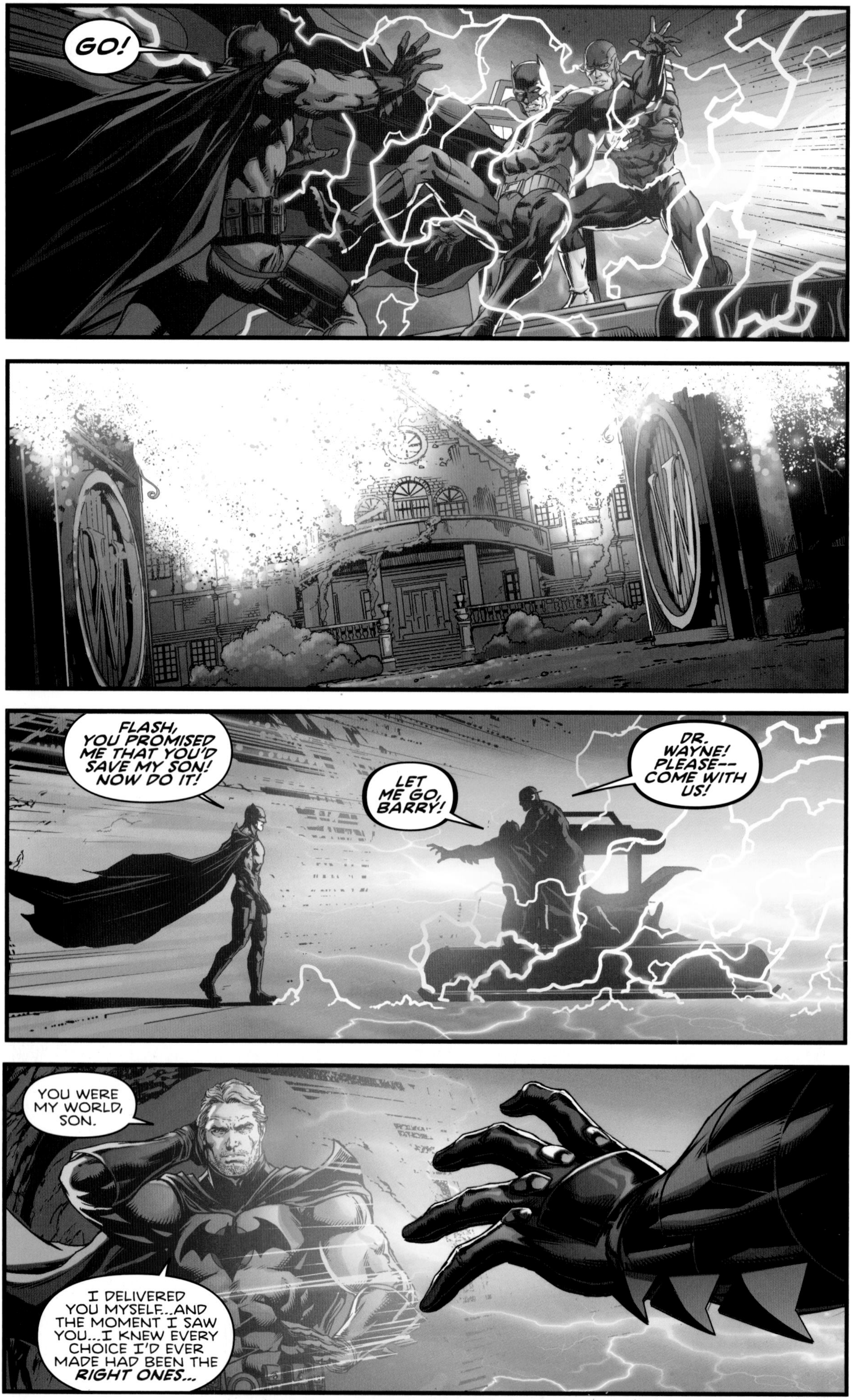
GO!
FLASH, YOU PROMISED ME THAT YOU'D SAVE MY SON! NOW DO IT!
LET ME GO, BARRY!
DR. WAYNE! PLEASE-- COME WITH US!
YOU WERE MY WORLD, SON.
I DELIVERED YOU MYSELF...AND THE MOMENT I SAW YOU...I KNEW EVERY CHOICE I'D EVER MADE HAD BEEN THE RIGHT ONES...

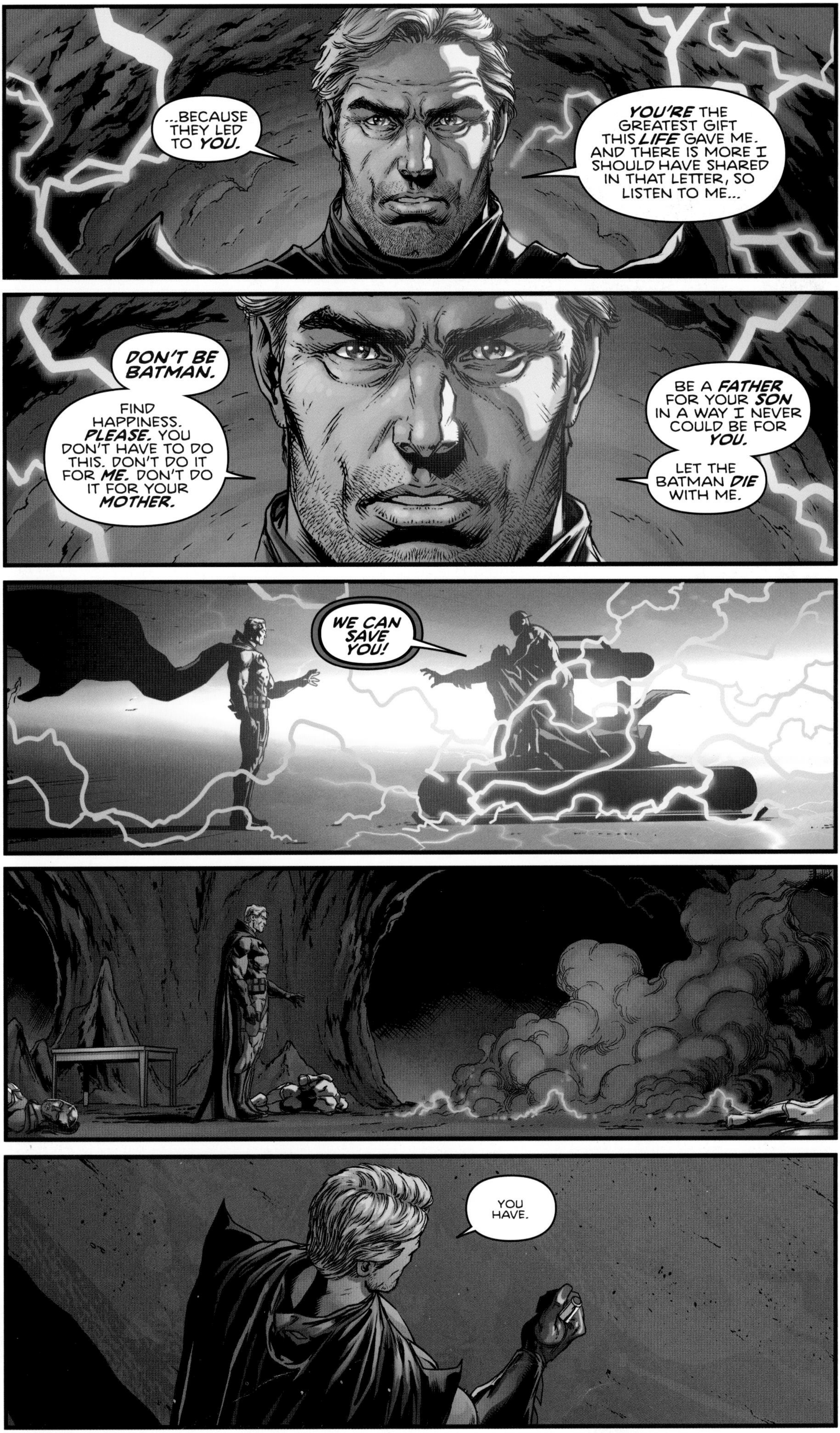
...BECAUSE THEY LED TO YOU.
YOU'RE THE GREATEST GIFT THIS LIFE GAVE ME. AND THERE IS MORE I SHOULD HAVE SHARED IN THAT LETTER, SO LISTEN TO ME...
DON'T BE BATMAN.
FIND HAPPINESS. PLEASE. YOU DON'T HAVE TO DO THIS. DON'T DO IT FOR ME. DON'T DO IT FOR YOUR MOTHER.
BE A FATHER FOR YOUR SON IN A WAY I NEVER COULD BE FOR YOU.
LET THE BATMAN DIE WITH ME.
WE CAN SAVE YOU!
YOU HAVE.

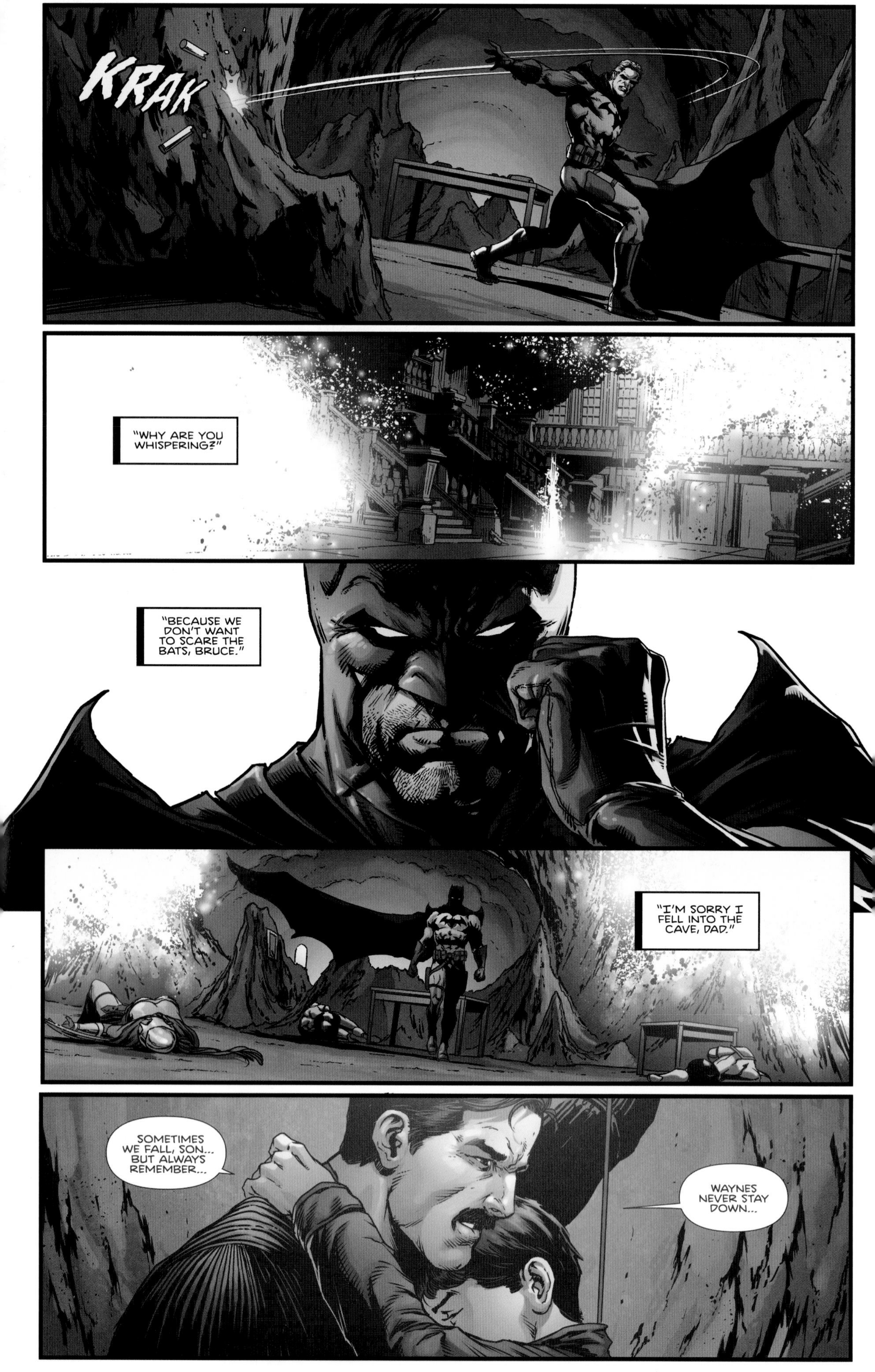
KRAK
"WHY ARE YOU WHISPERING?"
"BECAUSE WE DON'T WANT TO SCARE THE BATS, BRUCE."
"I'M SORRY I FELL INTO THE CAVE, DAD."
SOMETIMES WE FALL, SON... BUT ALWAYS REMEMBER...
WAYNES NEVER STAY DOWN...

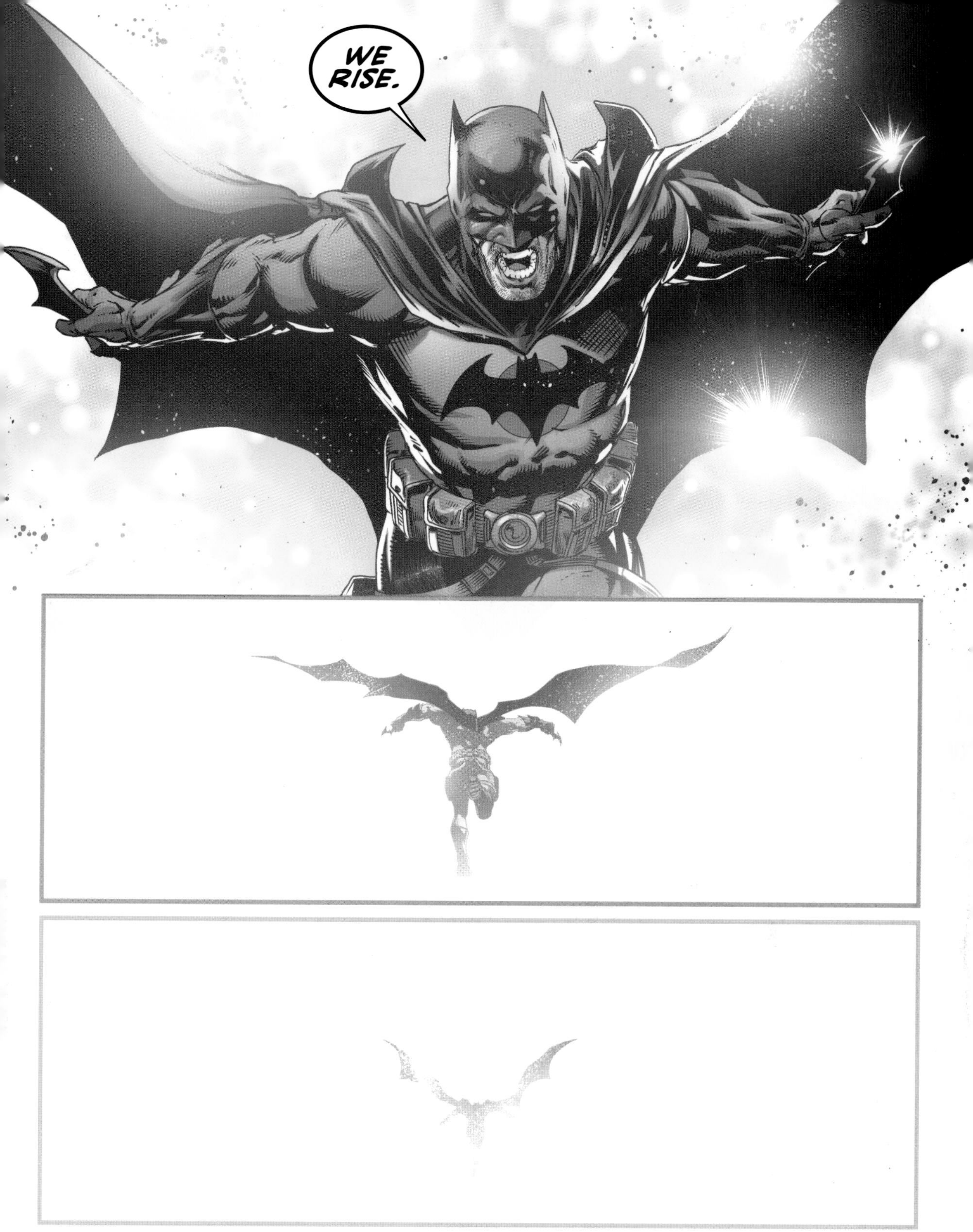
WE RISE.

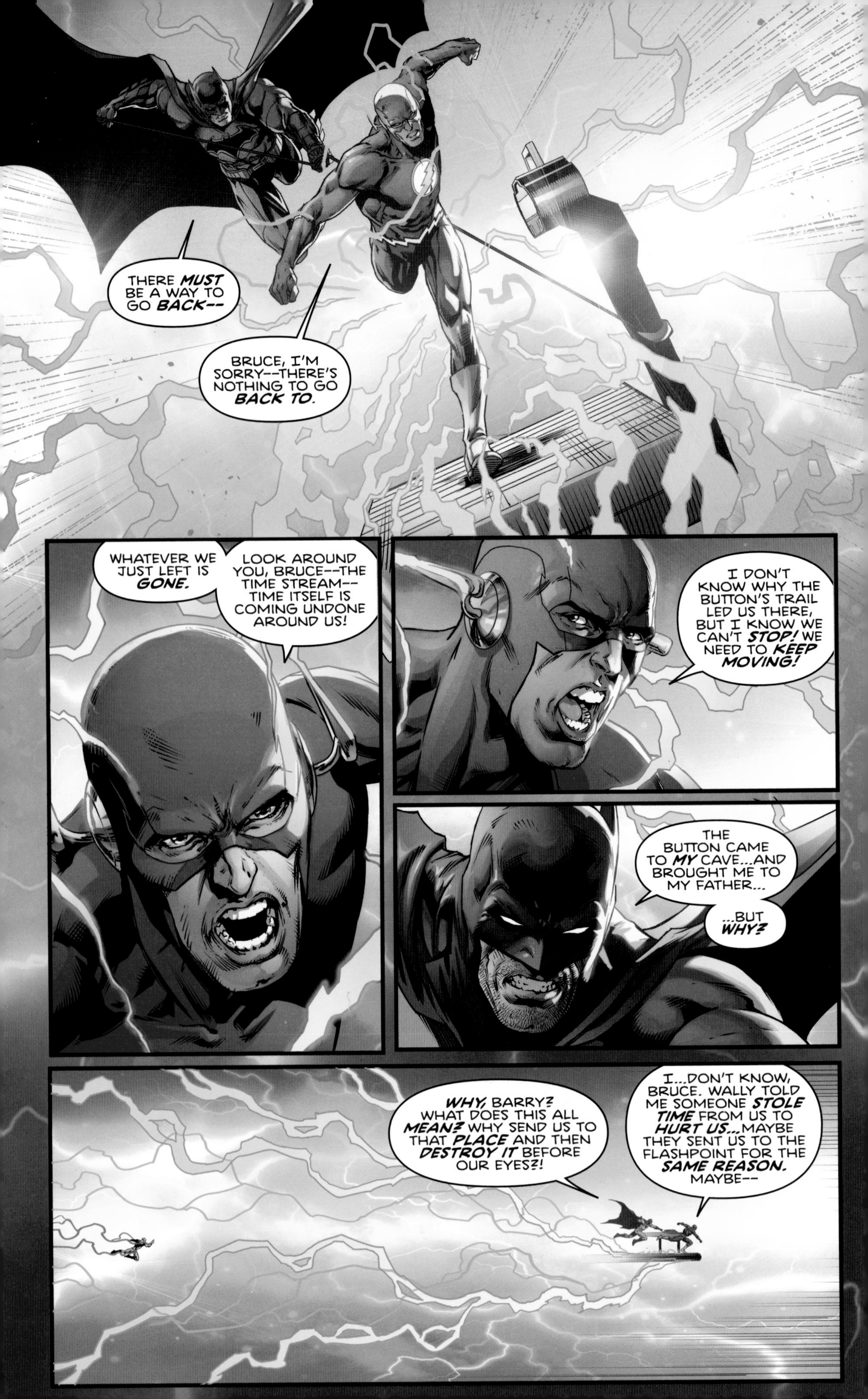
THERE MUST BE A WAY TO GO BACK--
BRUCE, I'M SORRY--THERE'S NOTHING TO GO BACK TO.
WHATEVER WE JUST LEFT IS GONE.
LOOK AROUND YOU, BRUCE--THE TIME STREAM--TIME ITSELF IS COMING UNDONE AROUND US!
I DON'T KNOW WHY THE BUTTON'S TRAIL LED US THERE, BUT I KNOW WE CAN'T STOP! WE NEED TO KEEP MOVING!
THE BUTTON CAME TO MY CAVE...AND BROUGHT ME TO MY FATHER...
...BUT WHY?
WHY, BARRY? WHAT DOES THIS ALL MEAN? WHY SEND US TO THAT PLACE AND THEN DESTROY IT BEFORE OUR EYES?!
I...DON'T KNOW, BRUCE. WALLY TOLD ME SOMEONE STOLE TIME FROM US TO HURT US...MAYBE THEY SENT US TO THE FLASHPOINT FOR THE SAME REASON. MAYBE--

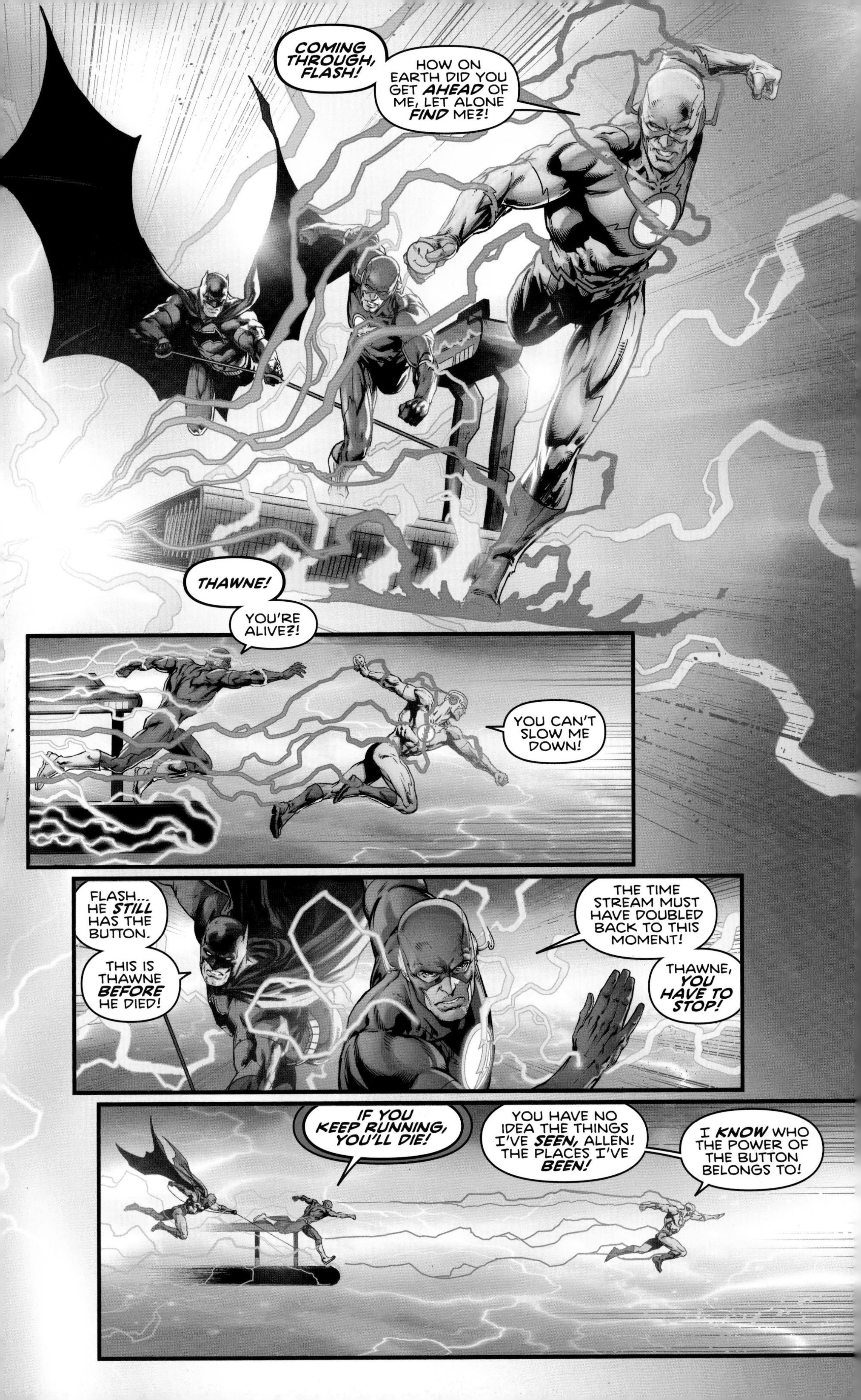
COMING THROUGH, FLASH!
HOW ON EARTH DID YOU GET AHEAD OF ME, LET ALONE FIND ME?!
THAWNE!
YOU'RE ALIVE?!
YOU CAN'T SLOW ME DOWN!
FLASH... HE STILL HAS THE BUTTON.
THIS IS THAWNE BEFORE HE DIED!
THE TIME STREAM MUST HAVE DOUBLED BACK TO THIS MOMENT!
THAWNE, YOU HAVE TO STOP!
IF YOU KEEP RUNNING, YOU'LL DIE!
YOU HAVE NO IDEA THE THINGS I'VE SEEN, ALLEN! THE PLACES I'VE BEEN!
I KNOW WHO THE POWER OF THE BUTTON BELONGS TO!

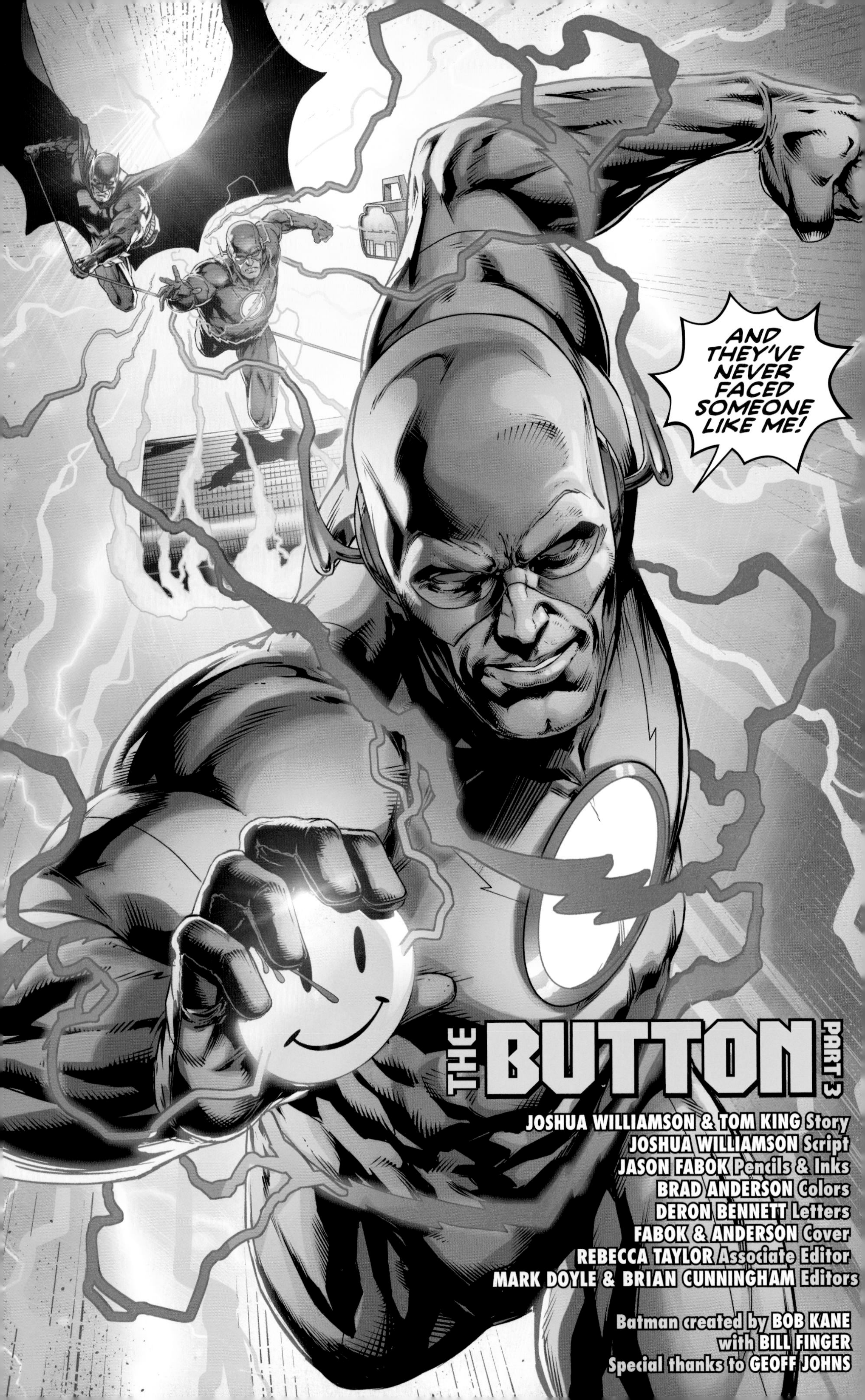
AND THEY'VE NEVER FACED SOMEONE LIKE ME!
THE BUTTON PART 3
JOSHUA WILLIAMSON & TOM KING Story
JOSHUA WILLIAMSON Script
JASON FABOK Pencils & Inks
BRAD ANDERSON Colors
DERON BENNETT Letters
FABOK & ANDERSON Cover
REBECCA TAYLOR Associate Editor
MARK DOYLE & BRIAN CUNNINGHAM Editors
Batman created by BOB KANE
with BILL FINGER
Special thanks to GEOFF JOHNS

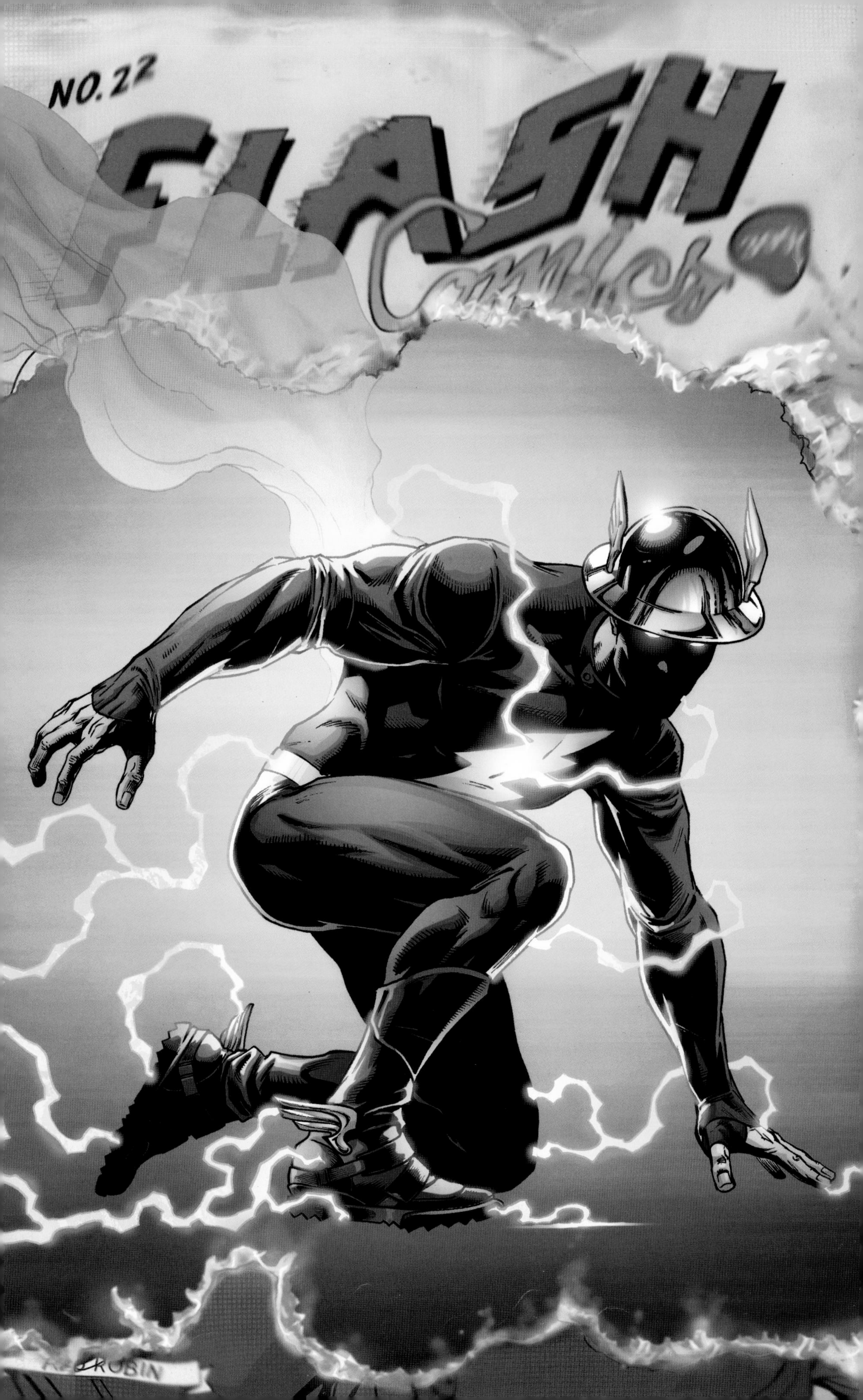
NO.22

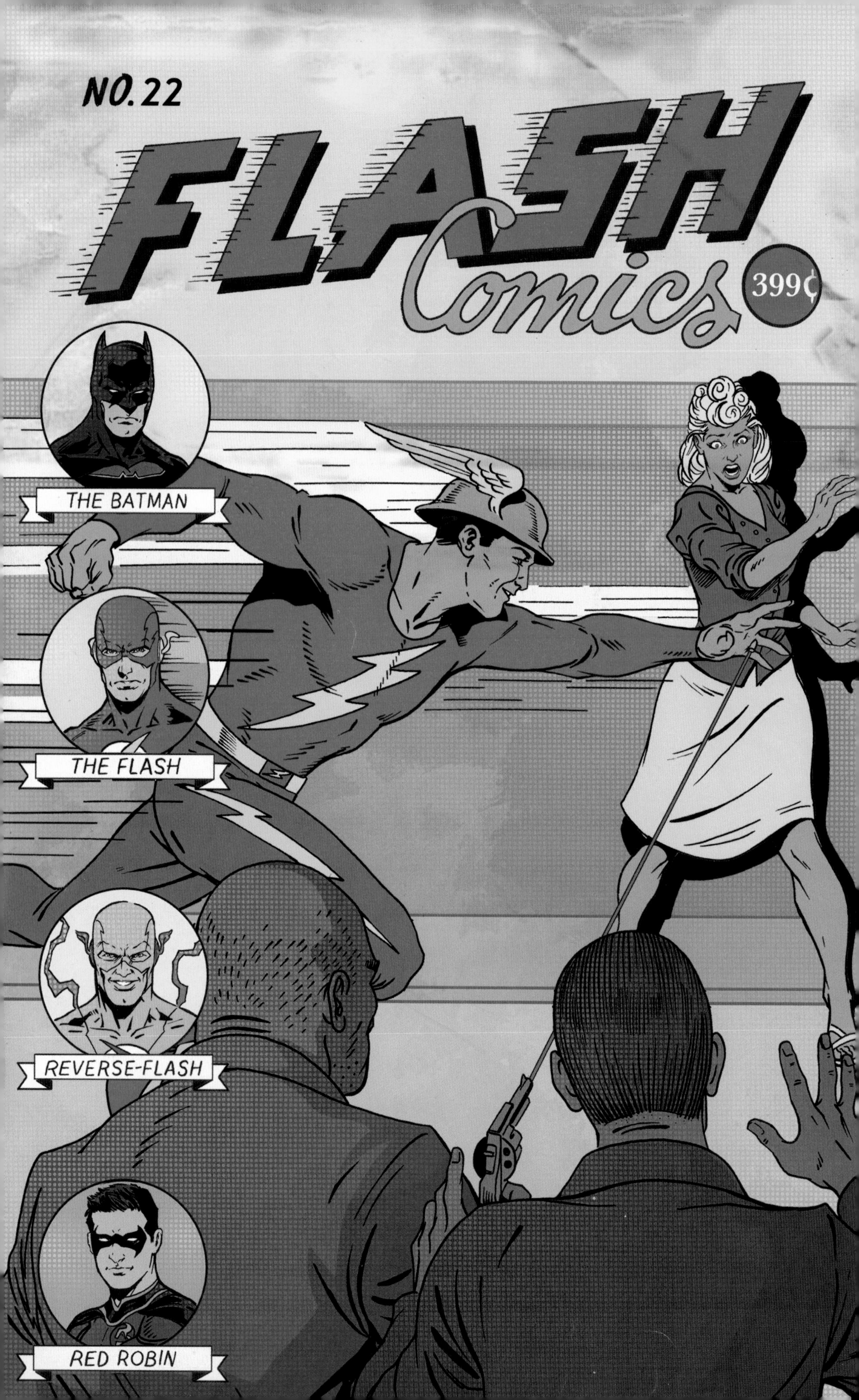

NO. 22
FLASH Comics
399¢
THE BATMAN
THE FLASH
REVERSE-FLASH
RED ROBIN

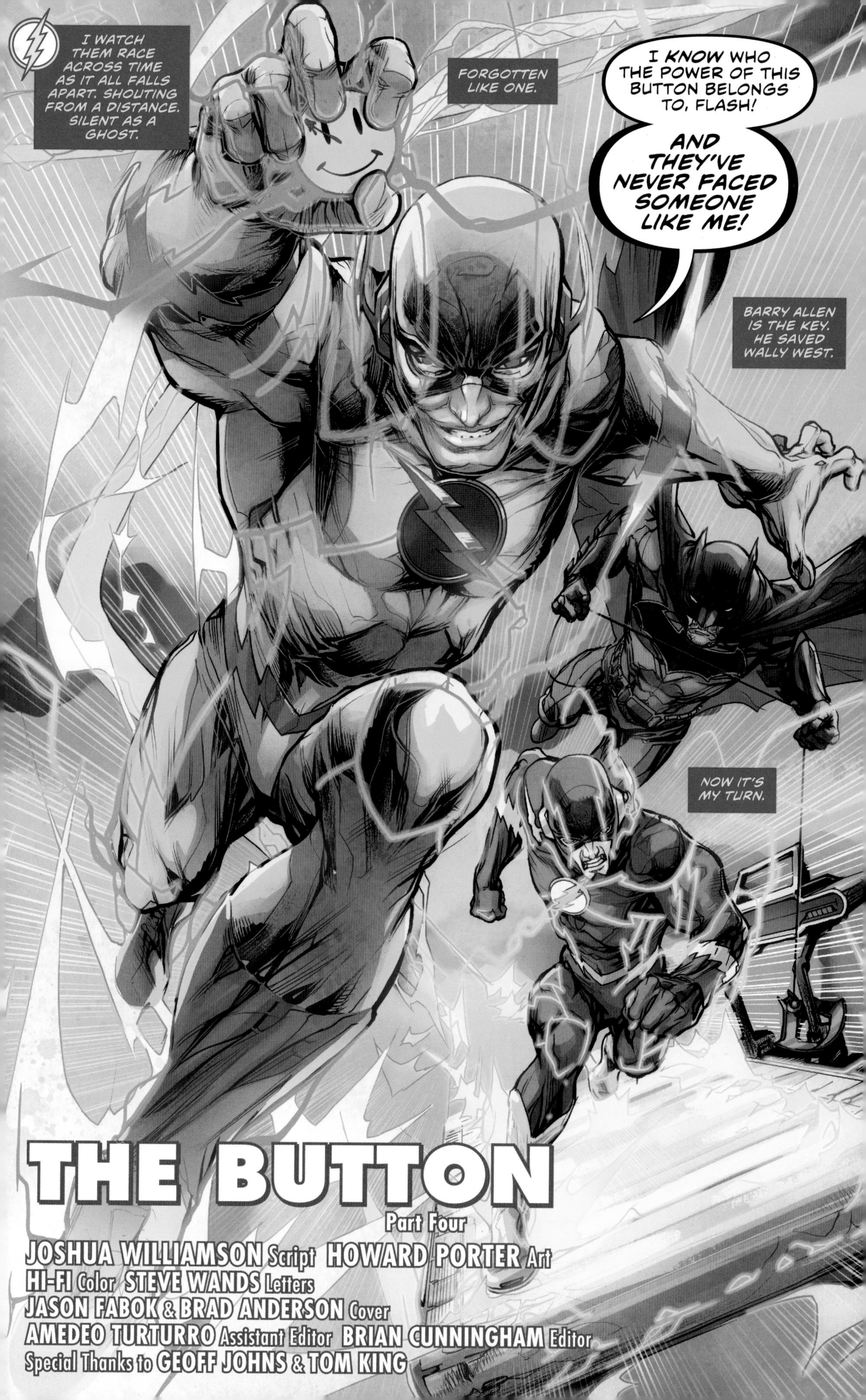
I WATCH THEM RACE ACROSS TIME AS IT ALL FALLS APART. SHOUTING FROM A DISTANCE. SILENT AS A GHOST.
FORGOTTEN LIKE ONE.
I KNOW WHO THE POWER OF THIS BUTTON BELONGS TO, FLASH!
AND THEY'VE NEVER FACED SOMEONE LIKE ME!
BARRY ALLEN IS THE KEY. HE SAVED WALLY WEST.
NOW IT'S MY TURN.
THE BUTTON
Part Four
JOSHUA WILLIAMSON Script HOWARD PORTER Art
HI-FI Color STEVE WANDS Letters
JASON FABOK & BRAD ANDERSON Cover
AMEDEO TURTURRO Assistant Editor BRIAN CUNNINGHAM Editor
Special Thanks to GEOFF JOHNS & TOM KING

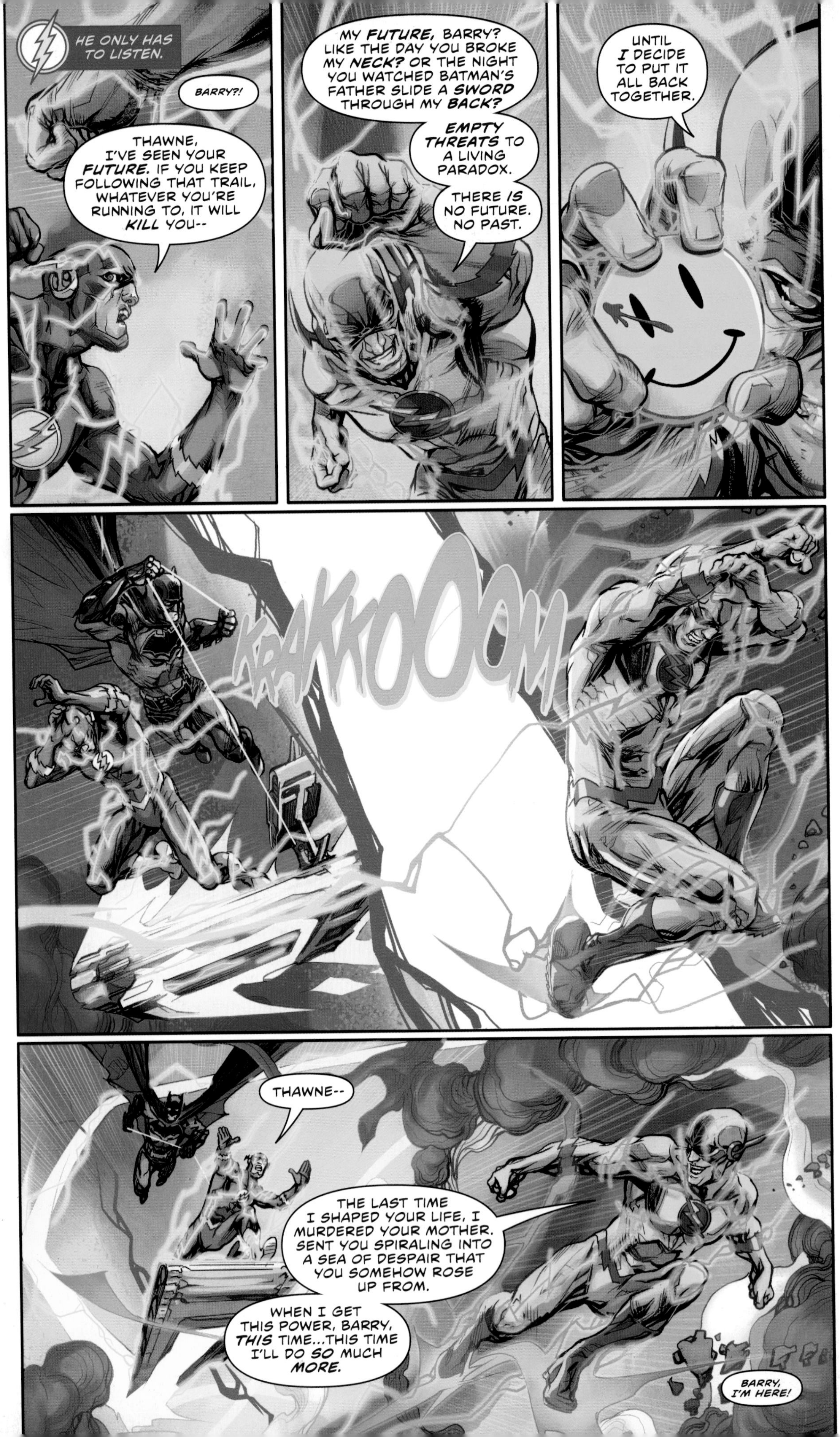
HE ONLY HAS TO LISTEN.
BARRY?!
THAWNE, I'VE SEEN YOUR FUTURE. IF YOU KEEP FOLLOWING THAT TRAIL, WHATEVER YOU'RE RUNNING TO, IT WILL KILL YOU--
MY FUTURE, BARRY? LIKE THE DAY YOU BROKE MY NECK? OR THE NIGHT YOU WATCHED BATMAN'S FATHER SLIDE A SWORD THROUGH MY BACK?
EMPTY THREATS TO A LIVING PARADOX.
THERE IS NO FUTURE. NO PAST.
UNTIL I DECIDE TO PUT IT ALL BACK TOGETHER.
KRAKKOOOM
THAWNE--
THE LAST TIME I SHAPED YOUR LIFE, I MURDERED YOUR MOTHER. SENT YOU SPIRALING INTO A SEA OF DESPAIR THAT YOU SOMEHOW ROSE UP FROM.
WHEN I GET THIS POWER, BARRY, THIS TIME...THIS TIME I'LL DO SO MUCH MORE.
BARRY, I'M HERE!

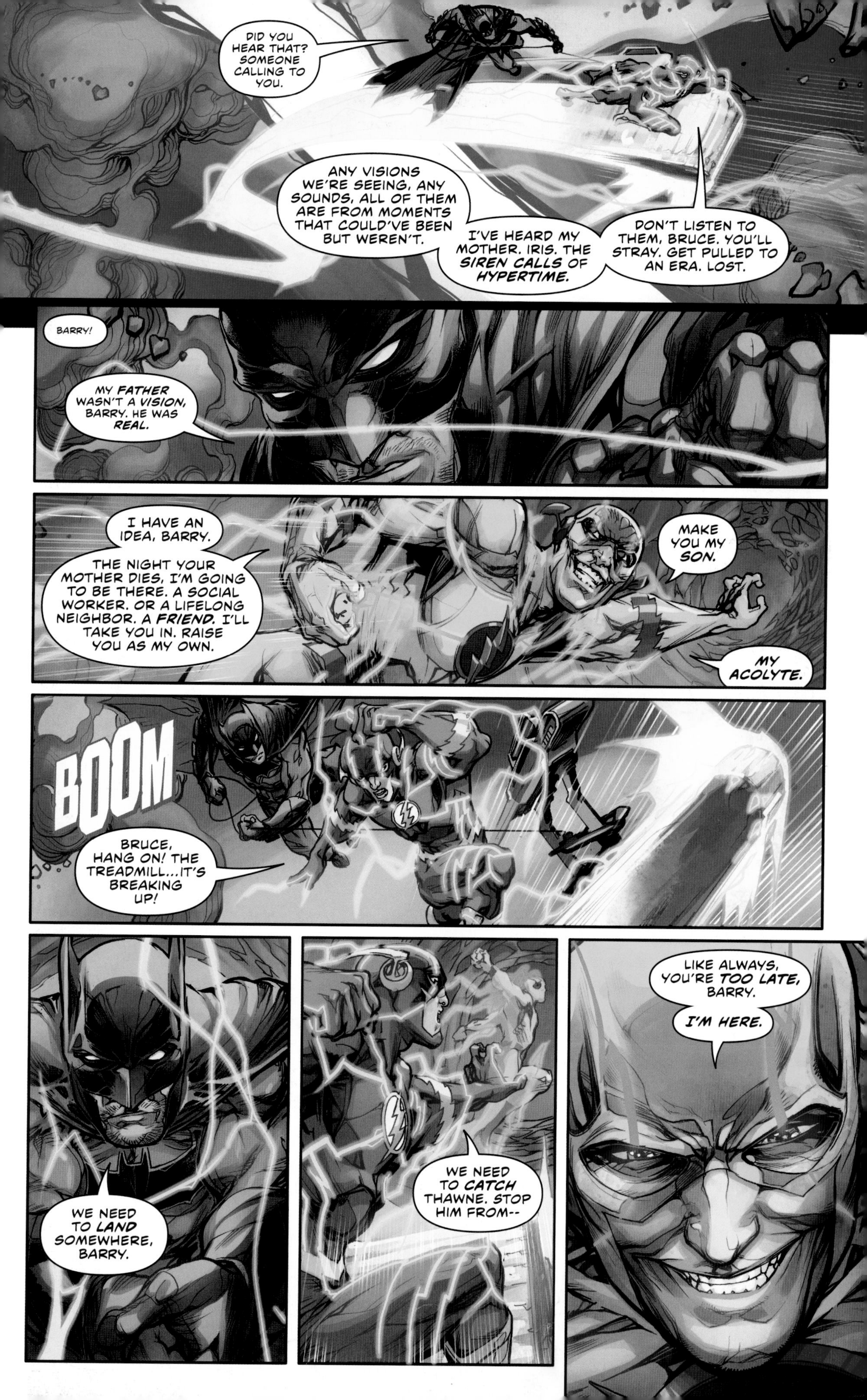
DID YOU HEAR THAT? SOMEONE CALLING TO YOU.
ANY VISIONS WE'RE SEEING, ANY SOUNDS, ALL OF THEM ARE FROM MOMENTS THAT COULD'VE BEEN BUT WEREN'T.
I'VE HEARD MY MOTHER. IRIS. THE SIREN CALLS OF HYPERTIME.
DON'T LISTEN TO THEM, BRUCE. YOU'LL STRAY. GET PULLED TO AN ERA. LOST.
BARRY!
MY FATHER WASN'T A VISION, BARRY. HE WAS REAL.
I HAVE AN IDEA, BARRY.
THE NIGHT YOUR MOTHER DIES, I'M GOING TO BE THERE. A SOCIAL WORKER. OR A LIFELONG NEIGHBOR. A FRIEND. I'LL TAKE YOU IN. RAISE YOU AS MY OWN.
MAKE YOU MY SON.
MY ACOLYTE.
BOOM
BRUCE, HANG ON! THE TREADMILL...IT'S BREAKING UP!
WE NEED TO LAND SOMEWHERE, BARRY.
WE NEED TO CATCH THAWNE. STOP HIM FROM--
LIKE ALWAYS, YOU'RE TOO LATE, BARRY.
I'M HERE.

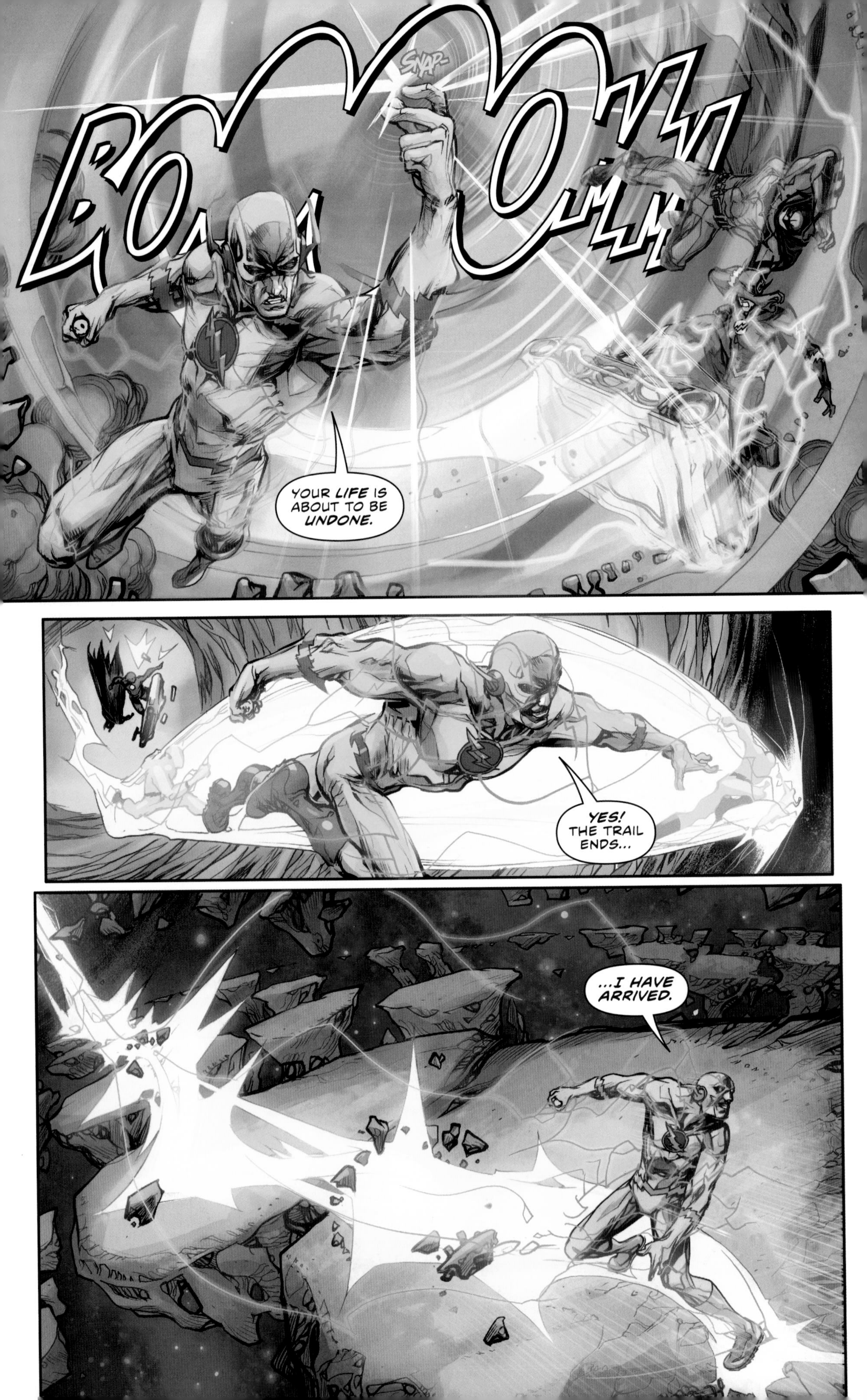
SNAP-
YOUR *LIFE* IS ABOUT TO BE *UNDONE.*
YES! THE TRAIL ENDS...
...*I HAVE ARRIVED.*

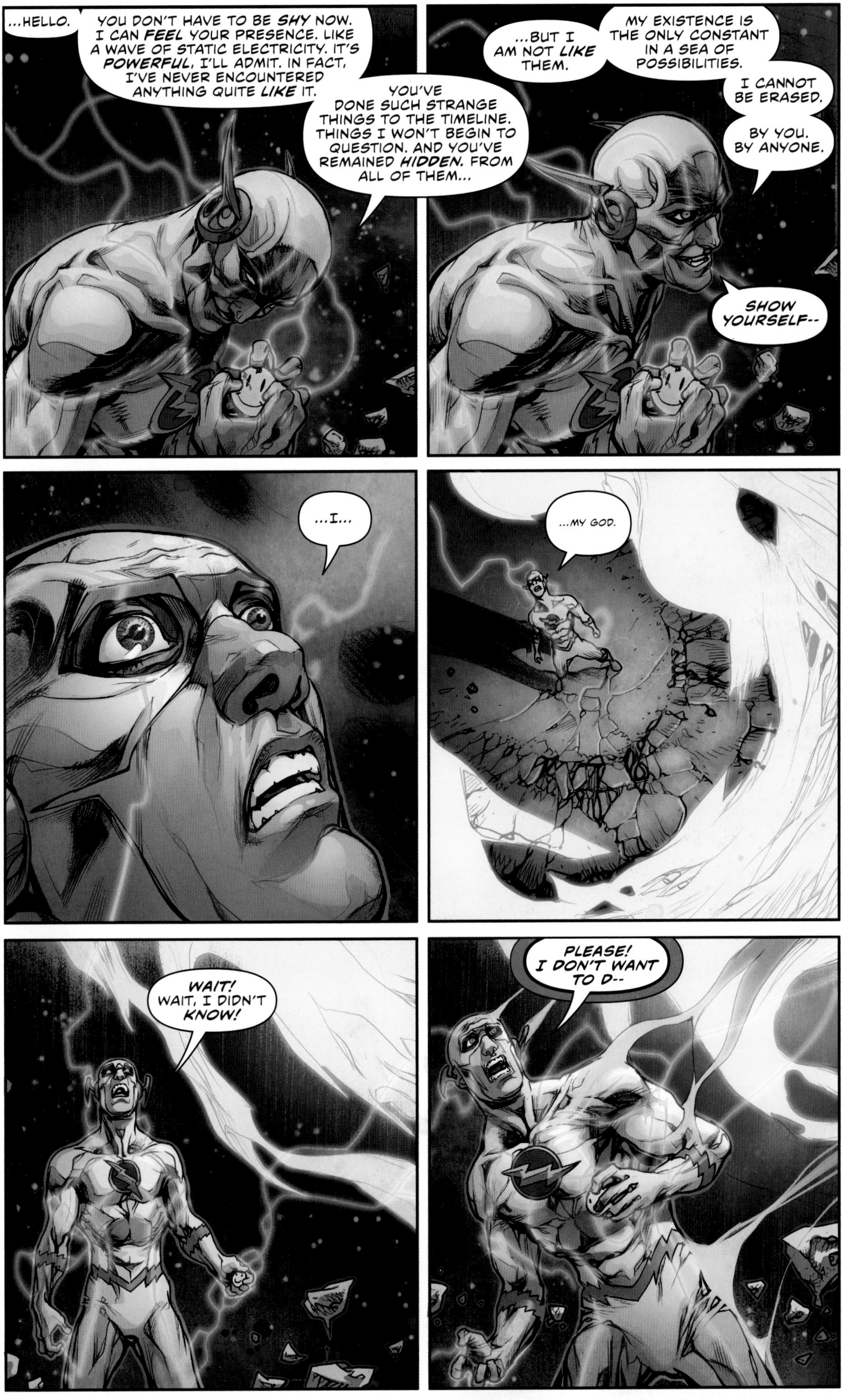

...HELLO.
YOU DON'T HAVE TO BE SHY NOW. I CAN FEEL YOUR PRESENCE. LIKE A WAVE OF STATIC ELECTRICITY. IT'S POWERFUL, I'LL ADMIT. IN FACT, I'VE NEVER ENCOUNTERED ANYTHING QUITE LIKE IT.
YOU'VE DONE SUCH STRANGE THINGS TO THE TIMELINE. THINGS I WON'T BEGIN TO QUESTION. AND YOU'VE REMAINED HIDDEN. FROM ALL OF THEM...
...BUT I AM NOT LIKE THEM.
MY EXISTENCE IS THE ONLY CONSTANT IN A SEA OF POSSIBILITIES.
I CANNOT BE ERASED.
BY YOU. BY ANYONE.
SHOW YOURSELF--
...I...
...MY GOD.
WAIT! WAIT, I DIDN'T KNOW!
PLEASE! I DON'T WANT TO D--

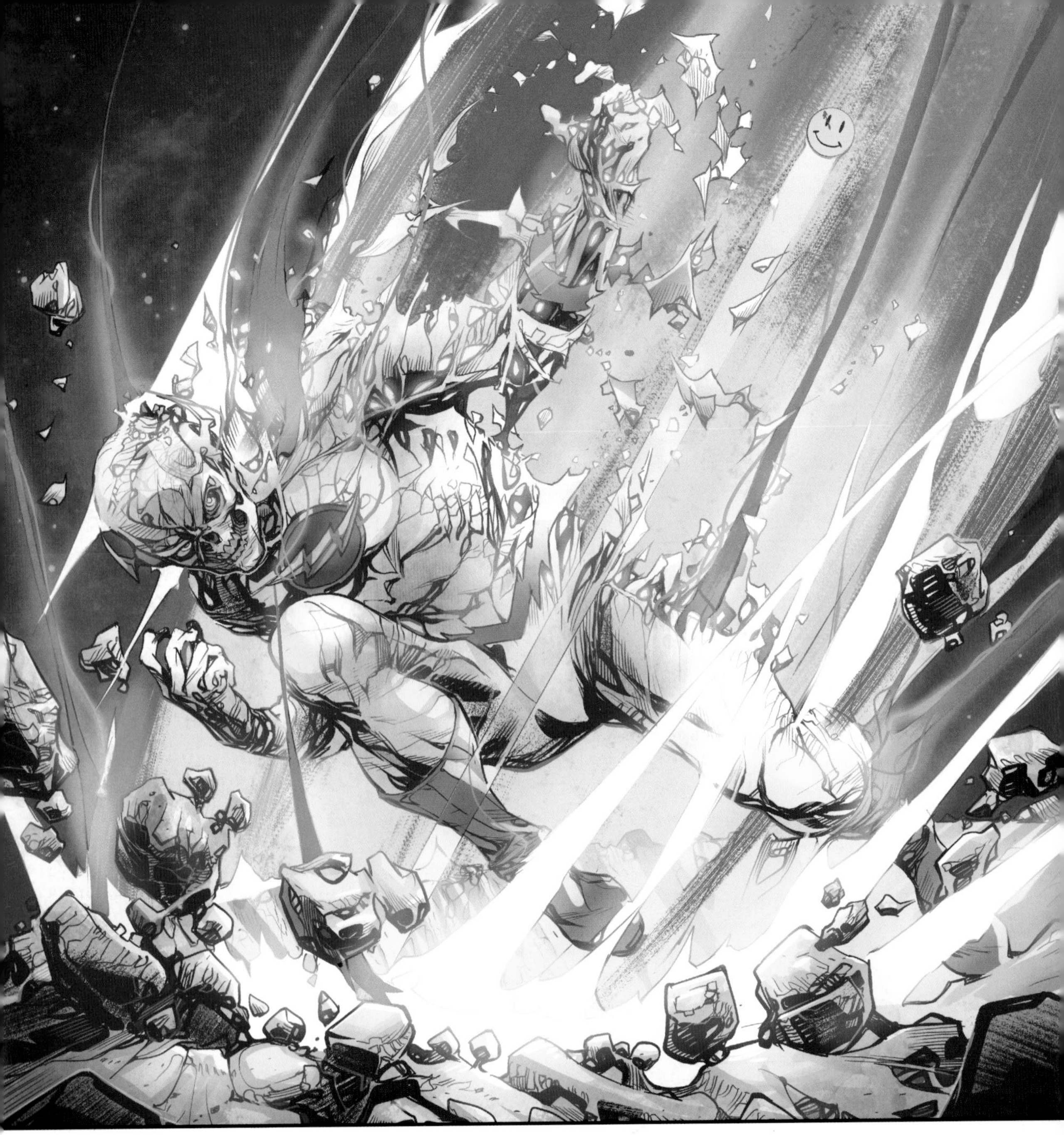

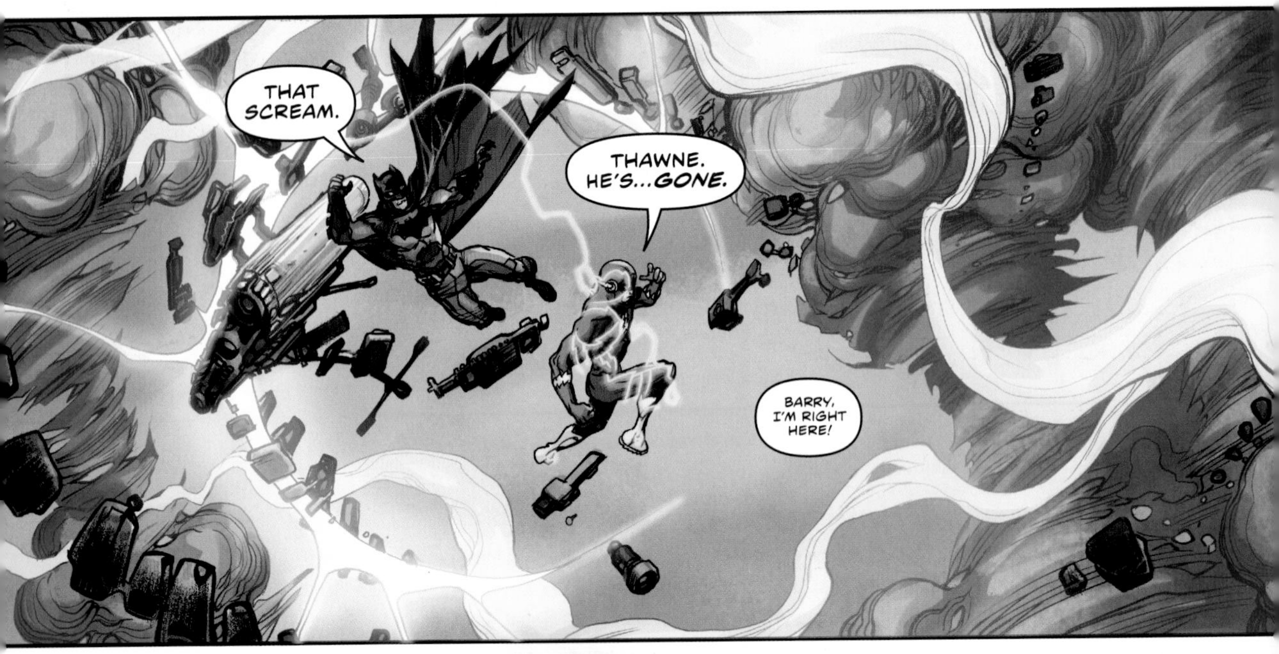
THAT SCREAM.
THAWNE. HE'S...GONE.
BARRY, I'M RIGHT HERE!

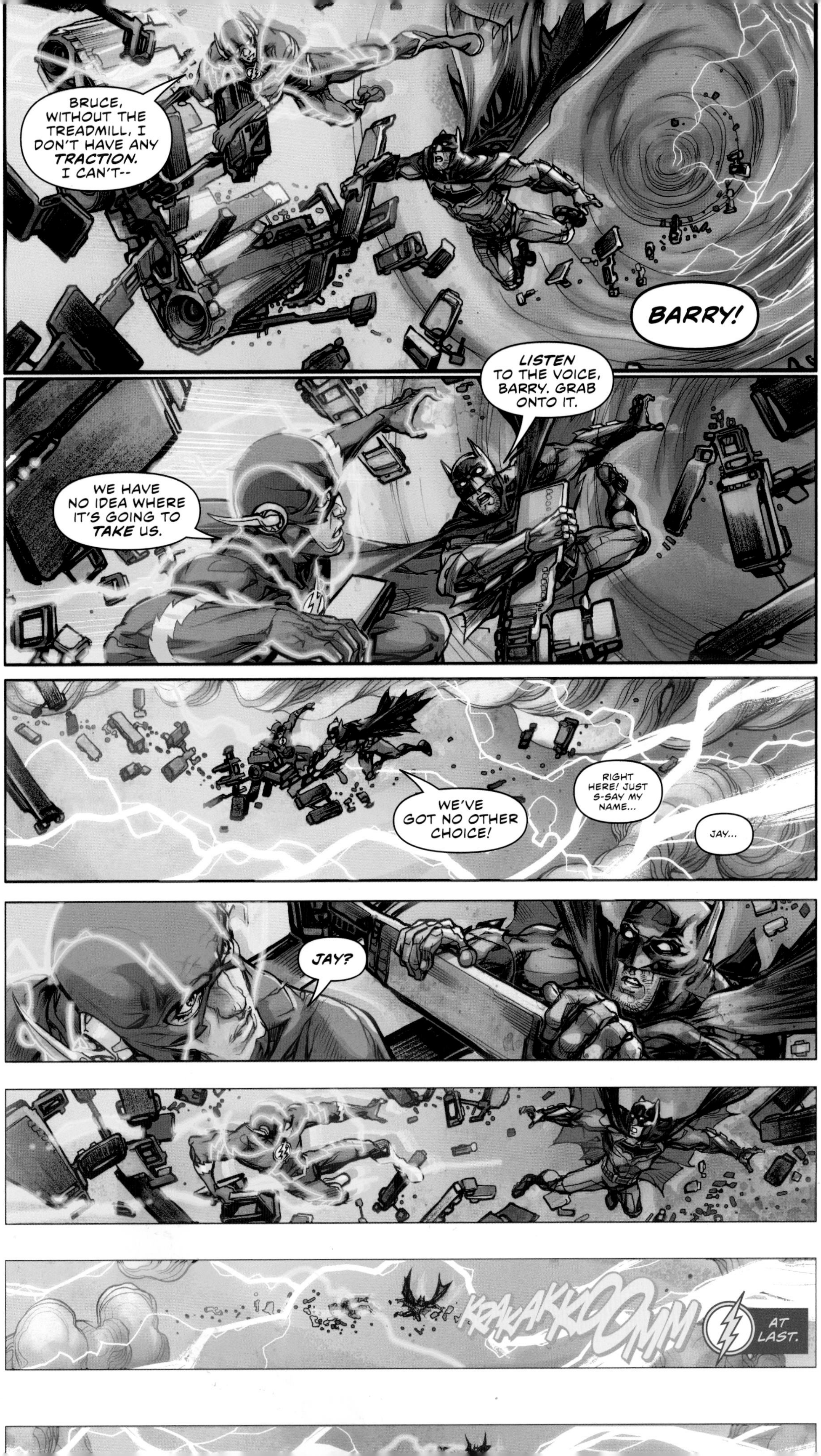
BRUCE, WITHOUT THE TREADMILL, I DON'T HAVE ANY *TRACTION.* I CAN'T--
BARRY!
LISTEN TO THE VOICE, BARRY. GRAB ONTO IT.
WE HAVE NO IDEA WHERE IT'S GOING TO *TAKE* US.
WE'VE GOT NO OTHER CHOICE!
RIGHT HERE! JUST S-SAY MY NAME...
JAY...
JAY?
KRAKAKKOOMM
AT LAST.

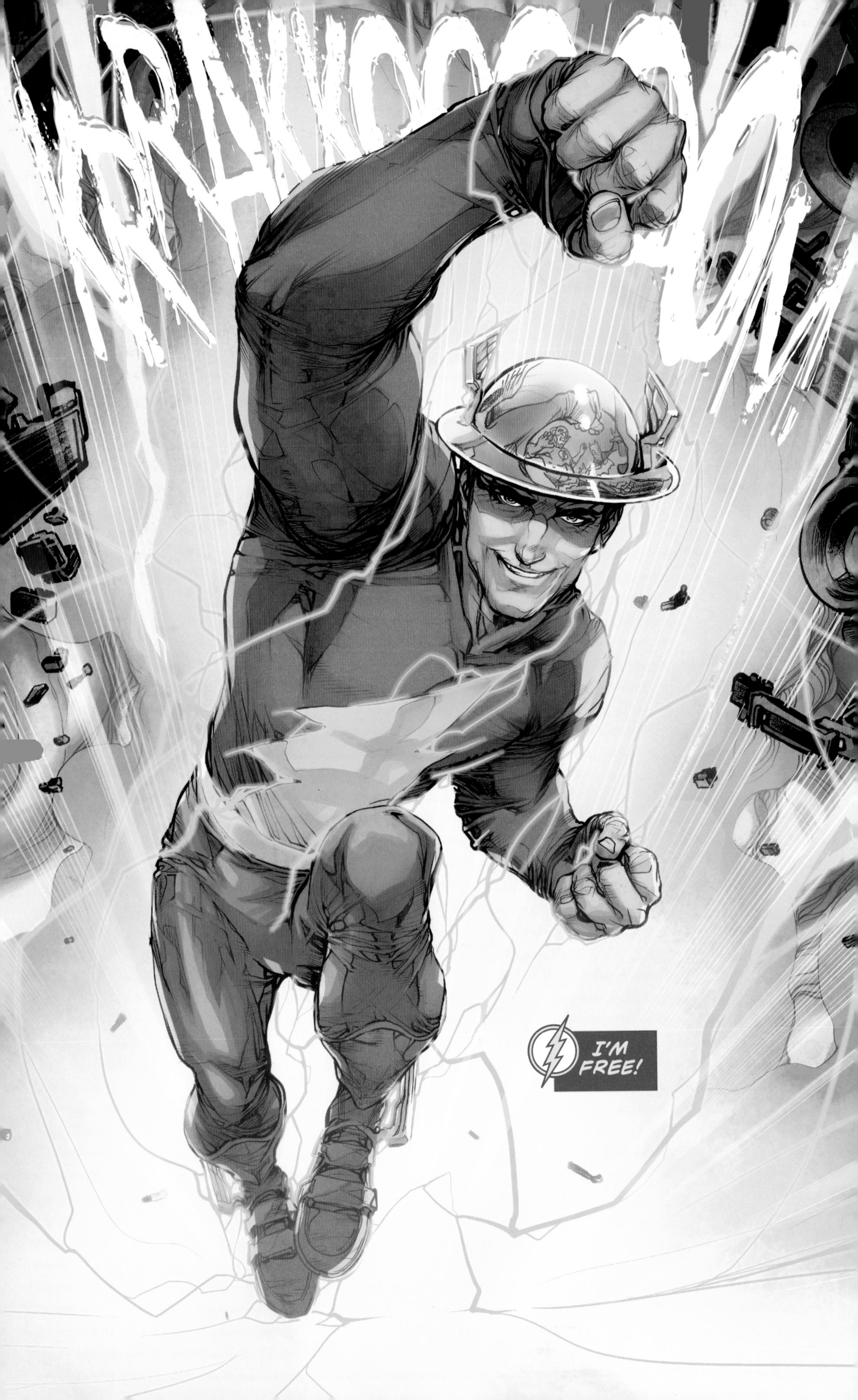
I'M FREE!

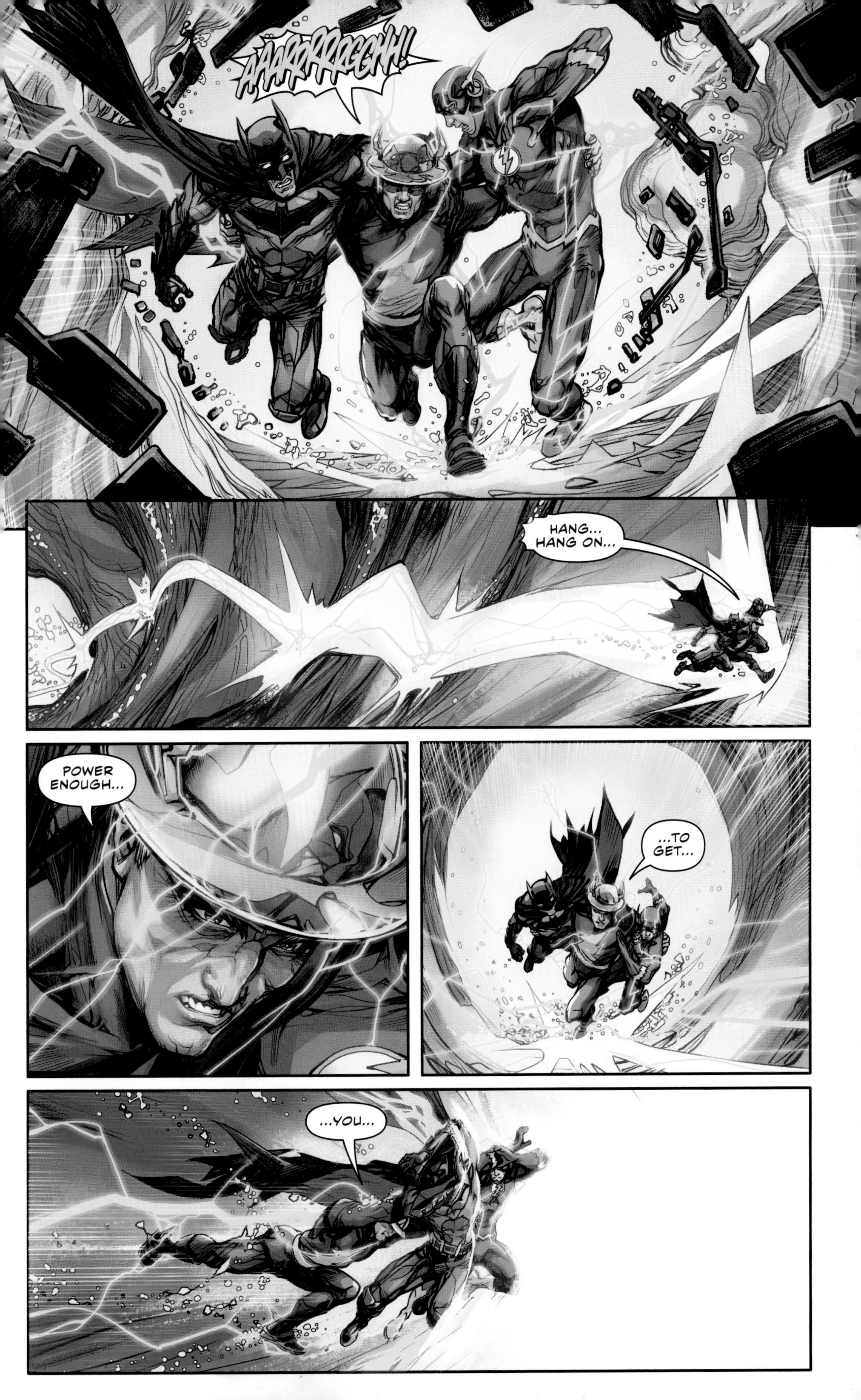
AAARRRRGGHH!
HANG... HANG ON...
POWER ENOUGH...
...TO GET...
...YOU...

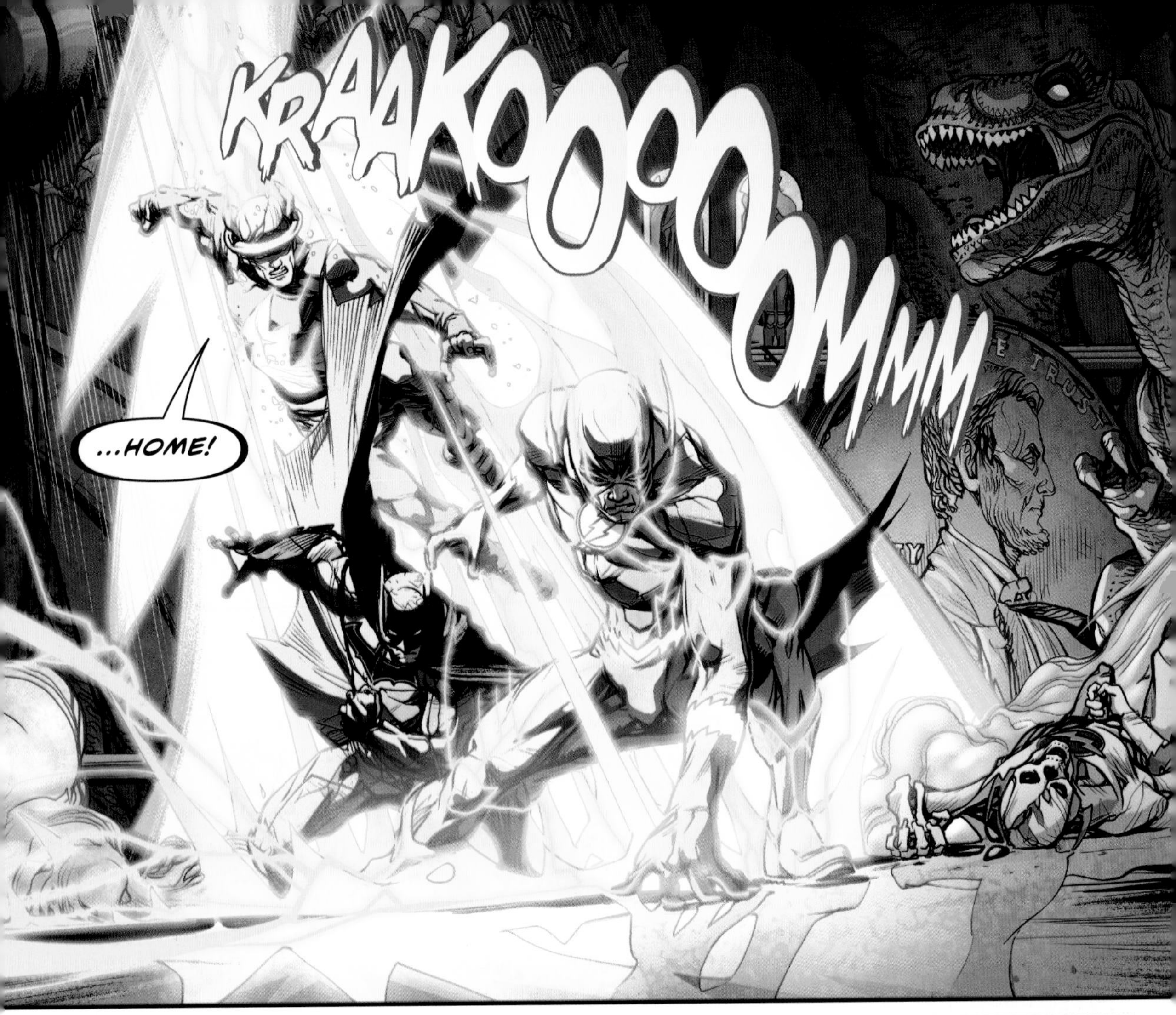
KRAAKOOOOOMMM
...HOME!

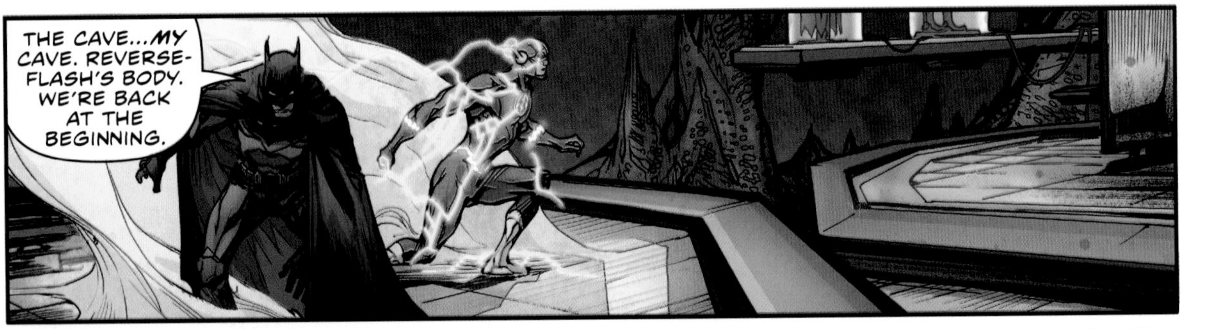
THE CAVE...MY CAVE. REVERSE-FLASH'S BODY. WE'RE BACK AT THE BEGINNING.

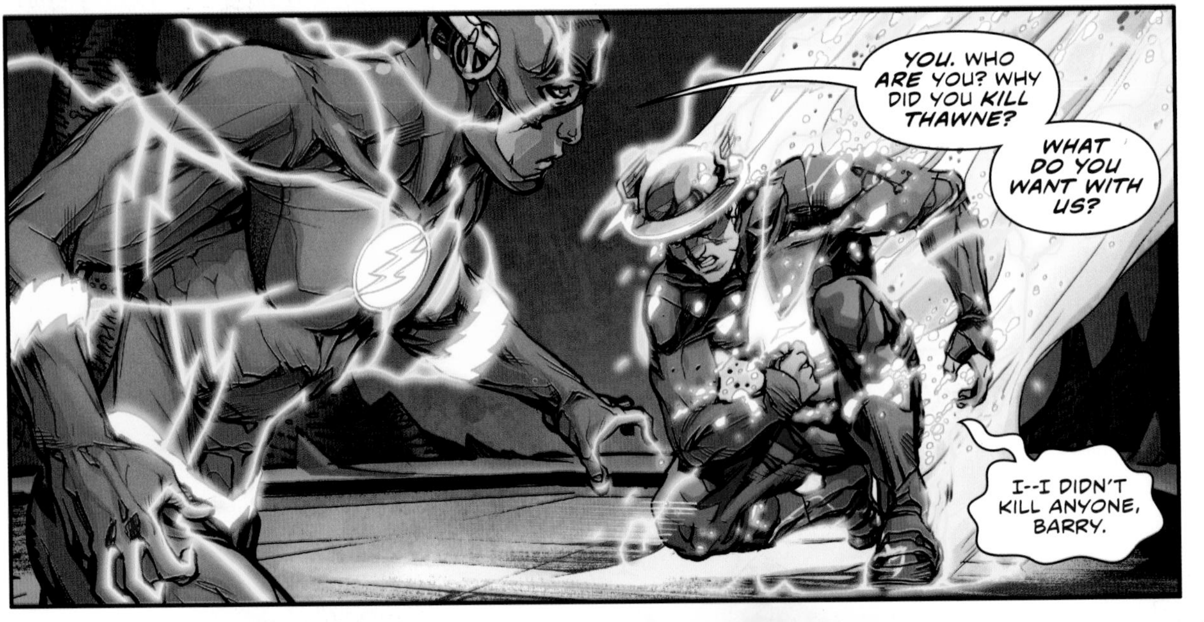
YOU. WHO ARE YOU? WHY DID YOU KILL THAWNE?
WHAT DO YOU WANT WITH US?
I--I DIDN'T KILL ANYONE, BARRY.

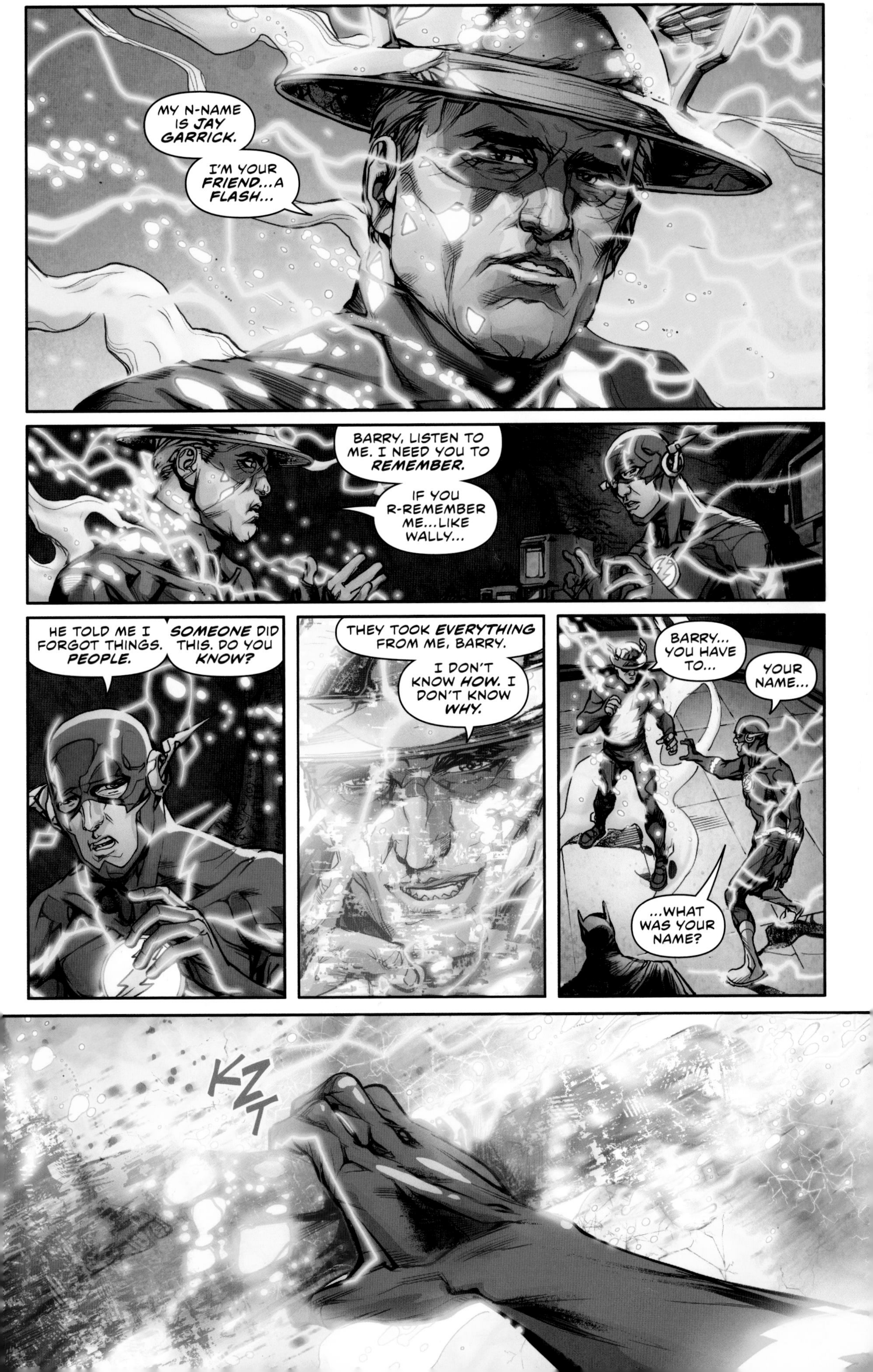
MY N-NAME IS JAY GARRICK.
I'M YOUR FRIEND...A FLASH...
BARRY, LISTEN TO ME. I NEED YOU TO REMEMBER.
IF YOU R-REMEMBER ME...LIKE WALLY...
HE TOLD ME I FORGOT THINGS. PEOPLE.
SOMEONE DID THIS. DO YOU KNOW?
THEY TOOK EVERYTHING FROM ME, BARRY.
I DON'T KNOW HOW. I DON'T KNOW WHY.
BARRY... YOU HAVE TO...
YOUR NAME...
...WHAT WAS YOUR NAME?
KZT

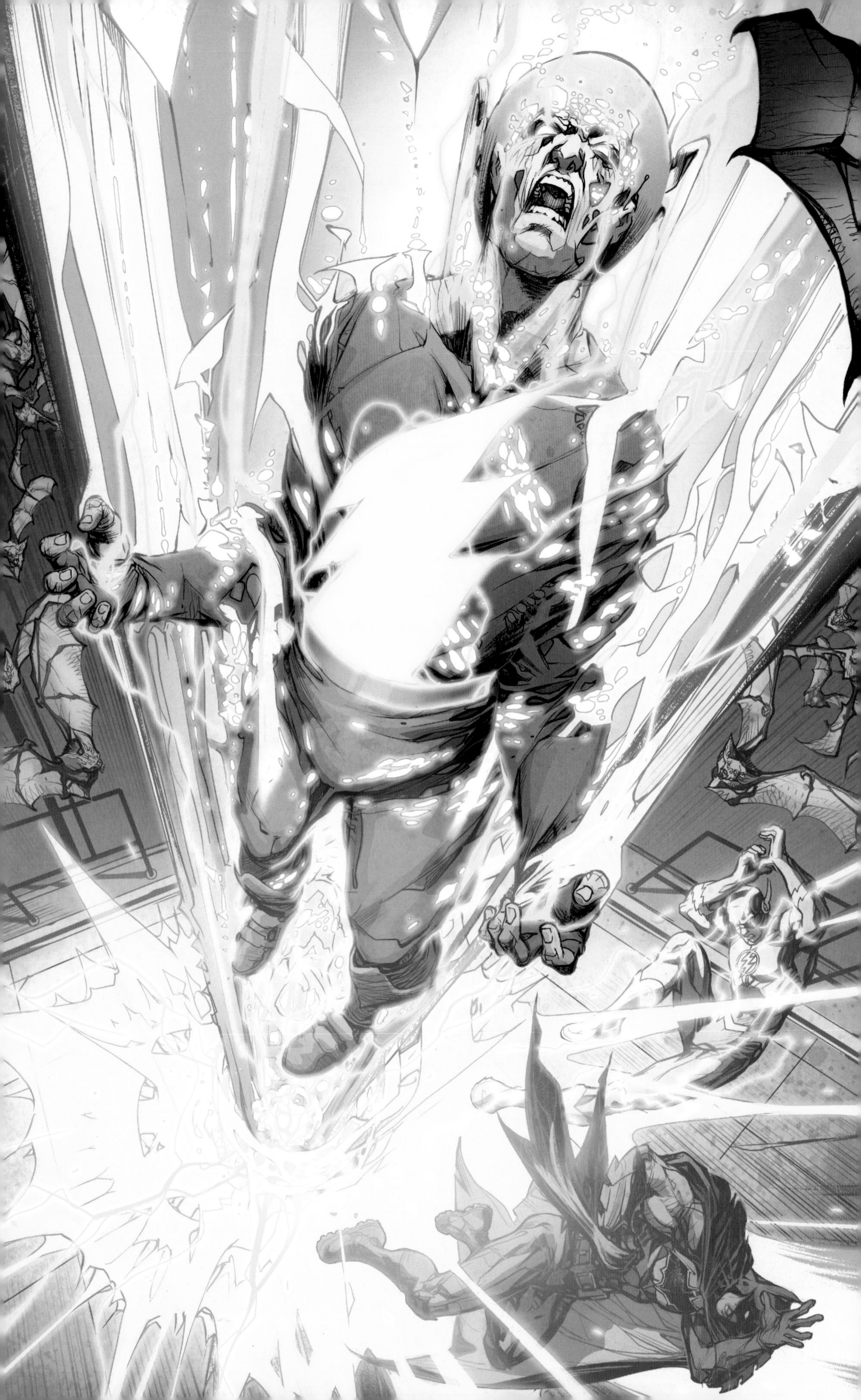

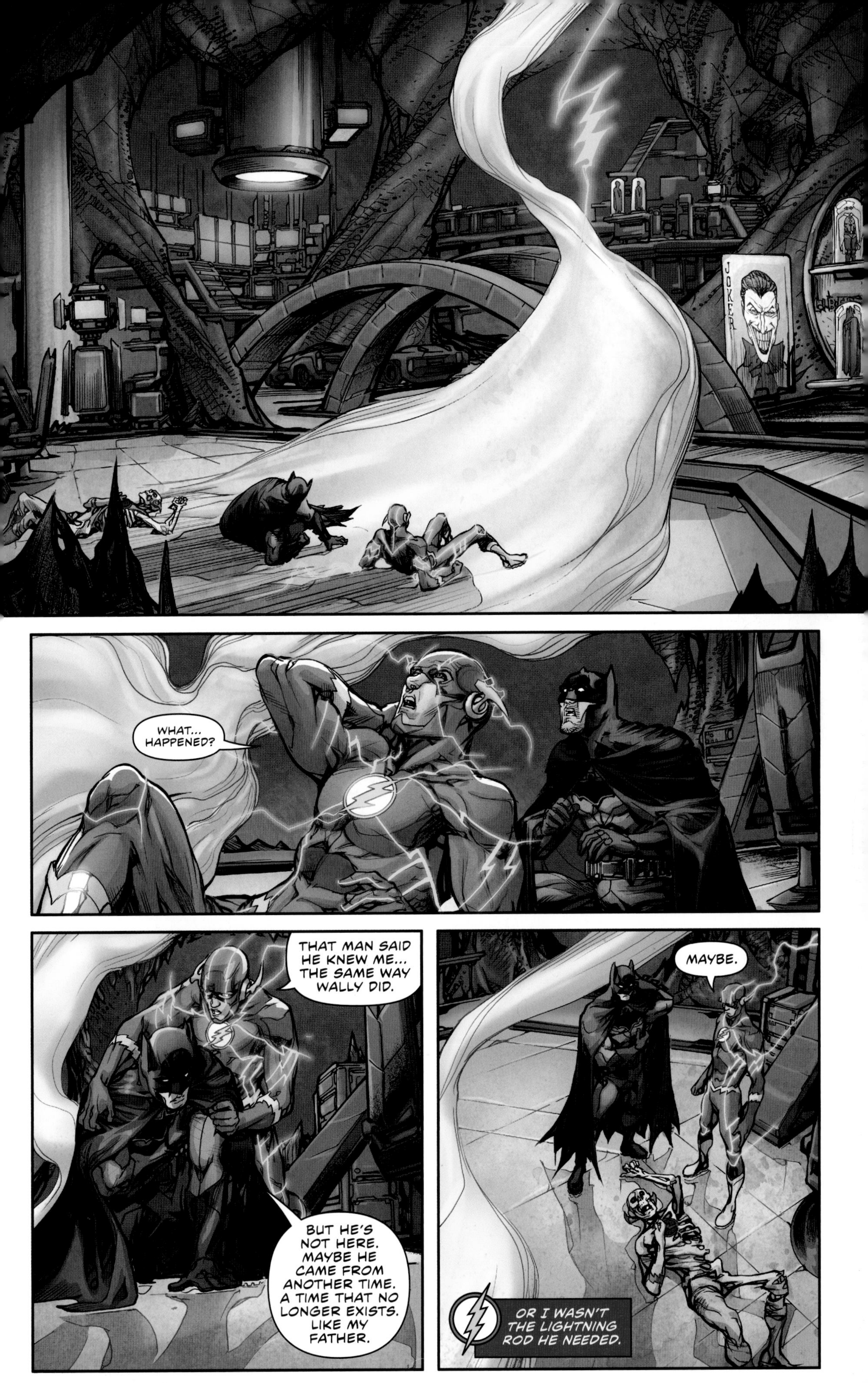
JOKER
WHAT... HAPPENED?
THAT MAN SAID HE KNEW ME... THE SAME WAY WALLY DID.
BUT HE'S NOT HERE. MAYBE HE CAME FROM ANOTHER TIME. A TIME THAT NO LONGER EXISTS. LIKE MY FATHER.
MAYBE.
OR I WASN'T THE LIGHTNING ROD HE NEEDED.

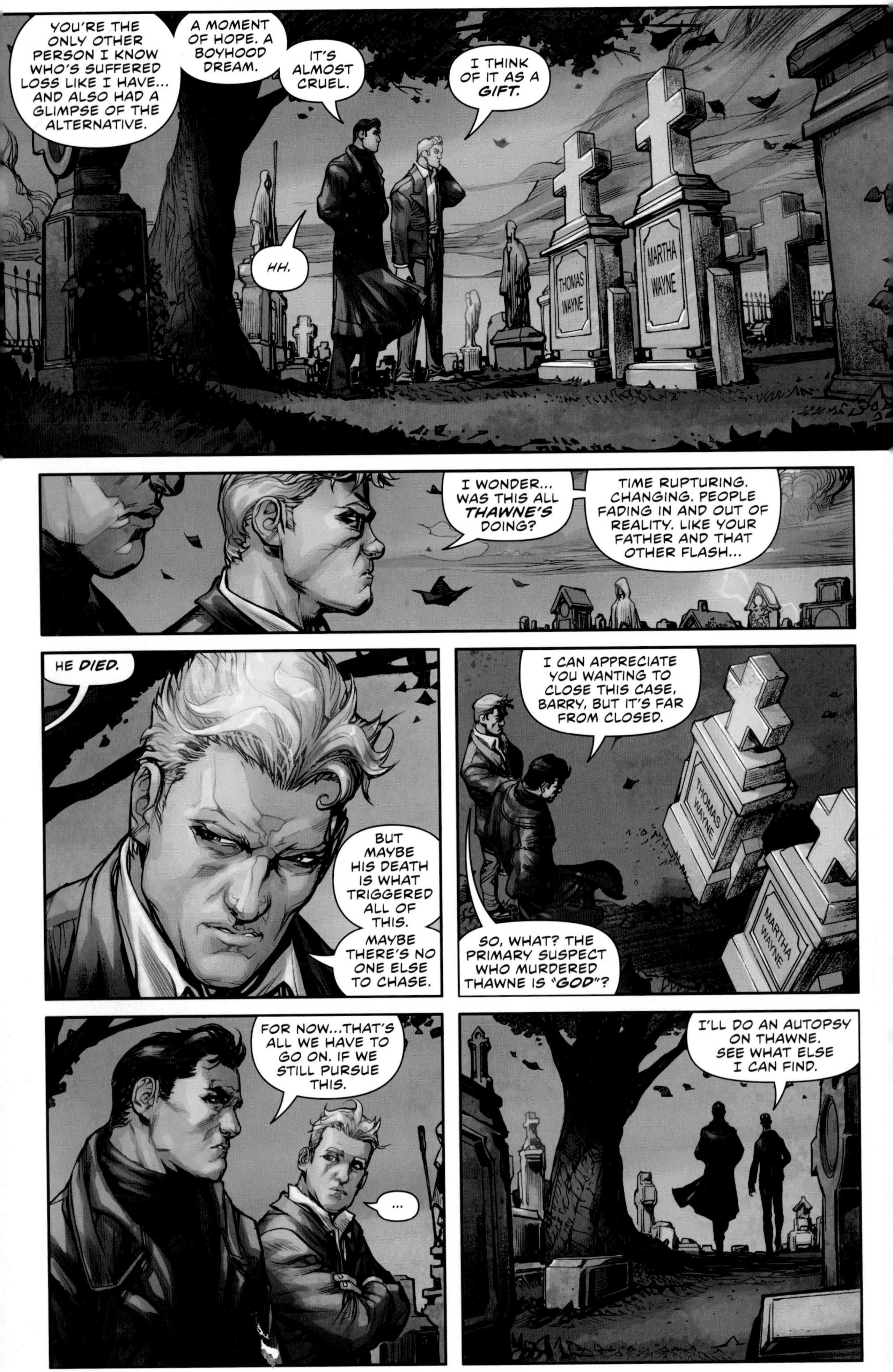
YOU'RE THE ONLY OTHER PERSON I KNOW WHO'S SUFFERED LOSS LIKE I HAVE... AND ALSO HAD A GLIMPSE OF THE ALTERNATIVE.
A MOMENT OF HOPE. A BOYHOOD DREAM.
IT'S ALMOST CRUEL.
I THINK OF IT AS A *GIFT.*
HH.
THOMAS WAYNE
MARTHA WAYNE
I WONDER... WAS THIS ALL *THAWNE'S* DOING?
TIME RUPTURING. CHANGING. PEOPLE FADING IN AND OUT OF REALITY. LIKE YOUR FATHER AND THAT OTHER FLASH...
HE *DIED.*
BUT MAYBE HIS DEATH IS WHAT TRIGGERED ALL OF THIS.
MAYBE THERE'S NO ONE ELSE TO CHASE.
I CAN APPRECIATE YOU WANTING TO CLOSE THIS CASE, BARRY, BUT IT'S FAR FROM CLOSED.
THOMAS WAYNE
MARTHA WAYNE
SO, WHAT? THE PRIMARY SUSPECT WHO MURDERED THAWNE IS "*GOD*"?
FOR NOW...THAT'S ALL WE HAVE TO GO ON. IF WE STILL PURSUE THIS.
...
I'LL DO AN AUTOPSY ON THAWNE. SEE WHAT ELSE I CAN FIND.

I DON'T PRETEND TO UNDERSTAND WHAT WE JUST WENT THROUGH, BARRY...BUT WHAT WE EXPERIENCED WASN'T AN ACCIDENT.

BEING GIVEN THE CHANCE TO SEE MY FATHER, ONLY TO LOSE HIM AGAIN... THAT OTHER FLASH WHO SAID HE WAS YOUR FRIEND, AND WE WERE POWERLESS TO HELP HIM... WHAT REVERSE-FLASH SAID RIGHT BEFORE HE DIED... HOW HE "SAW GOD"...

I DON'T KNOW, BARRY...

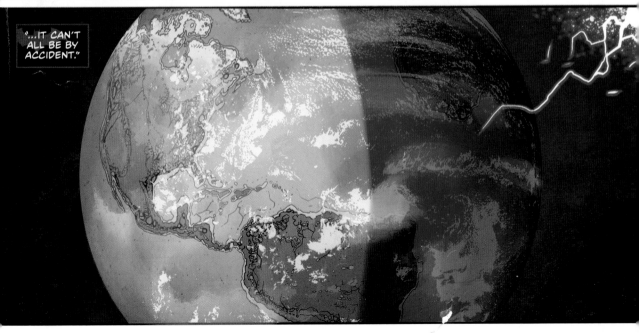

"...IT CAN'T ALL BE BY ACCIDENT."

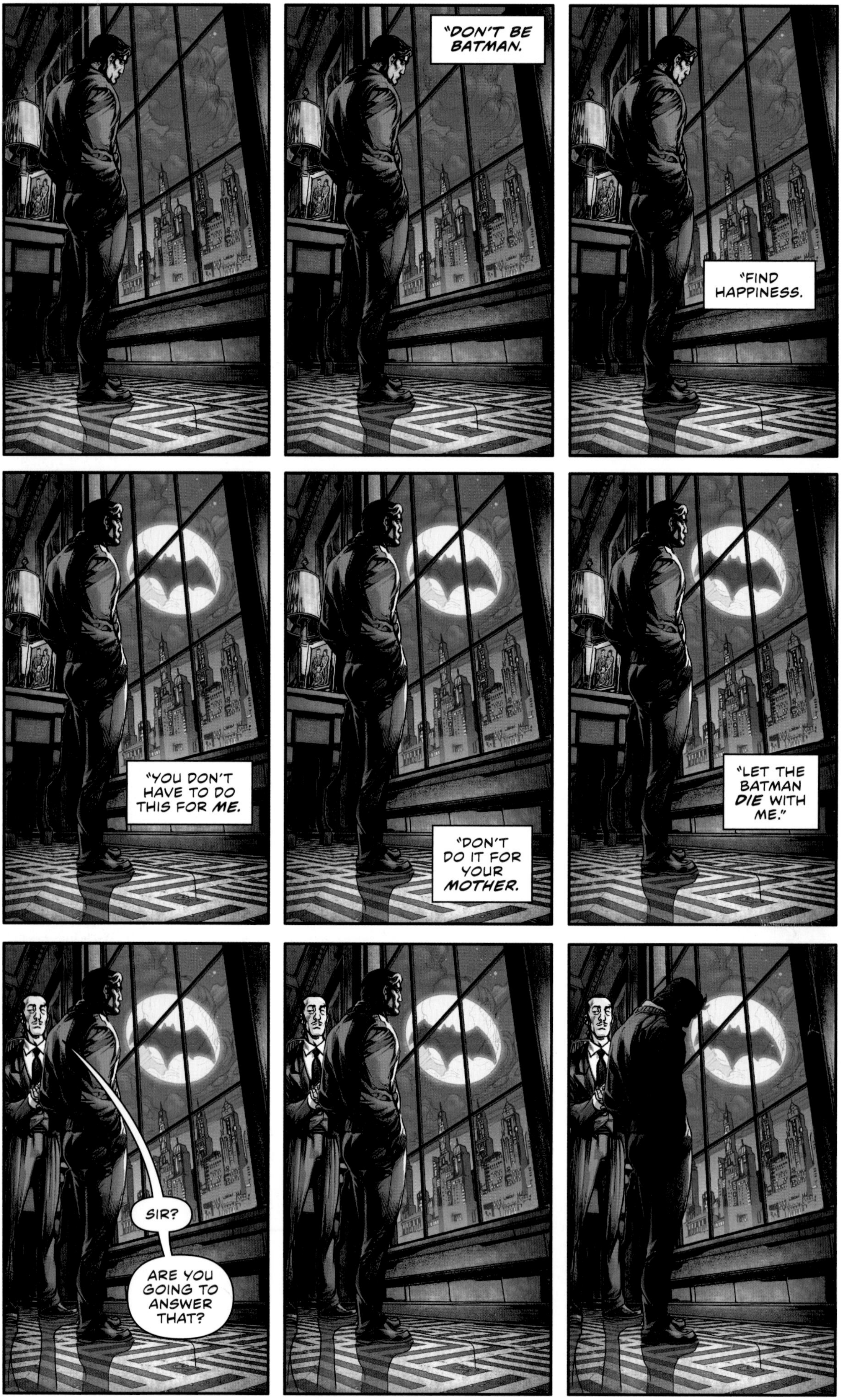
"DON'T BE BATMAN.
"FIND HAPPINESS.
"YOU DON'T HAVE TO DO THIS FOR ME.
"DON'T DO IT FOR YOUR MOTHER.
"LET THE BATMAN DIE WITH ME."
SIR?
ARE YOU GOING TO ANSWER THAT?

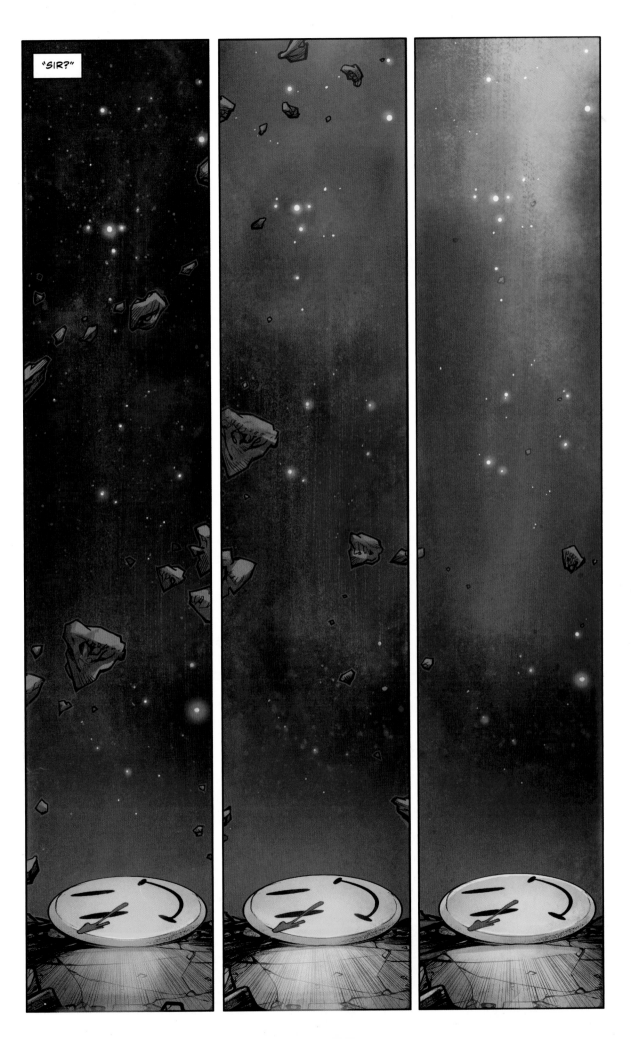

"SIR?"

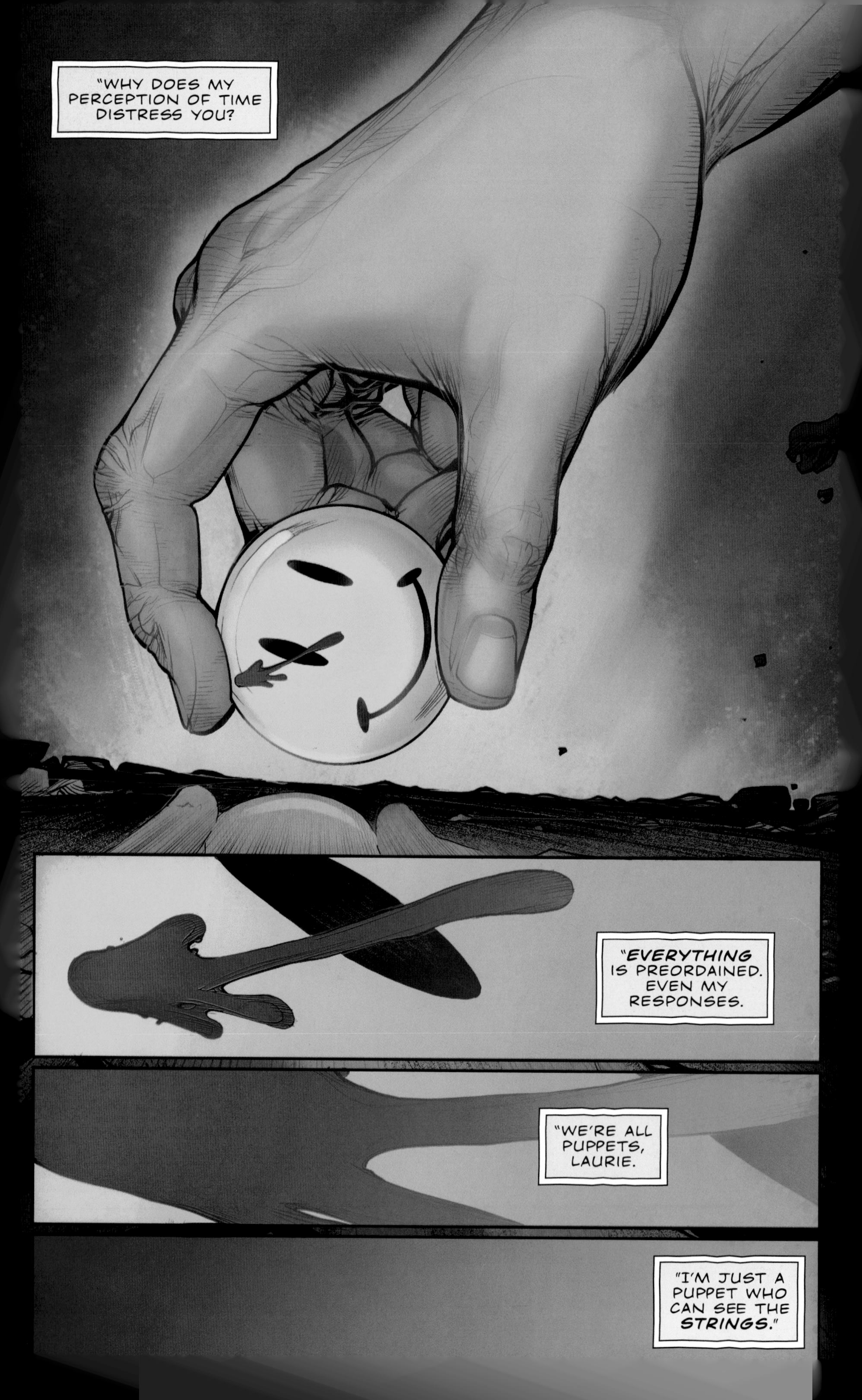
"WHY DOES MY PERCEPTION OF TIME DISTRESS YOU?
"EVERYTHING IS PREORDAINED. EVEN MY RESPONSES.
"WE'RE ALL PUPPETS, LAURIE.
"I'M JUST A PUPPET WHO CAN SEE THE STRINGS."

EPILOGUE

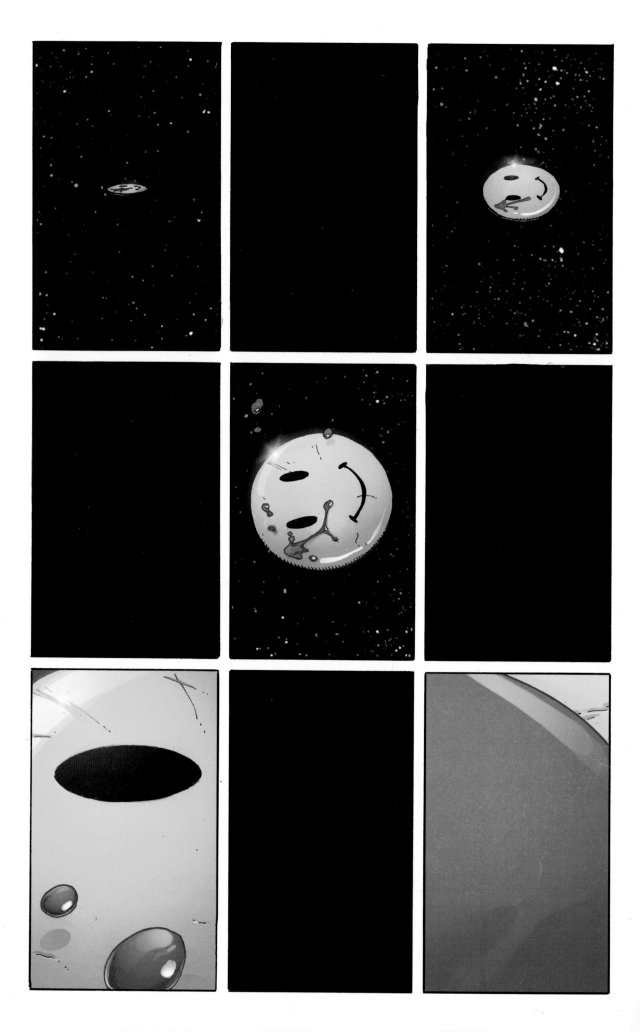

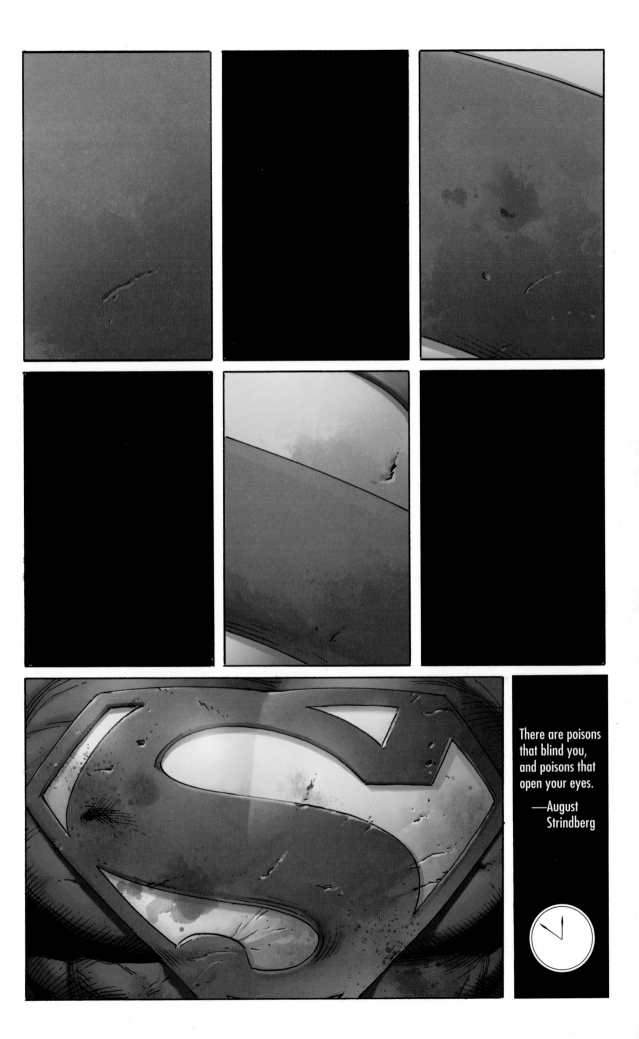

There are poisons that blind you, and poisons that open your eyes.

—August Strindberg

DOOMSD

Geoff Johns • Gary

COMIN

AY CLOCK

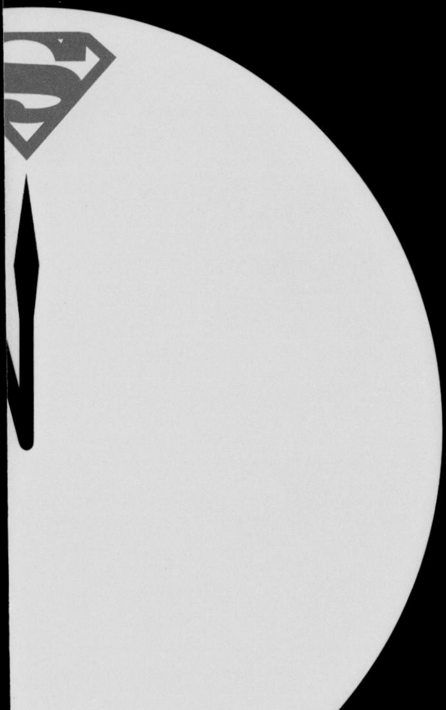

Frank • Brad Anderson

G SOON

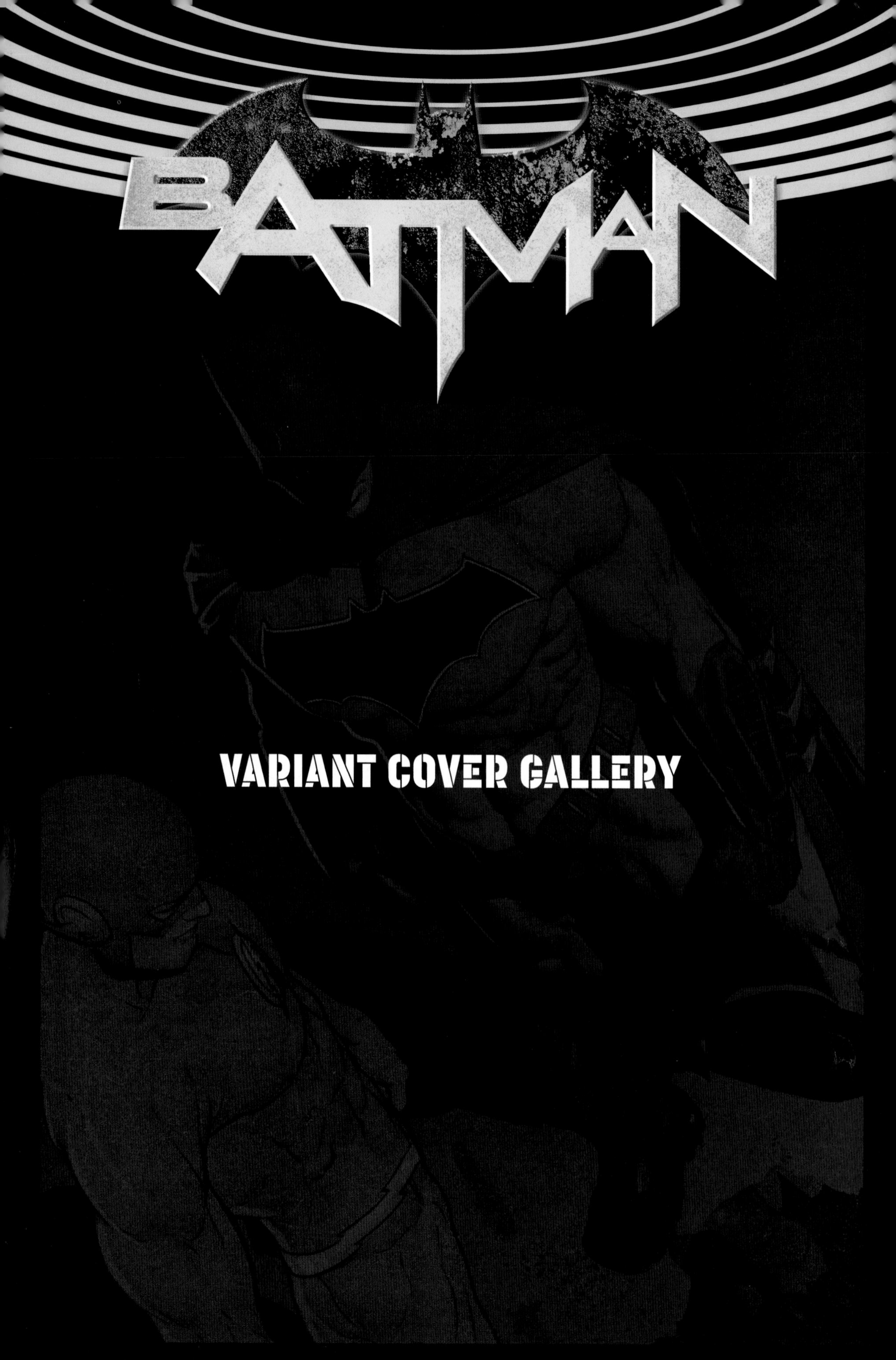

BATMAN

VARIANT COVER GALLERY

BATMAN #21 variant cover by Tim Sale & Brennan Wagner

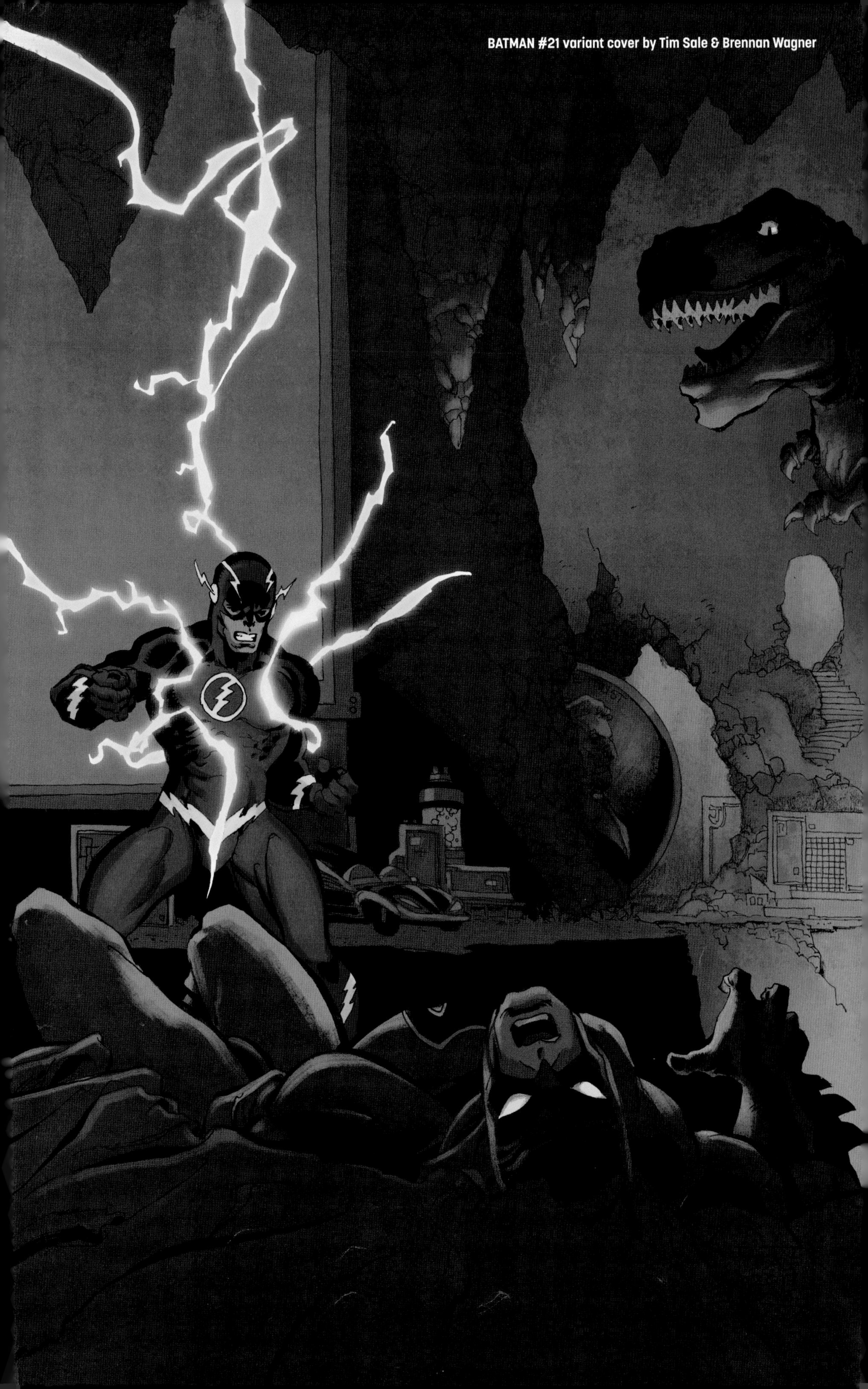

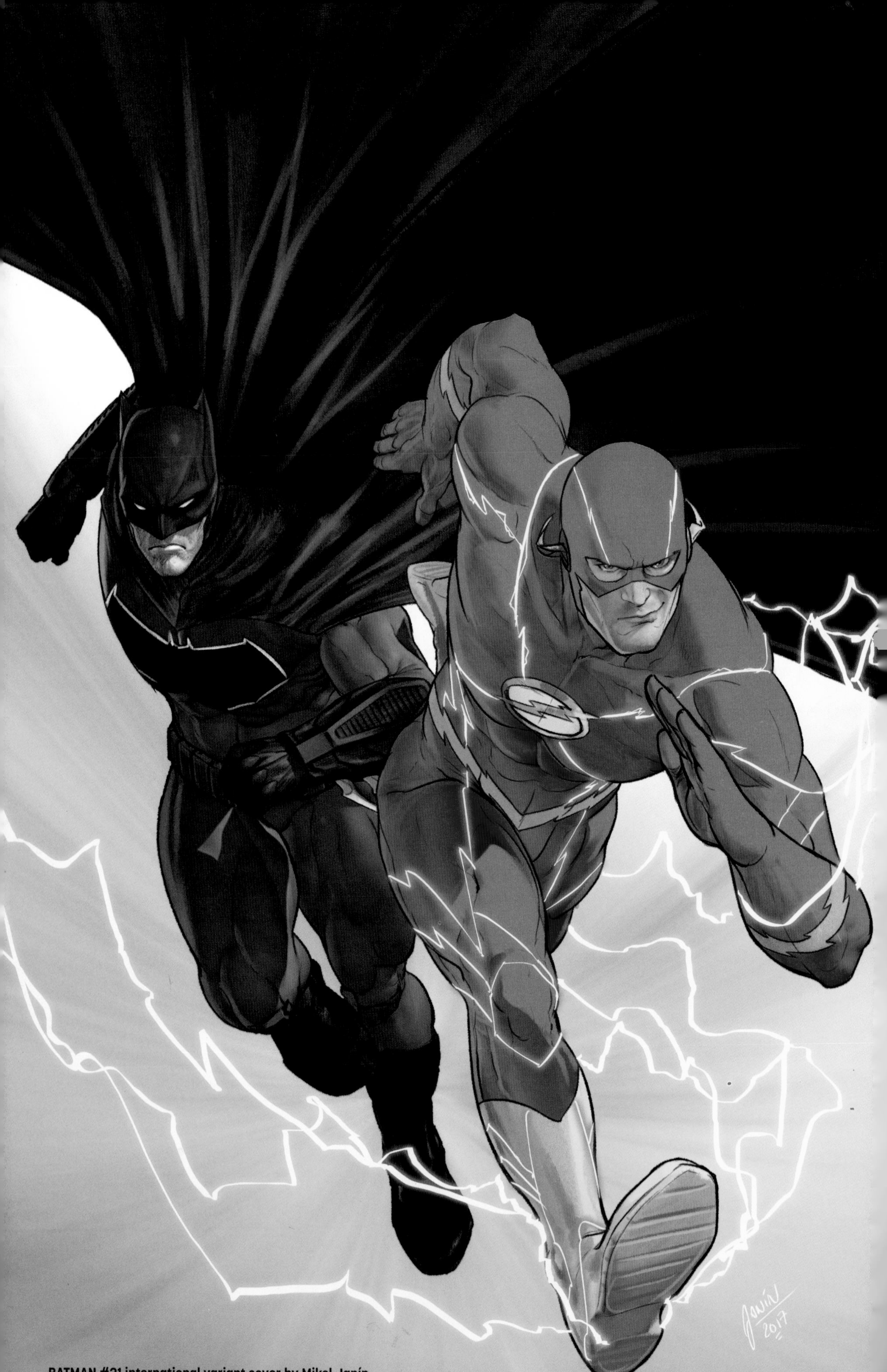

BATMAN #21 international variant cover by Mikel Janín

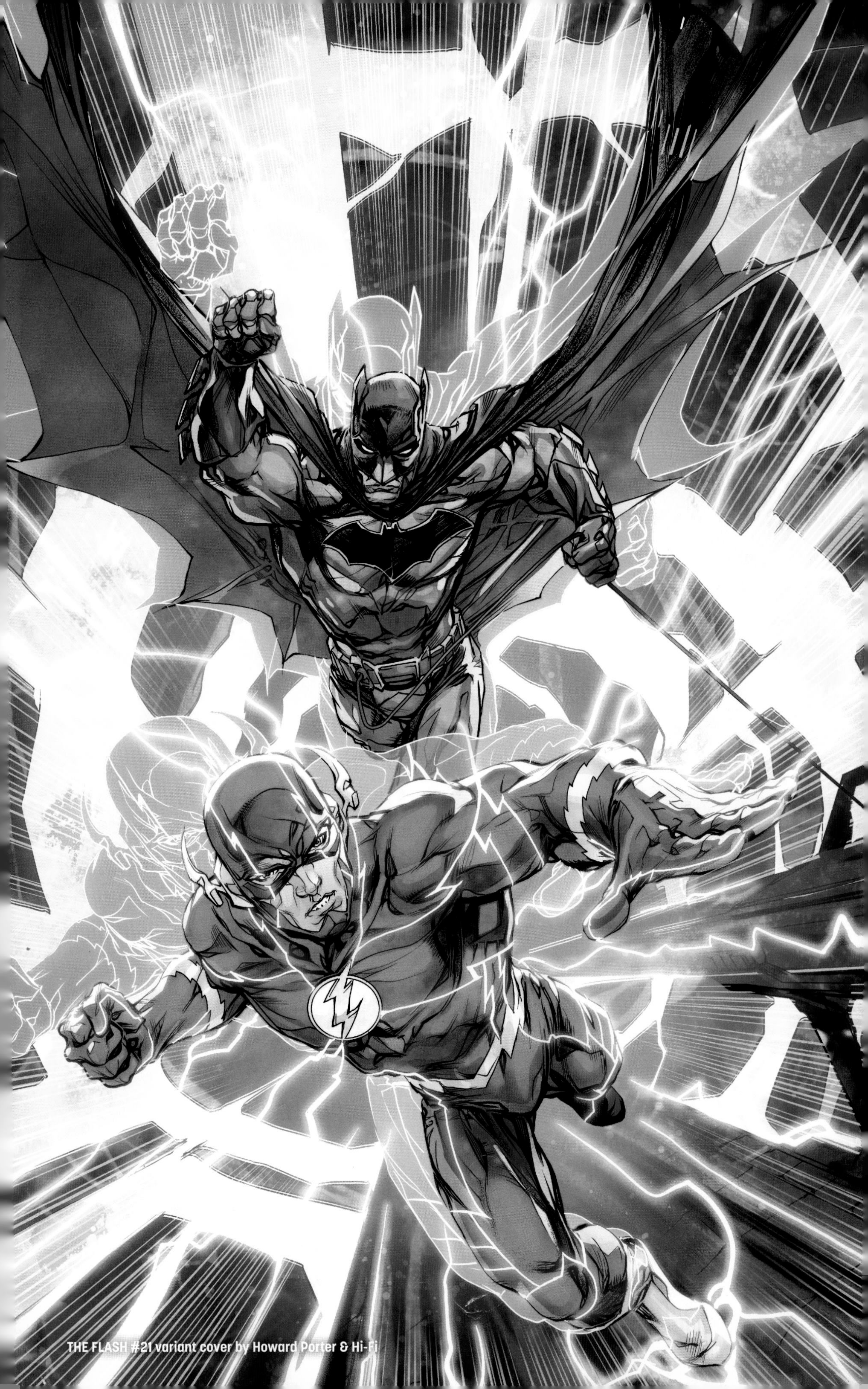

THE FLASH #21 variant cover by Howard Porter & Hi-Fi

THE FLASH #21 International variant cover by Mikel Janín

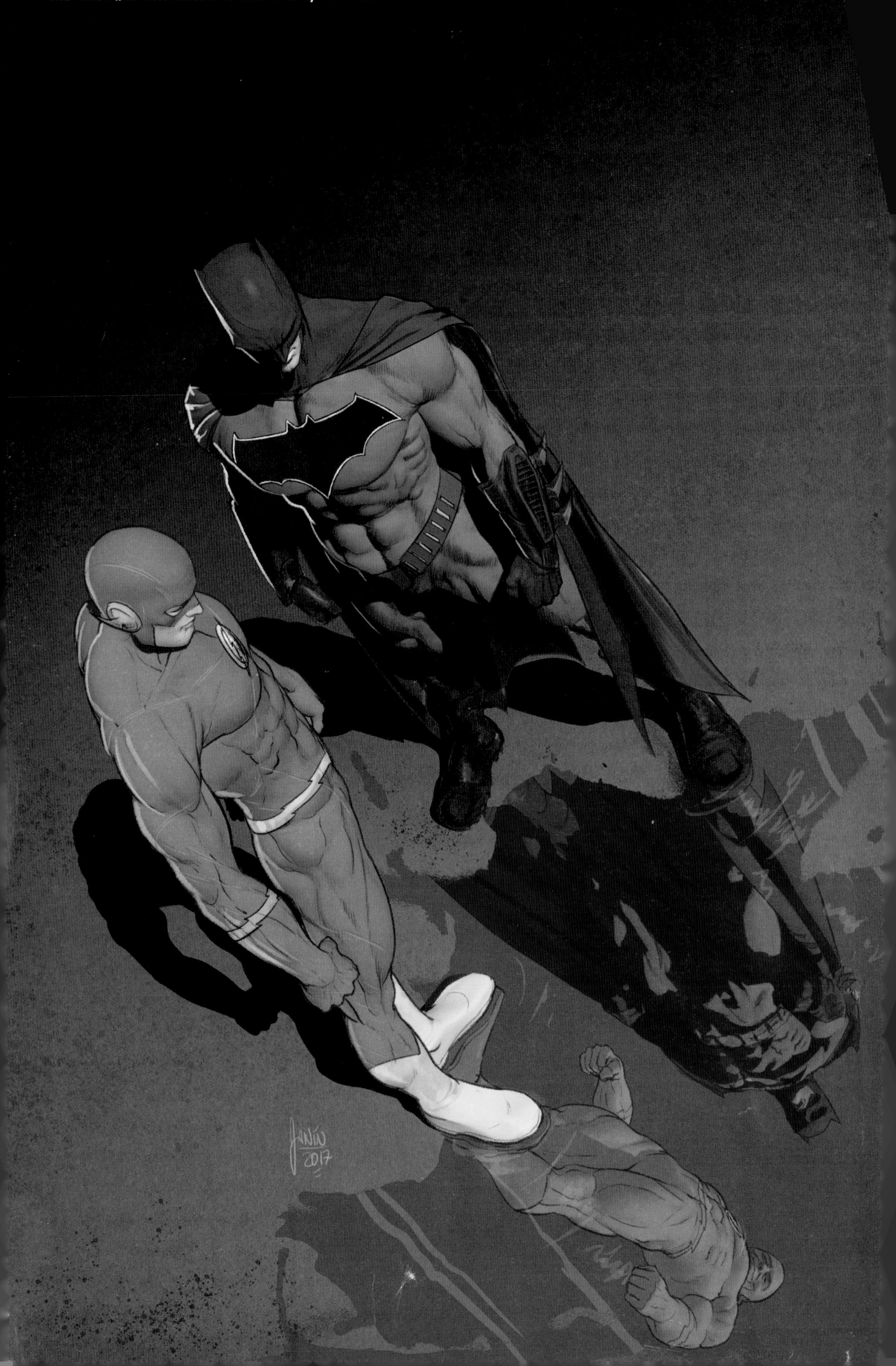

BATMAN #22 variant cover by Tim Sale & Brennan Wagner

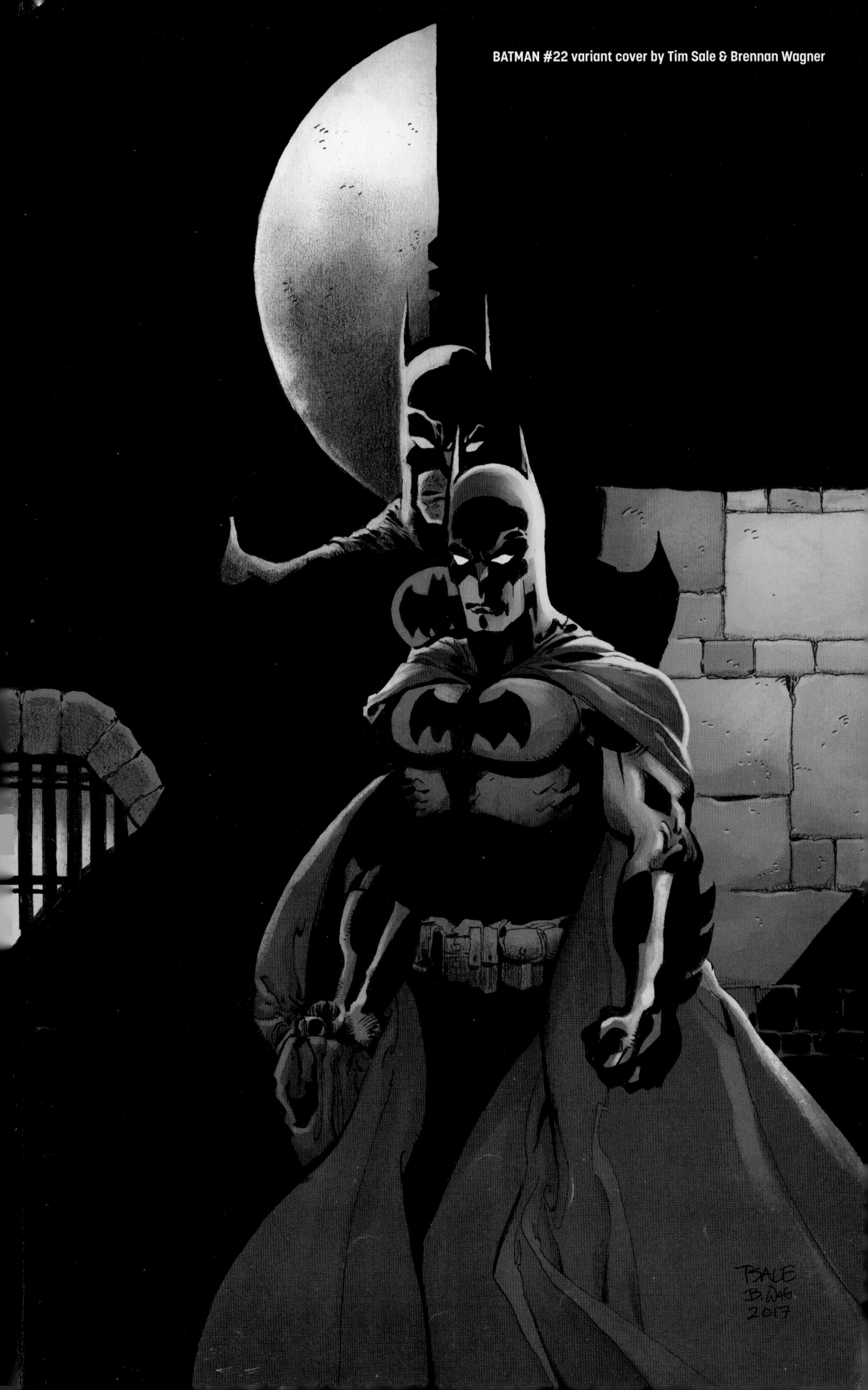
T SALE
B. WAG
2017

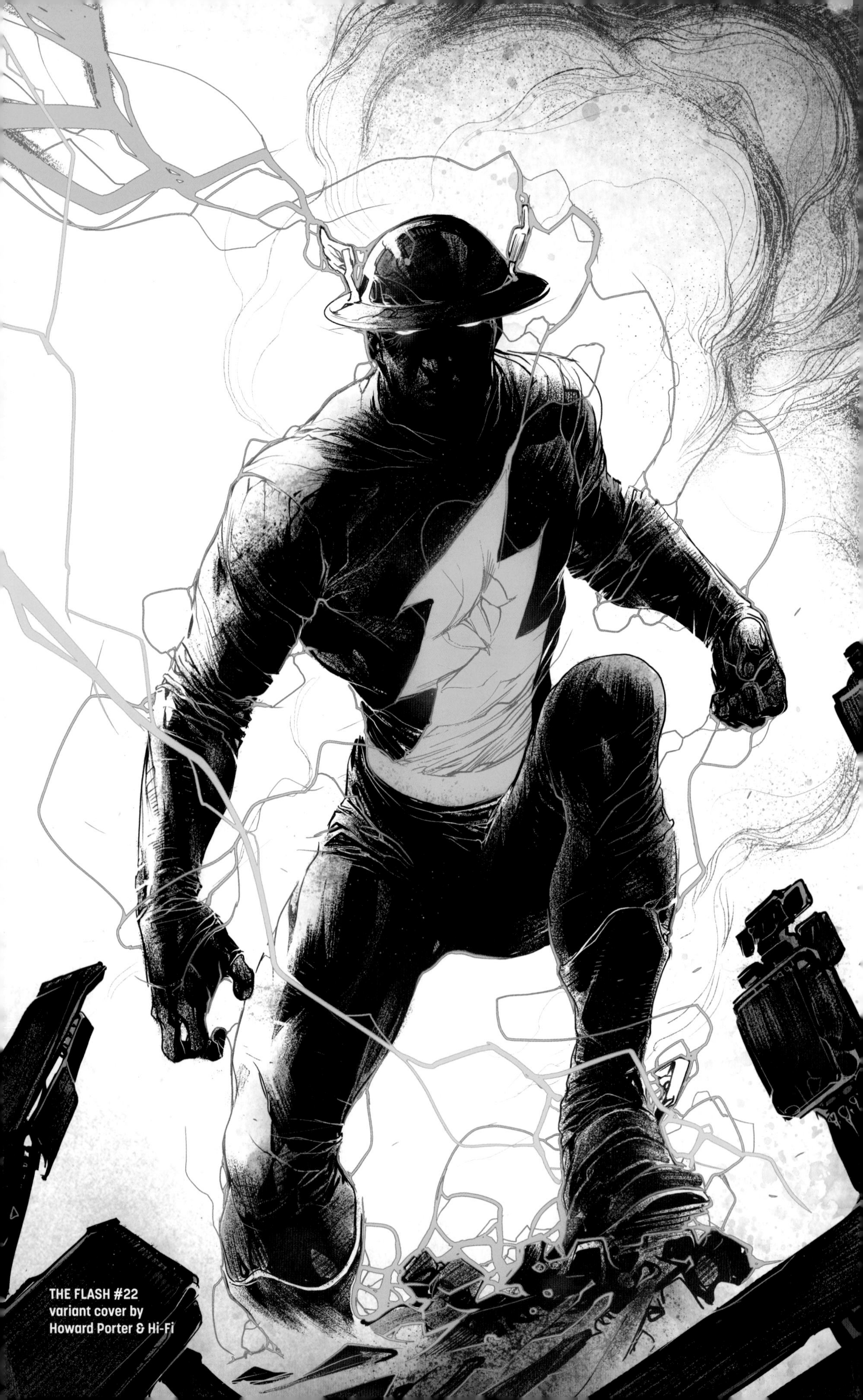

THE FLASH #22
variant cover by
Howard Porter & Hi-Fi

DC UNIVERSE REBIRTH

BATMAN

VOL. 1: I AM GOTHAM

TOM KING
with DAVID FINCH

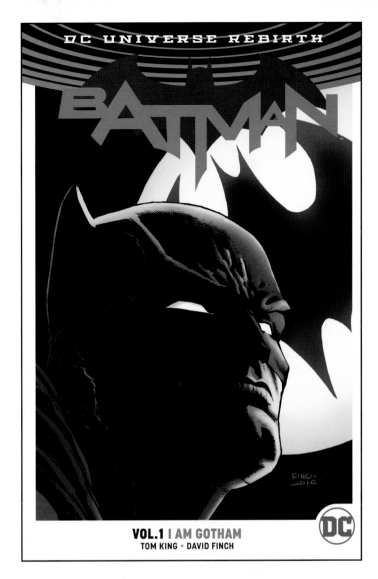

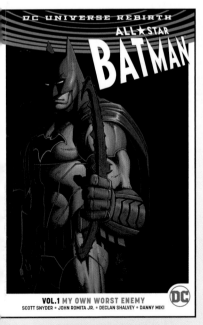

ALL-STAR BATMAN VOL. 1: MY OWN WORST ENEMY

NIGHTWING VOL. 1: BETTER THAN BATMAN

DETECTIVE COMICS VOL. 1: RISE OF THE BATMEN

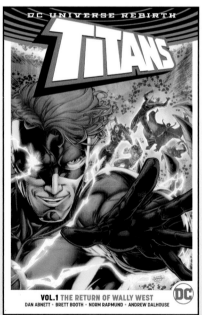
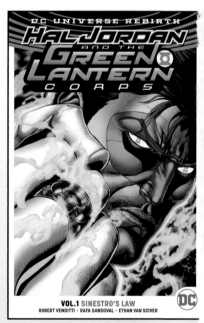